Ford Anglia 105E, Prefect 107E 1959-67 Autobook

By Philip H. Smith
C Eng F I Mech E M S A E
Member of the Guild of Motoring Writers.

Ford Prefect 107E 1959-61
Ford Anglia 105E 997cc 1959-67
Ford Anglia 105E 1198cc 1962-67

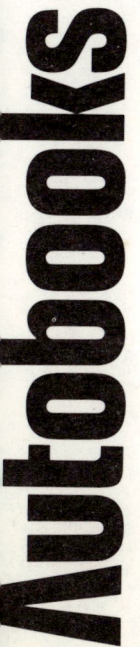

Autopress Ltd. Golden Lane Brighton BN1 2QJ England

The AUTOBOOK series of Workshop Manuals is the largest in the world and covers the majority of British and Continental motor cars, as well as all major Japanese and Australian models. For a full list see the back of this manual.

CONTENTS

ISBN 0 85147 150 1

First Edition   1969
Second Edition, fully revised   1969
Third Edition, fully revised   1969
Fourth Edition, fully revised   1970
Reprinted   1970
Reprinted   1970
Reprinted   1971
Reprinted   1972
Reprinted   1973
Reprinted   1974
Reprinted   1975

720

Printed and bound in Brighton England for Autopress Ltd by G Beard & Son Ltd   A

ACKNOWLEDGEMENTS

My thanks are due to The Ford Motor Co. Ltd., England, in its various Departments, for unstinted co-operation in supplying illustrative matter and data.

Appreciation is also extended to Iliffe Transport Publications Ltd. London, for permission to use their copyright illustrations which form Figs 1:2 and 1:3.

Ben Rhydding
Yorkshire   P.H.S.

INTRODUCTION

This do-it-yourself Workshop Manual has been specially written for the owner who wishes to maintain his car in first class condition and to carry out his own servicing and repairs. Considerable savings on garage charges can be made, and one can drive in safety and confidence knowing the work has been done properly.

Comprehensive step-by-step instructions and illustrations are given on all dismantling, overhauling and assembling operations. Certain assemblies require the use of expensive special tools, the purchase of which would be unjustified. In these cases information is included but the reader is recommended to hand the unit to the agent for attention.

Throughout the Manual hints and tips are included which will be found invaluable, and there is an easy to follow fault diagnosis at the end of each chapter.

In view of the specialized information now available (based on practical competition experience) of various modifications, no attempt has been made here to give advice on obtaining more power or altering performance in any way from standard. Nevertheless, the book will be found invaluable in enabling extensive dismantling operations to be tackled and the necessary inspection and rectification to be carried out prior to such modification, in cases where extra performance is the main object.

In this regard, it cannot be too strongly emphasized that before 'adding power' the owner should satisfy himself that his car in standard form is already giving of its best; this implies meticulous attention to all details of operation, as described in this book. For further reading, in the context of both good road performance as standard, and the improvement likely to accrue from the many and varied alterations which can be carried out using marketed components, the author feels justified in drawing attention to two of his other books— 'Tuning for Speed and Tuning for Economy', and 'Car Performance and the Choice of Conversion Equipment'.

Whilst every care has been taken to ensure correctness of information, it is obviously not possible to guarantee complete freedom from errors nor to accept liability arising out of such errors or omissions. Apart from such, it should further be noted that manufacturers' practice nowadays is to carry out minor design changes and improvements as experience dictates, without interruption of production runs, when such matters do not involve basic alterations to design.

CHAPTER 1

THE ENGINE

The Ford vehicles covered by this book are powered by four cylinder in-line engines having swept volumes of 998 and 1197 cc. The cylinder bore dimensions are identical, two lengths of stroke being used. Alternative compression ratios are also available. Performance data for all types is given in the Appendix, and also dimensional and other information. It is important to refer to the latter when carrying out overhauling and adjustment operations.

1 : 1 Engine construction

The engine is of the overhead valve type, a single row of valves being operated by pushrods and rocker-gear of conventional type. A general arrangement in perspective is shown on **FIG 1 : 1**, an end-section on **FIG 1 : 2**, and component details on **FIG 1 : 3**.

The main block casting and detachable cylinder head are of cast iron, the combustion chambers being fully machined. In-line vertical valves are used, with their guides directly machined in the head casting; the inlet valves are larger than the exhausts, and there are eight separate ports. The camshaft is located on the righthand side of the main block, and is driven by a single-roller chain which is provided with an automatic tensioning device. Three steel-backed white metal bushes support the camshaft, and its end float is controlled by a sintered

metal thrust plate bolted to the front face of the block. The camshaft has an integral skew gear for driving the ignition distributor and oil pump (both of which are on the righthand side of the engine) and also an eccentric for operating the AC diaphragm-type fuel pump.

The crankshaft is of a special cast iron, a material pioneered by Ford and with which they have had a wealth of experience. It has three main bearings of the white-metal steel-backed type; end float and thrust are controlled by half-washers fitted on either side of the centre bearing. The big-end bearings are also steel-backed with surfaces appropriate for the duty. The forged H-section connecting rods are split straight across the big-end eye, the caps being positively located by two dowels and bolts locked by tab washers. Steel-backed bronze bushes are used in the small-ends.

The aluminium-alloy pistons have solid skirts; two compression and one oil-control ring are situated above the gudgeon pin. The skirts have thermal slots extending from the scraper-ring groove towards the gudgeon pin bosses, to ensure that heat is transferred to the bosses rather than to the thrust faces. The piston is machined oval to compensate, so that it is circular at normal operating temperature. The gudgeon pins are fully floating and retained by circlips.

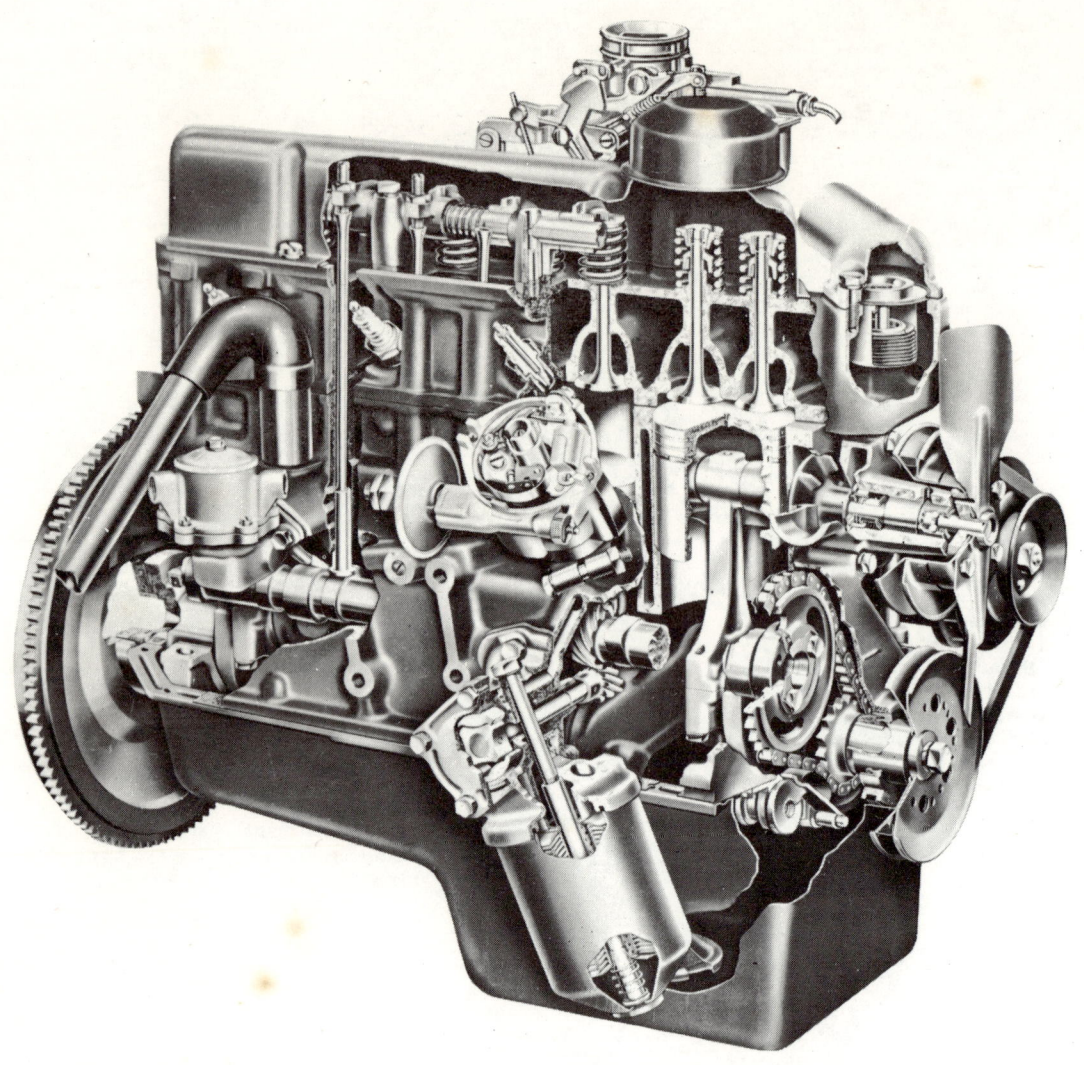

FIG 1 : 1   Part-section perspective view of engine

Two types of oil pump have been used, eccentric bi-rotor and sliding-vane. In each case a non-adjustable spring-loaded plunger relief valve is provided to maintain the oil pressure at the specified maximum.

1 : 2 Overhauling

The information which follows concerning dismantling and overhaul procedure will apply regardless of the purpose of such work, which may range from simple decarbonizing to complete renovation. Where special tuning and modification is required involving for example, replacement of the camshaft for one with greater lift and overlap, the applicable sequence will also apply.

It is possible to carry out quite extensive dismantling without removing the engine from the car, so long as a pit or ramp is available to give room for underneath working. However, for the probable majority who prefer

to operate in professional style at the bench, it will be useful to give brief details of the procedure for engine removal. This will necessarily vary somewhat according to the type of car and bodywork, but most points are covered by what follows.

It is recommended that the engine is parted from the gearbox before removal, leaving the latter in the car. First, remove the bonnet by disconnecting its support at the lower end, and taking out the pivot bolt and washer and two hinge bolts (one at either side) plus their flat washers. Drain off water and oil, and disconnect the battery. Jack-up the front of the car, supporting it on stands at the forward jacking locations. Take off the top and bottom radiator hoses and the four bolts securing the radiator core, and lift out the latter. Disconnect all pipes, wires and controls between the engine and its surrounding fittings. The handbrake primary cable is also disconnected at the relay lever.

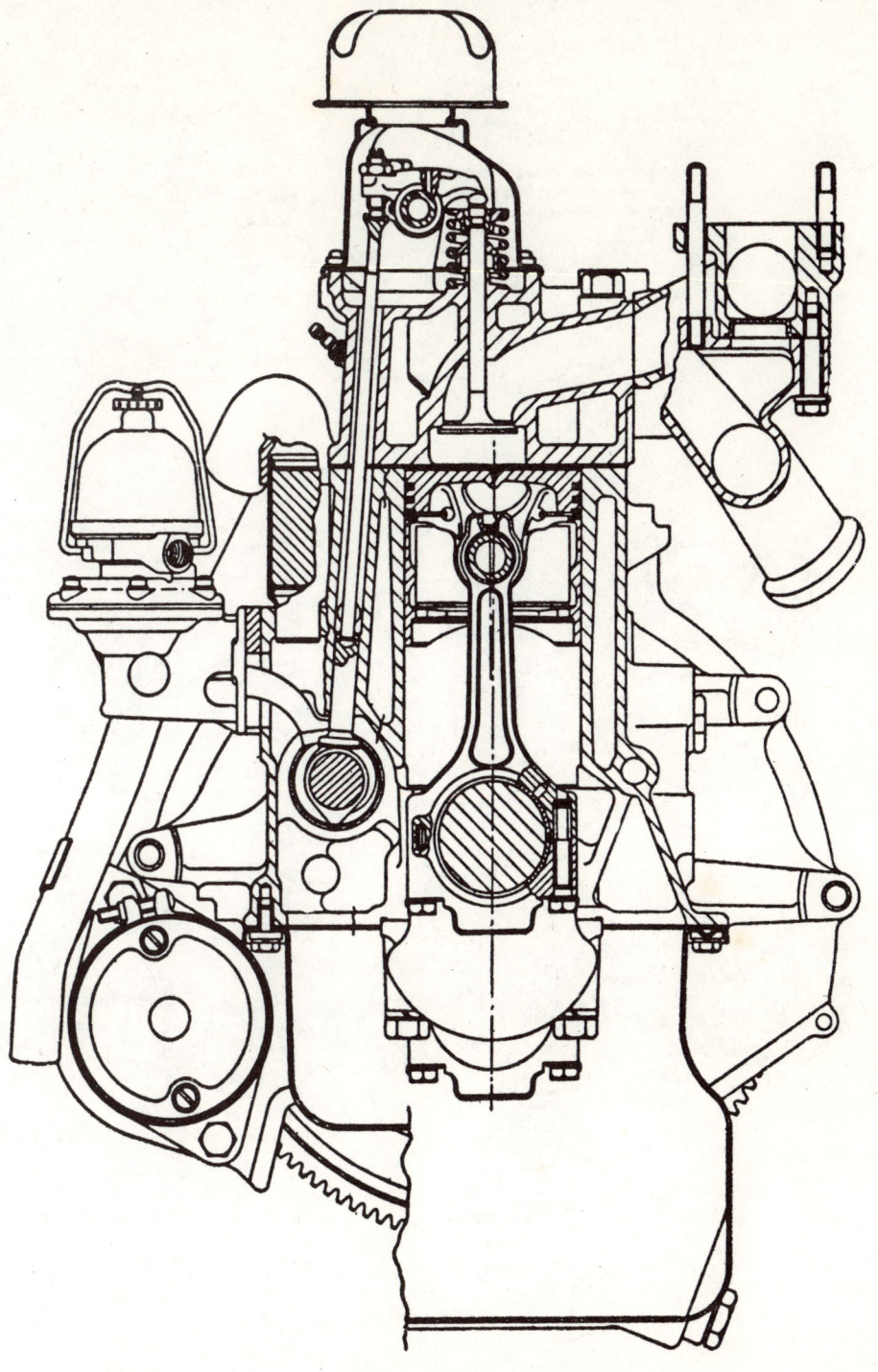

FIG 1 : 2   End sectional view of engine

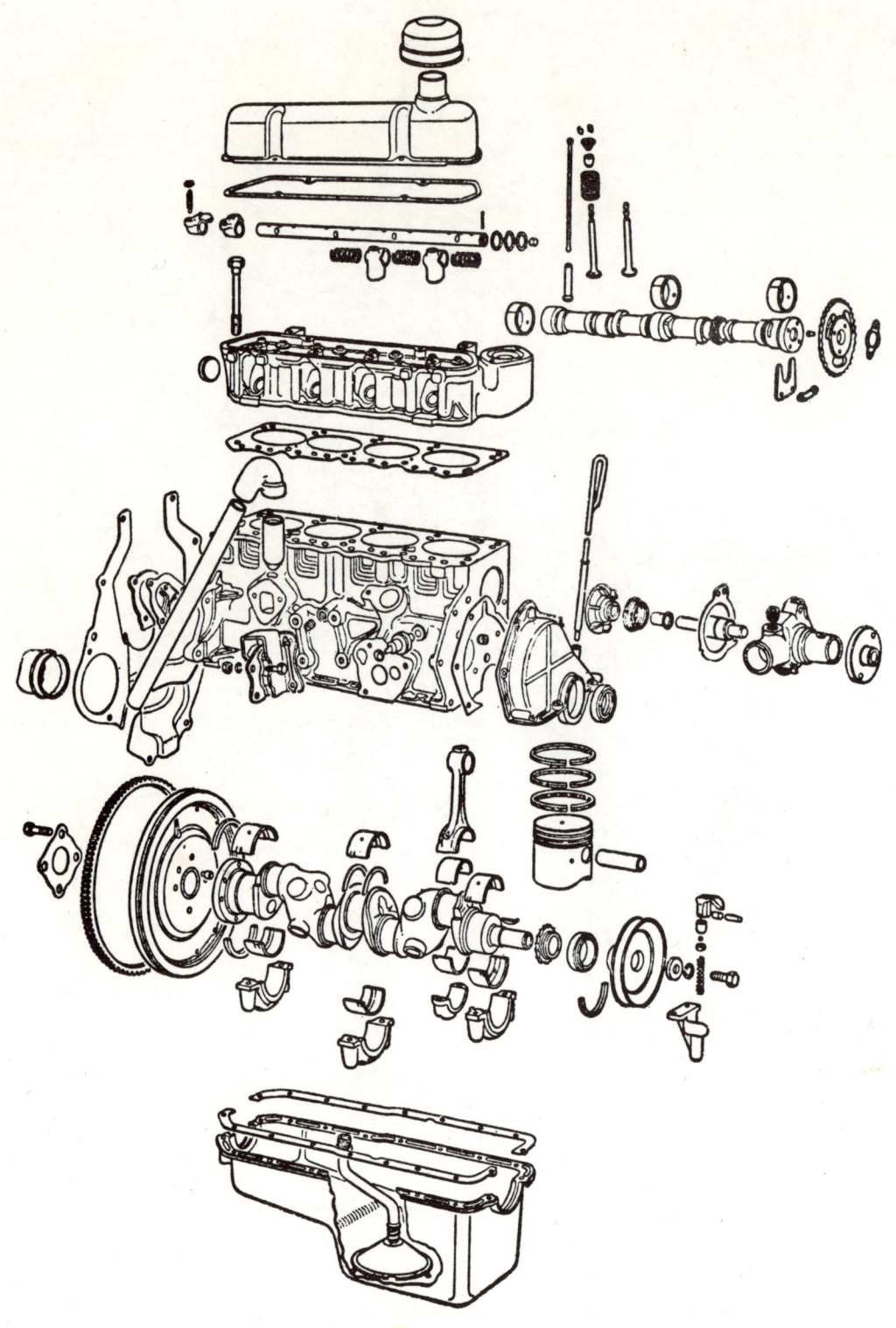

FIG 1 : 3   Component details of engine

Removing one of the clutch housing bolts will allow the breather pipe to be taken off; also remove the top bolt from the starter motor flange. Take out the spark plugs, unclip the distributor cap and remove it along with the plug leads. Take out the three securing bolts of the oil pump and filter, and withdraw the unit. Detach the heater hoses and air filter. Uncouple the exhaust pipe at its junction with the manifold, and remove the carburetter.

1 : 3 Lifting the engine

For taking the 'lift' of the engine the service tool makes use of long bolts inserted in place of the cylinder head bolts in the second and fourth holes on the lefthand side, which secure the bracket-end of the lifting tackle. If this is not available, a suitable sling must be arranged around the whole unit to take the weight. With this done, the sump shield (if fitted) should be removed from under the car, by taking out its four bolts. If the lower starter motor bolt and the cable are now removed the starter can be drawn forwards and away. The gearbox must now be supported from underneath and the eight remaining bolts taken out from the bell-housing flange. Finally, remove the bolts and nuts from the front crossmember to the engine mountings, pull the engine forwards off the clutch shaft, and lift upwards and out of the car.

In describing the various components of the engine, more specific details for dismantling will be given.

1 : 4 Oil pump

Oil pumps are of two types, eccentric bi-rotor and sliding vane. Both are driven in the same manner from skew (crossed-helical) gear from the camshaft. The pump draws the oil from the sump by way of a gauze screen located at the bottom of the suction pipe, the latter being screwed into the cylinder block and thence ducted to the pump. The plunger-type pressure relief valve which is incorporated in the pump returns surplus oil by another pipe, down to the sump bottom to prevent aeration. The pump delivery is through a filter built on to the pump body and then to a short gallery cast in the righthand side of the crankcase. Tapped into the gallery is a pressure-switch for the panel warning-light. A crossduct about halfway along the crankcase takes the oil from the rear end of the short gallery to a long gallery on the lefthand side. From this long gallery there are drillings to each main bearing, while further drillings from the main bearings take the pressure supply to the three camshaft bearings.

The rear thrust washer (on the centre bearing) is lubricated via a notch in the bearing liner combined with a chamfer on the bearing cap. The big-ends are lubricated by crankshaft drillings in the normal way. A small hole in the web of the connecting rod just below its junction with the shank provides an oil jet which impinges on the small-end and gudgeon pin, and the side of the bore, at each revolution. For lubricating the camshaft chain drive, the drilling between the main and camshaft bearings is tapped about halfway, from which point a metering jet sprays the drive.

The overhead valve gear is supplied by way of the rocker shaft. There is a flat machined on the camshaft front journal, which thereby pressurizes, at each revolution of the camshaft, a drilling that passes up through the block and head to the front rocker shaft pedestal. The rocker shaft is hollow, and this receives the oil from the pedestal

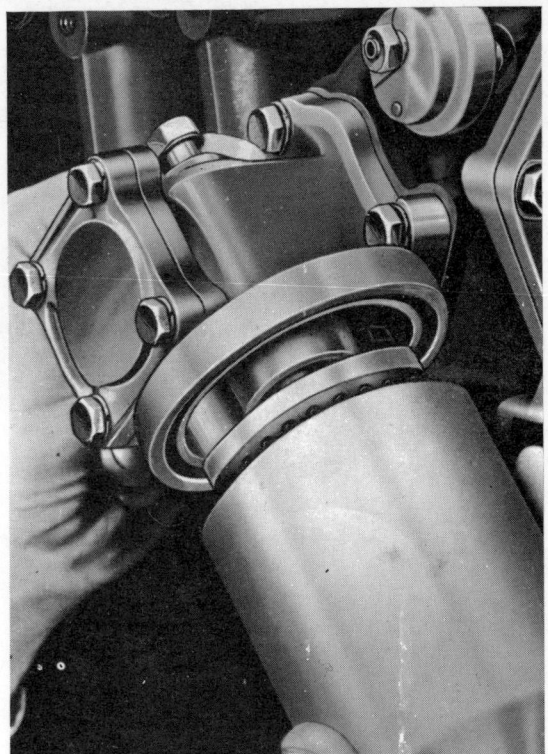

FIG 1 : 4 Oil filter showing location of sealing arrangement

and distributes it to the rocker bushes. Each rocker is drilled for passage of the oil to the valve stems and push-rod ends. Returning down the pushrod tunnels in the block, the lubricant serves the tappets and cams before passing by gravity back to the sump.

1 : 5 Oil filter

The renewable-element fullflow filter with its mounting flange integral with the body of the pump, is ducted through to the delivery side of the latter so that the oil passes through the filter element from outside to inside. An outlet duct then conveys the filtered oil to the gallery. If the pressure difference across the element is for any reason excessive, the oil bypasses through a relief valve located in the mounting flange and short-circuiting the inlet and outlet ducts.

The element is housed in a detachable canister which is held by a single long through-bolt unscrewed from below to detach the canister along with the element. The top rim of the canister seats against a rubber ring located in a groove in the top flange to ensure oil-tightness; an aluminium washer is fitted under the bolt head at the bottom end for the same reason. **FIG 1 : 4** illustrates how these items are arranged.

Crankcase ventilation is provided by way of a filtered air entry in the oil filler cap on the rocker-box. Through this, air enters the box and passes down the pushrod tunnels into the crankcase; some air also passes into the timing chain cover en-route. The breather outlet pipe

FIG 1 : 5   Components of bi-rotor oil pump

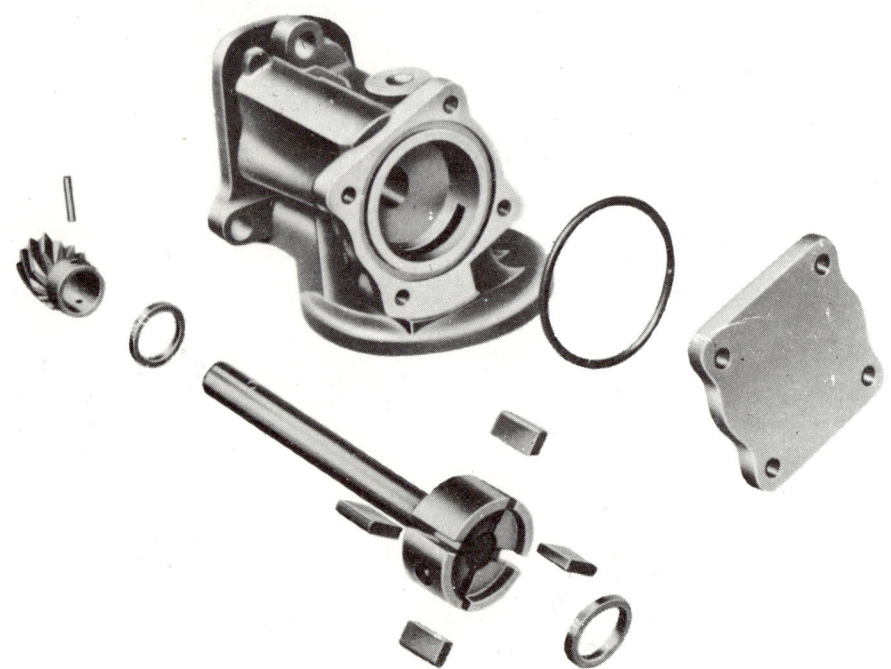

FIG 1 : 6   Components of vane-type oil pump

for exhausting the fume-laden air is attached to an elbow on the fuel pump mounting face, on the engine righthand side. In the breather pipe is a gauze for inhibiting the passage of oil droplets. To ensure free passage of ventilating air it is essential not to overlook the cleanliness of the filler cap filter. If of the oil-wetted gauze type, this is washed in petrol and reoiled every 5000 miles. Some are of oil bath type, in which case the filter is dismantled and the oil changed at a similar period.

Both types of oil pump are interchangeable with one another. They differ in their internal constructions but are identifiable by their end covers; the vane-type pump has a flat cover while that on the bi-rotor pump has four recesses thereon. Both types are self-priming and have a preset relief valve incorporated, which limits maximum pressure to 35-40 lb/sq in.

1 : 6 Bi-rotor type pump

This comprises internally two rotors; the outer rotor turns in the circular body interior, while the inner rotor is pinned to the driving shaft. Its four lobes engage five internal segments on the outer rotor, so that when the shaft rotates, the rotors gear into each other. At the same time the varying volume between the lobes and segments produces a pumping action at considerable pressure both positive and negative, so that the pump is inherently self-priming.

The pump body is held to the crankcase by three bolts, with a gasket between the faces. The filter canister and element can be dismantled by undoing the long centre bolt, and the rubber sealing ring taken out of its groove in the top flange. If the four bolts are now unscrewed from the sump endplate this can be removed, exposing a rubber sealing ring in the pump body; this ring should also be removed. The rotors can now be examined. Their clearance is checked by feeler gauge between the tips of the inner rotor lobes and the 'humps' of the outer segments; this must not exceed .006 inch. The diametrical clearance between the outer circle of the outer rotor and its corresponding bearing surface in the pump body should also be checked, and this must not exceed .010 inch.

Rotors are supplied only in matched pairs, and excessive clearance can only be remedied by fitting a new pair; if the body-to-outer rotor clearance is at fault the wear may be in the pump body, in which case this should be renewed. A straightedge is next placed across the face of the body which takes the cover plate. There should be a maximum of .005 inch between the end faces of the rotors and this straightedge. If this amount is exceeded the body face can be lapped on a flat surface plate to correct.

If the rotors require dismantling further to the extent shown on **FIG 1 : 5,** the skew gear must be removed from its shaft by driving out the retaining pin. The gear can then be pulled off, and the shaft and inner rotor withdrawn, also the outer rotor.

It is not usual for either the pump or filter relief bypass valves to need attention, but if required the pump valve and spring can be taken out after the spring seat has been extracted. This is a press-fit, and care is required when removing. A similar method is used for the filter valve.

After the pump components have been inspected and replaced as necessary, assembly is mainly a reversal of procedure. With all parts thoroughly cleaned and oiled the rotors are replaced into the pump body. Press back the skew gear on to the shaft, avoiding damage to the rotor when doing so by supporting the shaft at this end, on a spacer. Repin the gear, carefully peening-over the pin-ends. If there is any doubt about the pin condition, replace it with a new one, as it can cause serious damage if loosened. The outer rotor is correctly positioned when its chamfered face is not visible, i.e. it should face the interior of the body.

Replace the rubber sealing ring in the body groove, fit the end cover with its machined face inwards to the pump and secure it firmly with the four bolts, tightening them diagonally and not forgetting the lockwashers.

1 : 7 Vane-type pump

In this type of pump (see **FIG 1 : 6**) the body contains a rotor which with its shaft is mounted eccentrically to the body axis. In the rotor are four slots containing vanes, the latter being positioned by rings on either side of the rotor. In operation, the vanes are urged outwards by centrifugal force, to seal against the body bore. The vanes slide in and out of the rotor slots as the shaft revolves, creating suction and pressure due to the varying volume between the vanes. The pump is removed in the same way as for the previous type; the endplate and its sealing washer are also similar and after taking it off, the rotor and vanes are exposed.

The clearance from the face of the body and the rotor is measured as before with a straightedge, and should not exceed .005 inch. If excessive, lap the body face until it is correct. Because of the centrifugal action the vanes are self-adjusting for wear to some extent. However, the vane-to-slot clearance should not exceed .005 inch. If this clearance is too great new vanes and possibly a new rotor will be required.

To remove the rotor and drive shaft, the skew gear is unpinned in the same way as before and the gear pulled off. The rotating component can then be withdrawn, along with the inner ring locating the vanes. The relief valve is of the same type as used in the bi-rotor pump.

When reassembling the pump the vane-locating inner ring is first placed in the body, and then the drive shaft and rotor inserted. The skew gear is replaced and pinned, with the same precautions as detailed for the other type of pump. Put the vanes in the grooves with the curved edges outwards, and replace the vane locating outer ring.

The sealing ring and endplate are then replaced and the filter dealt with on precisely the same lines as before.

When replacing the filter canister in either type of pump (with a new element if called for) the rubber sealing ring should be replaced. This should be inserted into the groove at say four equal points and then pushed firmly home all the way round. If it is seated at only one point, attempts to work it in circumferentially will probably stretch the ring so that it no longer holds the pressure. The aluminium washer under the centre bolt head should also be renewed if it is at all doubtful. When replacing the pump and filter unit on the engine, ensure that the mounting faces are absolutely clean, and use a new gasket on the joint; tighten the three bolts securely and evenly.

1 : 8 The manifold system

The cast iron inlet and exhaust manifolds have separate ports to match up with the eight valve ports. On the inlet manifold there is a tapered plug below the carburetter riser, for insertion of a vacuum test gauge; a pressed steel hot-spot plate occupies a bore just below the carburetter, this plate receiving heat from a similar bore cast on the exhaust manifold.

The exhaust manifold is of a freeflow contour, and its single outlet is cone-shaped to form a flange for the clip-fitting to the downpipe.

When assembled, the inner carburetter retaining stud which is specially long, clamps the two manifolds firmly together at the centre hot-spot, a bolt being inserted upwards at the front for a like purpose. Before uniting the joint faces at this point they should be smeared with a good heat-resisting jointing compound. The attachment of the manifolds to the head is by four bolts and two end studs, a steel-reinforced asbestos gasket being interposed between the faces. The outer pair of inlet branches have a larger internal diameter than the inner pair to receive locating sleeves.

1 : 9 Valves and gear

In some cases pressed-in valves guides are used, but generally the guides are formed by the bores machined directly in the casting. The pressed guides can be replaced if worn, new ones being fitted with the plain end flush with the spot-faced boss inside the port. The integral guide bores can be reamed .015 inch oversize to take the valves having the corresponding oversize stems; this over-sizing can also be done on detachable guides. It is essential after renovation of guides, that the valve seats are recut to make sure that the seat is concentric with the new guide-bore.

It is best to entrust recutting of seats to a competent Ford dealer with the correct equipment. If the seats are badly worn, inserts may be fitted and this again is a job to be 'put out'. If an insert is discovered to be loose or in any way damaged it must be renewed and properly reseated in the casting. Oversize inserts are provided for this purpose.

The valves have 45 deg. faces, the respective head diameters for inlet and exhaust being 1.262 and 1.183 inch. The stems are phosphate-coated for improved wear qualities. There is a diffused aluminium coating on the inlet valve head to increase resistance to wear, oxidisation, and the effect of high temperatures. This face must on no account be ground-in, as such action removes the coating. Pitted or worn faces cannot be rectified and the valves must be replaced. The seats, however, can be corrected, if not bad enough to recut, by grinding-in with a non-coated valve used for this purpose only. The exhaust valves may, of course, be ground in by the normal process.

Two oversizes of stem are available for both inlets and exhausts, these being .0015 and .003 inch.

Below the valve spring retainer is an umbrella-type oil seal to prevent oil leakage down the guides into the combustion chamber. The seals, valve springs, retainers and collets, are identical on all engines, the springs being blue-coloured for identification.

The rocker shaft is supported in four detachable pedestals, with the rocker arms in pairs one on either side of each pedestal. The end rockers are overhung and retained by splitpins while between the others, spacer compression springs are threaded on the shaft for correct locating. Each pedestal is secured by a $\frac{3}{8}$ inch bolt, which also locks the shaft in the pedestal.

The integral cylinder block and crankcase has three internal webs for the main bearings. When removing bearing caps it should be noted that they are identical, with the exception of the front one. The caps should therefore be marked for replacement in their correct positions; the arrow on each cap must also point forwards. The bearing-shell bore in the crankcase may be either standard or .015 inch oversize; in the latter case there are white paint-spot identification markings on both the caps and the case. The camshaft bores may also be oversized .020 inch, but no marking is used in this case.

1 : 10 Cylinder bores

The cylinder bores are graded for size in production, the grade number of each bore being stamped on the top face of the block; the pistons are correspondingly selected. (Further information regarding this is given in the Appendix). It is possible to fit pressed-in cylinder liners, standard and .020 inch oversize bores being listed. Replacing liners in an engine already so fitted is again a job for an expert with the necessary equipment; the liner bore has to be finished to the correct clearance after pressing in.

The steel pushrods are $\frac{1}{4}$ inch dia. When dismantled they should be checked for straightness both with a straightedge and by rolling on a flat surface. Bent rods must be replaced. The tappets are of the chilled cast iron headed type, and can only be removed from below after withdrawing the camshaft.

The latter runs in three whitemetal steel-backed bushes having a standard or oversize external diameter as mentioned earlier. The bushes are suitable for fitting as routine service, as they do not require machining in position. Single bushes should not, however, be replaced, as this may affect correct shaft alignment; if necessary as a result of wear, all three should be changed.

The cams are offset rearwards from the centres of the tappets so as to induce rotation of the tappets to spread the wear; the cams are also tapered slightly for the same effect. In the front shaft bush there is an oil hole leading to the rocker shaft oil-feed drilling which in conjunction with the flat on the shaft journal gives an intermittent supply at each revolution. When assembling the bushes, they must be fitted with all oil holes registered with those in the block casting; that is, with the butt joint 'upwards and outwards' at 45 deg. to the vertical.

The camshaft end float is controlled by a sintered-iron thrust fork which runs in a groove behind the front flange of the shaft; the fork is bolted to the block casting by two bolts. The camshaft chainwheel has 34 teeth of .375 inch pitch in a single row. There is a timing mark on each sprocket to indicate correct relationship of crank and camshafts.

1 : 11 Bearings

The bearing liners carrying the crankshaft are supplied in undersizes for use when the shaft is reconditioned, these being available as .010, .020 and .030 inch under standard size. Standard diameter liners having an oversize on the exterior diameter of .015 inch can be obtained for use with the oversize bearing-web bores mentioned earlier.

Several different thicknesses of half-washer can be fitted at the centre main bearing to obtain the required accuracy of end float on the crankshaft. Sizes (over standard thickness) are .0025, .005, 0075 and .010 inch.

The rear oil seal comprises two graphite impregnated rubber-bonded synthetic fibre packings, one located in a retainer attached to the rear face of the block, and the other in the sump flange. These operate in conjunction with a scroll on the shaft. At the front an oil seal is provided around the boss of the V-belt pulley. It is located in the timing chain cover, and has two lips; an inner one preventing oil from passing out, and an outer one to keep out water and dirt. The seal can be removed without taking off the cover (after removing the radiator and pulley) by using a special tool which is also used for replacing the seal. When sliding the new seal along the shaft the oil-sealing lip should face the engine.

The H-section forged steel connecting rods have their caps located by two hollow dowel pins pressed into the rod, and are secured by two $\frac{11}{32}$ inch bolts with locking plates. At each end of the forging is a machined pad which can be 'shaved' to obtain a set of rods within a specified weight tolerance. Either end can be corrected by attention to its pad.

The big-end shells have their bearing surfaces of a material to suit the duty of the engine. The upper liner (in the rod itself) has an oil hole to match up with the squirt hole in the rod forging, the lower shell (held in the cap) being plain; this is clarified by **FIG 1 : 7.** Each pair of liners must obviously have the same material specification and no mixing as between bearings is permissible. For renovated journals, undersized shells can be obtained, the sizes under standard being .002, 010, 020, 030 and .040 inch. The small-end is a steel-backed bronze bush, not replaceable.

1 : 12 Pistons

Markings on the piston give a good indication of connecting rod accuracy; a heavy skirt marking above the gudgeon pin on one side, along with a similarly heavy marking below the pin on the other side, means that the rod is probably bent. It must either be straightened, or a replacement rod fitted. When rods are assembled with their pistons, the word 'front' on the web of the rod must face accordingly. The rods are also numbered when installed in manufacture, and this numbering must be followed when replacing after attention. The number is on the big-end at the side facing the camshaft, and of course, the cap must be kept to its original rod. The pistons are of aluminium alloy, flat-topped and with solid skirts. Each piston has two compression and one oil control ring above the gudgeon pin. The use of thermal slots and special machining to ensure correct clearance under working conditions has already been mentioned. Cast pads are provided inside, at the bottom of the skirts, for machining to the correct weight tolerance. The gudgeon pin is offset .04 inch towards the thrust side of the bore, to minimize piston slap when 'changing sides' at the dead centres. For this reason it is important to install the pistons the right way round, i.e. with the arrow-

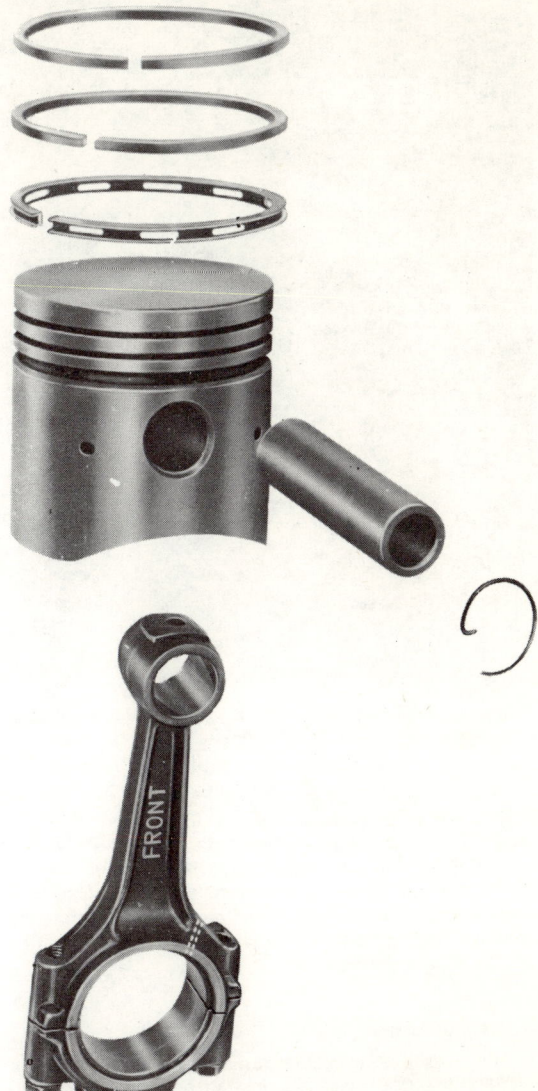

FIG 1 : 7 Piston and connecting rod assembly. Note marking on connecting rod, and oil squirt-hole at big-end

head on the crown pointing forwards. The gudgeon pins are hollow, fully floating and located endways by circlips seated in grooves in the piston bosses. The bosses have their holes graded during manufacture, paint spots on the bosses indicating the grading; the pins are then selected for correct fit in the bosses and the small-end bush.

The maximum variation in weight as between complete piston and connecting rod assemblies in an engine is 8 grams. When changing the parts making up the assembly it is a good idea to check this complete weight, and then select parts so that the variation does not exceed the above amount.

FIG 1:8 Flywheel with clutch in position, and plate-locating mandrel inserted at centre

Of the two compression rings the lower one is stepped externally on the bottom face, and the upper one is chromium plated and tapered. Both rings are marked TOP and must be fitted properly. The upper ring also has a reddish-brown compound on the outer edge which helps running-in; this must not be removed. Oil control rings can be fitted either way round.

1:13 Oversizes

The oversizes available for pistons and rings are .0025, 005, 015 and .030 inch. During initial engine assembly the bores and pistons are graded. As already stated, the bore number can be found adjacent to the bore on the top face of the block at the pushrod side; a corresponding number is stamped on the piston crown, which ensures that the fitted clearance is .0008 to .0014 inch at a point $\frac{3}{4}$ inch from the bottom of the skirt when measured between the skirt and the cylinder bore.

When pistons of standard size are selected each cylinder should be measured at a point $1\frac{9}{16}$ inch from the top face of the block, at right angles to the engine axis, and reference made to the table for the correct piston grade; the piston must have a grade number corresponding to the bore number.

When reboring either to an oversize or for fitting standard-bore liners, each bore must be machined for the correct individual piston fit. The piston skirt diameter is measured at right angles to the gudgeon pin, $\frac{3}{4}$ inch from the skirt bottom, this dimension being used because of the ovality of the skirt.

Alternatively a pull-scale tool can be used, which consists of a feeler gauge $\frac{1}{2}$ inch wide and .0015 inch thick, anchored to a graduated spring scale. The gauge is inserted into the bore for its full length from the top, and the piston is pushed in crown first, so as to trap the blade between the skirt (at its largest diameter) and the wall. Holding the piston stationary, put a steady withdrawing pressure on the gauge, and observe the pull recorded on the scale. 3 to 7 lbs. should be needed to pull out the blade from a new piston in an unused bore. With an engine that has run, the polished surfaces will reduce the grip on the blade and the pull is correspondingly lessened.

1:14 Flywheel

The flywheel shown complete with clutch in **FIG 1:8**, is an iron casting and is concentrically located by a sleeve at its centre, which registers in the spigot bearing bore in the end of the crankshaft. There is a dowel in the crankshaft flange to ensure that the flywheel is always fitted in the same position so as to maintain the correct balance of shaft combined with wheel. The gear-tooth ring for the starter is shrunk on and registers with a groove. The wheel has an undercut on its edge, to give a lead into the groove, which facilitates replacement of the ring. Earlier wheels do not have this undercut, and servicing is only carried out on the complete assembly.

An unserviceable starter ring can be removed by cutting it with a hacksaw in one of the tooth-roots and then splitting off with a chisel. On no account should attempts at repositioning circumferentially be made (as was sometimes done in the past when tooth wear was largely confined to the engagement points on the ring).

A new ring gear is heated to a temperature of not more than 204°C and then fitted with its chamfered inner edge to the shoulder. No quenching is used; the ring must cool naturally. It is essential when heating that this is carried out evenly, and the temperature is correct when a section of the ring (which must be polished for the purpose) turns a light yellow. Too great a temperature will prejudice the wear-resisting properties of the teeth.

The assembly is initially balanced dynamically to close limits, and any heavy point remaining is marked with paint on the wheel. A similar mark will be found on the clutch, and when this is assembled the mark should be positioned to be diametrically opposite to the mark on the wheel. There are three dowels and six bolts for positioning and securing the clutch.

1:15 General dismantling

The method of dismantling various assemblies will be evident from the foregoing descriptions but the following additional information will cover other items.

The generator and its bracket can be removed by taking out the water pump bolt holding the generator support strap, and the two bracket bolts.

The distributor can be withdrawn after disconnecting the vacuum pipe and unscrewing the single bolt holding the clamp plate to the block.

The oil pressure tell-tale switch is a screw-fit in the gallery casting. The thermostat is accessible after detaching the water elbow and gasket; it can be lifted out of its register.

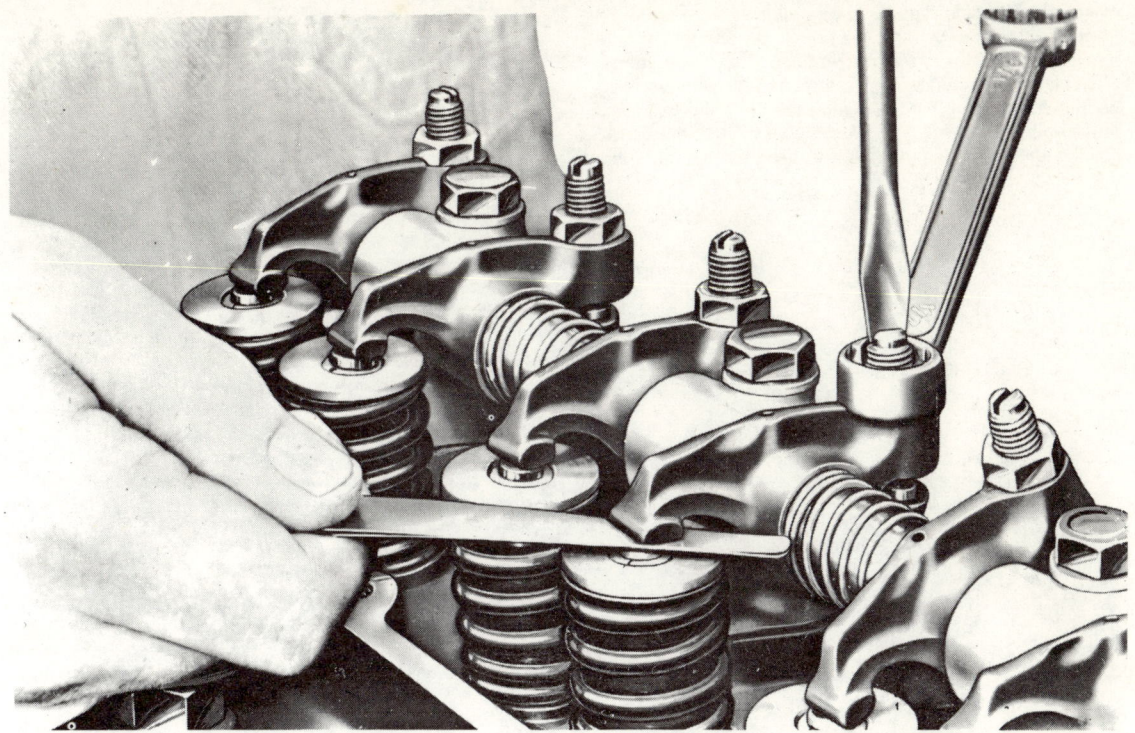

FIG 1:9 Rocker shaft assembly in position, showing location of pedestal bolts, and method of gauging clearance

The rocker shaft assembly is removed by taking out the bolts securing the pedestals to the head which can be seen in **FIG 1:9.** Slacken these a little at a time, alternatively and evenly, so as not to bend the shaft under spring pressure; with the bolts right out, the shaft can then be lifted off. The rocker shaft can be dismantled by removing the splitpin from one end and detaching the flat washer, crimped spring washer and second flat washer which contacts the overhung rocker arm. The pedestals, rockers and spacing springs can then be slid off the shaft but care must be taken to keep them in the correct order for refitting. The pushrods are next lifted out, and these again must be put back in their same locations.

The cylinder head bolts can then be removed in the sequence shown in **FIG 1:10** and the head and gasket lifted off.

1:16 Valve removal

To remove the valves a normal G-clamp type of compressor can be used, but a special Ford type is available which locates in one of the rocker support bolt holes. In this case, the valves have to be kept in the closed position from inside the head, by using a support plate which is part of the equipment. With the spring compressed the split collets can be extracted, followed by the collar and valve spring. The rubber umbrella seal has to be slid off the stem before the valve can be withdrawn.

If the three retaining bolts of the water pump are taken out the pump can be removed; one of the bolts

also anchors the dynamo support strap, and another secures the timing cover; the bolts must therefore not be mixed.

The crankshaft pulley is removed by unscrewing the front bolt along with its washers, after which the pulley can be drawn off with a suitable drawer.

When removing the sump, note that the two rear bolts are longer than the rest; also, remove the cork packing strip from the timing cover and the gaskets from the flange faces.

If it is desired to remove the sump with the engine in the chassis, the starter and radiator hoses are taken off. The front of the engine has then to be raised to clear the crossmember, which necessitates removal of the nuts and bolts from the front mounting brackets and the

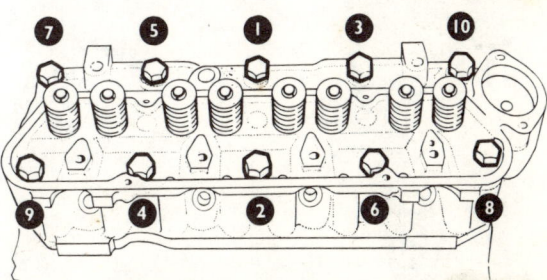

FIG 1:10 Sequence of removal and tightening of cylinder head bolts

use of lifting tackle. The setscrews can then be removed from the sump flange, and the crankshaft rotated to give clearance for the crankwebs, allowing the sump to be lifted clear. The timing cover is attached by bolts and can be withdrawn from the shaft after taking these out. Two of the bolts are dowel-type, identifiable by their machined shanks; therefore keep the bolts to their respective holes.

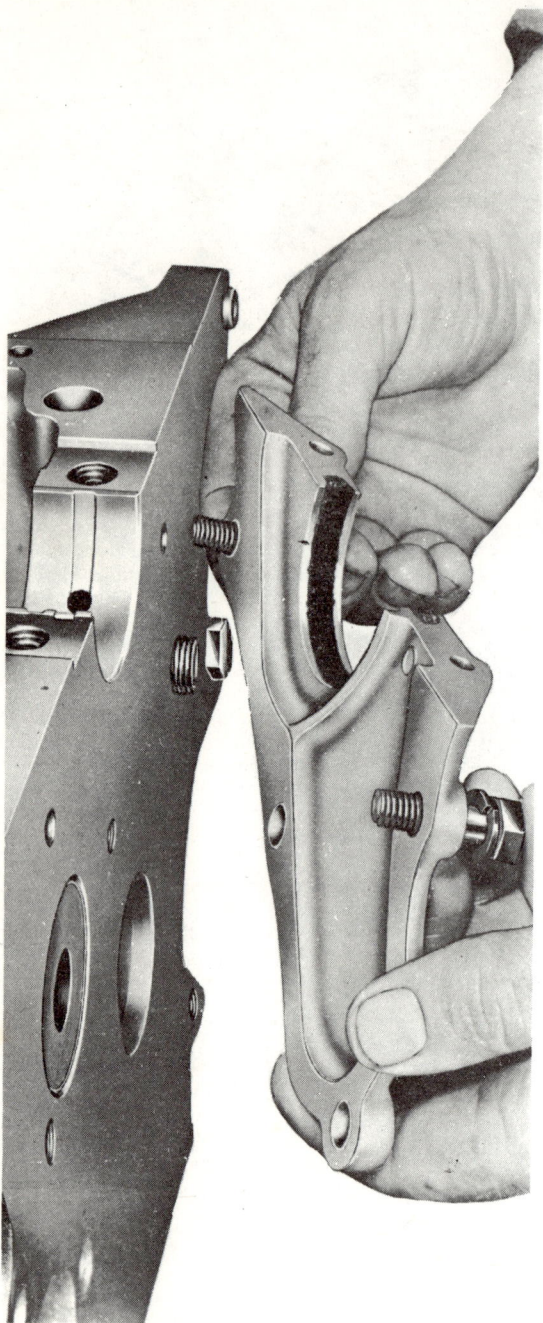

FIG 1:11 Rear oil seal carrier with seal in position

1:17 Crankshaft removal

The clutch assembly (see **FIG 1:8**) can be taken off (without using any kind of compressor tool) by unscrewing the bolts holding the pressure unit to the flywheel; the unit and also the driven plate can then be lifted off. The timing chain tensioner is held by two bolts and after removing as a unit its tensioner arm can be detached from the pivot pin.

The two pipes from the oil pump intake and pressure relief valve can also be detached; the former is a screwed fit, the tab washer over the nut being straightened first and then the nut unscrewed allowing the pipe to be withdrawn. The relief valve return pipe is pressed in, and requires drifting out, using a drift of correct size with light hammer blows.

When dismantling the big-ends the bolts should be unscrewed a few turns after bending the locking tabs to clear. Then tap each bolt head to release the rod from the cap, and remove the bolts completely. The pistons can then be pushed out of the cylinder bores; if there is difficulty in getting them to emerge, it is likely that carbon around the top of the bore is causing sticking, and this must be carefully scraped away. The gudgeon pins can be withdrawn after detaching both circlips, using suitable pliers. The pin may be rather tight, but will be released by warming the piston in hot water.

To remove the flywheel, the locking plate tabs are bent back and the four bolts unscrewed. The wheel can then be tapped off its flange evenly all round.

The camshaft sprocket wheel is secured by two retaining bolts which can be removed after bending the locking plate clear; there is a dowel locating the wheel on its flange. The endless chain is then detached from the crankshaft sprocket, which can be pulled off using the appropriate tool, and its key removed from the shaft.

Having marked each main bearing cap for repositioning correctly, the cap bolts can be taken out and the caps removed. The two thrust half-washers, one on each side of the centre bearing, are also removed; the shaft can then be lifted out and also the bearing shells, noting their correct positions.

The rear oil seal for the crankshaft is in a housing retained by four bolts to the block, as illustrated in **FIG 1:11,** the two lower bolts being of dowel type for correct alignment.

The camshaft thrust plate registers in a groove behind the shaft flange as shown on **FIG 1:12,** it is removed by undoing the two retaining bolts. The engine must now be inverted so that the tappets are clear of the camshaft, and the shaft can then be withdrawn. Lift out the tappets, keeping them in correct order for refitting.

Should the camshaft bearing brushes require replacement, a special tool is necessary for withdrawing and replacing them.

1:18 Inspection

The power unit is now completely dismantled; all parts must be thoroughly cleaned and checked for condition. The various oilways in the block and head can be cleared by use of a high-pressure petrol squirt, and finally blown through. When replacing blanking plugs in oilways, first apply a good plastic sealer to the screw threads to prevent leakage or loosening. Examine all tapped holes to ensure that the threads are sound and that there is no possibility of studs or bolts 'bottoming'. This can be caused by hard-packed dirt at the base. Doubtful threads can be corrected and cleared, by running-down the appropriate size of tap.

Components may be checked dimensionally against the data given in the Appendix. If the engine has been dismantled at a 'major overhaul' period, renewal of all gaskets, joint washers, locking plates and oil seals will be required. If, however, it is relatively new, but has been stripped for a special purpose, e.g. inspection prior to modification, it is possible that some of these parts will be quite serviceable even after removal. However, if at all doubtful, renewal is most advisable.

Assuming that the block is serviceable and with any required renovation carried out to cylinder bores, camshaft bushes, etc., assembly is largely a reversal of the dismantling procedure.

1 : 19 Reassembly

The valve tappets are inserted with the engine block upside down in correct order of removal. After ensuring that the tappets are fully raised, slide the camshaft through the bushes; rotate the shaft to make sure of its freedom of motion. Fit the thrust plate with its fork in the flange groove and bolt it to the block; check the end float, which should be between .002 and .007 inch. If this is not correct the thrust plate must be renewed; if all is well, bend the locking plate over the bolt heads, neatly and squarely. Oil the main bearing shells and fit into their locations in the block and bearing caps. Register the rear oil seal upper half in its carrier, and press it fully and evenly into the groove. Then trim the ends of the seal, leaving $\frac{1}{32}$ inch protrusion of the seal above the carrier end face. Fit the carrier (see **FIG 1 : 11**), using good jointing compound on the gasket. Make sure that the spring washers are on the bolts, and that the two dowel bolts (adjacent to the sump flange) are correctly positioned; these should also be nipped tight first, so that the carrier aligns properly. The four bolts are then pulled tight, diagonally and evenly.

1 : 20 Crankshaft replacement

Oil the crankshaft main journals and position the shaft in the crankcase shells. The centre thrust half-washers are put into their recesses on either side of the bearing (see **FIG 1 : 13**), with their oil grooves facing the adjacent crankshaft webs. Next fit the main bearing caps, noting the positioning marks already referred to, and tighten them to 55-60 lb ft torque reading. Check that the shaft rotates freely.

The shaft is next pushed rearwards in the bearings to its fullest extent, and a feeler gauge inserted between the shaft and the rear thrust washer (at the centre main). The clearance should be between .003 and .011 inch. If it exceeds this, remove the centre bearing cap and fit oversize thrust washers to correct the float.

Check that the input-shaft spigot bearing at the flywheel end of the crankshaft is clean, and that the flywheel flange and face are free from burrs. Fit the wheel squarely on the flange dowel and tap it into place. Then fit the locking plate and four bolts, and tighten the latter to a torque reading of 45-50 lb ft.

The flywheel run-out should not exceed .004 inch measured on the face adjacent to the wheel rim. If correct,

FIG 1 : 12   Location of camshaft thrust plate

FIG 1 : 13   Location of crankshaft thrust washers

bend back the locking plate squarely and neatly over the bolt heads. Locate the timing sprocket key in its keyway at the front of the shaft, and press the sprocket home, with the timing-mark facing the front. The slightly differing sprockets for engine sizes are identified by the groove in the boss, and this should be checked if renewing.

Time the shafts by first turning the crankshaft until the sprocket tooth is pointing at the camshaft centre line.

Push on the camshaft sprocket temporarily, and turn it until the mark on its related tooth is in line with the other sprocket mark and the crankshaft centre line. Now take off the camshaft sprocket, wrap the endless chain around both sprockets without disturbing their circumferential relative positions, and refit the camshaft sprocket. Fit the locking plate and sprocket retaining bolts. Check that the timing marks are still correct, and if all is well tighten up the bolts and secure with the plate.

1 : 21 Piston selection

The pistons are selected in accordance with previous remarks. The ring gap should measure .009 to .014 inch, while the clearance of ring-side to groove should be .0016 to .0036 inch on the compression rings and .0018 to .0038 inch on the oil control ring. Remove the rings after checking. The pistons must now be assembled to the connecting rods, by fitting a circlip in one of the boss grooves, and locating the rod inside the piston with the word 'front' on the same side as the arrowhead on the piston crown, the assembly being shown on FIG 1 : 7. Plunge the piston in hot water, and couple it to the small end of the rod by sliding the gudgeon pin through the bosses and bush until it abuts firmly against the circlip; then fit the second circlip. Oil the pin freely after shaking off any surplus drops of water.

The rings can now be refitted noting the marking TOP on the compression rings. Bear in mind also the previous comment regarding the running-in compound on the top ring. Fit the big-end bearing shells to their correct rods and caps, ensuring that the tongues engage with the locating grooves. Also check that the oil hole in the top shell registers with the squirt hole in the rod.

To refit the pistons and rods, access is necessary to both top and bottom of the block, which must be positioned in the best way for this purpose; (it is usual to rest the block on its end). Space the ring gaps at equal circumferential distances of 120 deg. and push the piston into the bore from the top, noting that the arrow on the crown faces the front of the block. A ring squeezer is highly desirable for giving an easy passage of the rings into the bore. Carefully ease the piston and connecting rod down the bore, and at the same time rotate the crankshaft until the appropriate crankthrow aligns with the big-end of the rod. Push the rod-end over the big-end crankpin, and fit the cap, carefully aligning it with the dowels. Fit the bolts and locking plates, and nip the bolts. Fit all the pistons and rods in this manner, turning the shaft as required between each fitting; the cylinder bores and big-ends must now be liberally oiled.

The crankshaft can then be turned and all motions checked. If all is well, tighten all the big-end bolts to a torque reading of 20-25 lb ft, and carefully lock the bolts with the tab washers.

The chain tensioner-arm is next repositioned on its hinge-pin, and the tensioner bolted to the block. The cam spring is tensioned by rotating it about $2\frac{1}{2}$ turns from its free position, this being done on initial assembly.

1 : 22 Oil seals

The return-oil pipe from the relief valve is next reinserted into its hole in the block, the narrow end protruding into the crankcase; the pipe is driven fully home with a hammer and drift. The oil pump suction pipe should have a new tab washer fitted to the nut, and then positioned so that the gauze filter housing does not foul either the relief valve pipe or the crankthrow of No. 2 cylinder. When this is correct, tighten up the nut, and lock with the washer.

If a new front oil seal is being fitted, the timing cover must be supported properly around the seal housing when pressing-in, as the cover is easily distorted under this pressure. The oil-thrower on the crankshaft is fitted with its dished face outwards, i.e. towards the pulley. The timing cover can then be refitted. Its gasket is positioned on the cover flange using jointing compound, and then fitted over the shaft-end and bolted to the block face. Remember the spring washers, and also that the two bolts adjacent to the sump are dowel bolts, and will align the cover correctly, if lightly nipped first. Subsequently all the bolts must be tightened evenly.

The crankshaft rear oil seal half, which is located in the sump flange, can now be inserted in its groove and pushed home evenly all round. The ends of the seal are then cut so that they protrude $\frac{1}{32}$ inch above the flange face. The seal must then be well oiled.

The oil pump and filter assembly can next be refitted to the block, using a new gasket and tightening the bolts evenly. Before replacing the sump fit new gaskets to the flange on the block, applying jointing compound at the front end on the timing cover, and at the rear end on the oil seal carrier. Make sure that the gaskets fit into the recess for the cork packing in the timing cover (at the base of the groove), and then press the cork strip into the groove using jointing compound. Accuracy in fitting these packings is important to avoid oil leaks, but when all is correct the sump will be found to seal absolutely tightly at both this point and at the rear bearing. It can then be bolted in position, tightening all the bolts evenly and firmly.

When replacing the water pump, note that the timing cover is held by one of the bolts, and the generator support strap by another; therefore ensure that the correctly-sized bolts are in their proper positions.

The crankshaft pulley is next aligned with the key and pushed on the shaft, securing it with the bolt along with its flat washer and lockwasher. To refit the clutch assembly it is necessary to centralize the driven plate by means of a mandrel through the centre of the pressure unit. (A special locating tool is available, this being shown in position on FIG 1 : 8.) This ensures that when the unit is in position the gearbox input shaft can be entered into the unit, without any trouble from misalignment of the driven plate. The pressure unit with the driven plate thus aligned, is offered up to the flywheel, noting the position of the three dowels and the balancing paint-mark positions, which must be diametrically opposite on pressure unit and flywheel rim. Push the pressure unit over the dowels in this position, insert the six bolts and tighten them to a torque reading of 12-15 lb ft. The driven plate mandrel or locating tool can then be withdrawn.

1 : 23 Valve replacement

The cylinder head components can be assembled to the head after the latter has been dealt with as required, i.e. decarbonized, rectified or modified. The exhaust valves may be ground in if necessary, but the strict warning previously given regarding the special coating on the

FIG 1 : 14   Cylinder head in position with valves fitted

inlet valve must be adhered to. Each valve can then be refitted by first lubricating its stem and then inserting into the correct guide. If the Ford tool is used, the packing is put inside the head to hold up the valve; then with the head normally placed, the umbrella seals can be fitted, large diameter downwards. The spring is now put over the stem and positioned correctly on the head. Replace the top collar, compress the spring with the tool, and fit the split collets, positioning them carefully. Then release the tool slowly noting that the collets 'wedge' properly and that the spring collar is quite level.

If a horseshoe-type spring compressor is used the procedure is similar except that the head has to be laid on its side so that the tool can abut against the valve-head. Thus, all the parts must be assembled on the stem before the compressor is applied. After all the valves have been refitted, test each one for operation by pressing down with a vertical push on the end of the stem; **FIG 1 : 14** shows the head in this condition.

The cylinder head gasket can now be fitted to the block, ensuring that it is correctly in place by noting the lining-up of the various water holes, etc. Two special locating studs are then screwed into diagonally opposite bolt holes to ensure that all the holes line-up with those in the head. (If these are not available, close fitting mandrels will serve quite well, so long as care is taken.) The head is then placed over the locating studs or mandrels and gently eased down on to the gasket. Insert the head bolts and remove the mandrels. The bolts must be tightened until they just nip and then finally tightened in the correct order 'inwards to outwards' (see **FIG 1 : 10**) to a torque reading of 65-70 lb ft. Go over the tightening sequence several times so that tightening is even all the way. It is necessary to check for tightness after the first road-trial, and again at about 500 miles running.

The rocker shaft is reassembled in the order of dismantling, after ensuring that it is thoroughly clean internally and that all oilways are perfectly clear. Align the pedestals so that the bolt hole is on the adjustment side of the rockers. The shaft-end splitpins should have their heads upwards and the legs well splayed out.

The pushrods can next be replaced in their tunnels, making sure that their ball-ends engage in the cup-ends of the tappets. Then fit the rocker shaft to the head; see that each rocker adjusting screw is properly engaged in the cup at the top end of its pushrod. Tighten the pedestal bolts gradually to take up the uneven spring pressure. Finally, pull up the bolts to a torque reading of 17-22 lb ft.

1 : 24 Rocker adjustment

The rocker adjustment must now be set to give a feeler gauge clearance between rocker-end and valve stem, of .008 to .010 inch on the inlet valves and .018 to .020 inch on the exhausts, this being of course with a cold engine. The valves numbered from the front are, inlets 2, 3, 6 and 7, and exhausts 1, 4, 5 and 8. A well known simple method of adjustment using the valve numbering as above, and giving the minimum amount of engine rotation for the purpose, is to adjust certain closed valves when others are fully open. The following table shows the sequence, the engine being turned until the valves numbered at the left are fully open.

Valves fully open	*Valves closed (to adjust)*
Nos. 1 and 6	Nos. 3 and 8
Nos. 2 and 4	Nos. 5 and 7
Nos. 3 and 8	Nos. 1 and 6
Nos. 5 and 7	Nos. 2 and 4

It should be borne in mind that as the righthand column contains one closed valve of each type, the correct feeler gauge size must be used between operations. The clearance is right when the gauge is just 'nipped' in the gap as indicated on **FIG 1 : 9**, and a certain knack is necessary to ensure that the clearance is not altered when the locknut on the rocker is tightened. The

FIG 1:15 Timing mark on pulley for static ignition setting. Later engines have 2 marks

clearance should therefore be checked to ensure that nothing has shifted after finally tightening. It is worth while taking a good deal of trouble on this point, as consistency of clearance throughout the eight valves can mean quite a lot in terms of engine smoothness and quiet running.

The clearance should be checked after the engine has reached normal operating temperature. In this case the readings are .010 inch for inlet and .017 inch for exhaust valves.

1 : 25 Ignition timing

The ignition can now be retimed, the first requirement being to turn the crankshaft to the correct position. On early cars there is a single mark on the timing cover, as shown on **FIG 1:15,** and the crankshaft must be turned until the arrow on the pulley is in line with this. On later engines there are two marks, the one nearest the car centre giving a static setting of 10 deg. advance, while the other gives 6 deg. advance. For the intermediate 8 deg. advance, a position midway between the two marks must be selected. The various static settings are given in the Appendix. When suitably lined-up, the piston of No. 1 cylinder should be near the top of the compression stroke. This can be checked by noting that both its valves are closed. If this is not so, turn the engine through another complete revolution. Ensure that the oil seal on the distributor body is serviceable and then fit the unit so that its rotor is pointing towards the segment in the cap which is wired for No. 1 cylinder; the contact breaker points should also be just opening. As the skew-drive gears engage, the rotor will turn slightly. To allow for this, first position the distributor with the rotor tip adjacent to the low tension terminal, and the vacuum diaphragm spindle about parallel with the cylinder block, before finally pushing the unit down and engaging the gears. When fully down, the rotor position should be correct. The clamp bolt on the body is now slackened and the body turned until the contact points are just opening;

the clamp bolt may then be tightened in this position. (Refer also to Chapter 3 for information on distributor scale markings.)

The fuel pump can be replaced using a new gasket if necessary, also the oil pressure warning light, thermostat, and water outlet elbow flange. The generator is next fitted with about ½ inch total side movement on the belt between the pulleys on the water pump and generator. Tighten the bolts securely so that the adjustment does not shift in service.

The manifold gasket should be coated on both sides with good heat-resisting jointing compound. The manifold unit is then located on the studs at front and rear of the head, and the other bolts (with their flat and lockwashers) inserted. New self-locking nuts should be used on the front and rear studs. These along with the bolts are then tightened firmly and evenly. This completes assembly of the engine.

1 : 26 Fault diagnosis

(a) Engine will not start

1 Defective coil
2 Faulty distributor capacitor (condenser)
3 Dirty, pitted or incorrectly set contact breaker points.
4 Ignition wires loose or insulation faulty.
5 Water on spark plug leads
6 Corrosion of battery terminals or battery discharged
7 Faulty or jammed starter
8 Spark plug leads wrongly connected
9 Vapour lock in fuel pipes
10 Defective fuel pump
11 Overchoking
12 Underchoking
13 Blocked petrol filter or carburetter jets
14 Leaking valves.
15 Sticking valves.
16 Valve timing incorrect
17 Ignition timing incorrect

(b) Engine stalls

Check 1, 2, 3, 4, 10, 11, 12, 13, 14 and 15 in (a)
1 Spark plugs defective or gaps incorrect
2 Retarded ignition
3 Mixture too weak
4 Water in fuel system
5 Petrol tank vent blocked
6 Incorrect valve clearance

(c) Engine idles badly

Check 1 and 6 in (b)
1 Air leak at manifold joints
2 Slow-running jet blocked or out of adjustment
3 Air leak in carburetter
4 Over-rich mixture
5 Worn piston rings
6 Worn valve stems or guides
7 Weak exhaust valve springs

(d) Engine misfires

Check 1, 2, 3, 4, 5, 8, 10, 13, 14, 15, 16, 17 in (a); 1, 2, 3 and 6 in (b)
1 Weak or broken valve springs

(e) Engine overheats. See Chapter 4

(f) Compression below normal (or varying between cylinders)

Check 14 and 15 in (a), 5 and 6 in (c) and 1 in (d)
1 Worn piston ring grooves
2 Scored or worn cylinder bores

(g) Engine lacks power

Check 3, 10, 11, 13, 14, 15, 16 and 17 in (a), 1, 2, 3 and 6 in (b), 5 and 6 in (c) and 1 in (d). Also check (e) and (f)
1 Leaking joint washers
2 Fouled spark plugs
3 Automatic advance not operating

(h) Burnt valves or seats

Check 14 and 15 in (a), 6 in (b) and 1 in (d). Also check (e)
1 Excessive carbon around valve seat and head

(j) Sticking valves

Check 1 in (d)
1 Bent valve stem
2 Scored valve stem or guide
3 Incorrect valve clearance

(k) Excessive cylinder wear

Check 11 in (a) and see Chapter 4
1 Lack of oil
2 Dirty oil
3 Piston rings gummed up or broken

4 Badly fitted piston rings
5 Connecting rods bent

(l) Excessive oil consumption

Check 5 and 6 in (c) and check (k)
1 Ring gaps too wide
2 Oil return holes in piston choked with carbon
3 Scored cylinders
4 Oil level too high
5 External oil leaks
6 Ineffective valve stem oil seals

(m) Crankshaft and connecting rod bearing failure

Check 1 in (k)
1 Restricted oilways
2 Worn journals or crank pins
3 Loose bearing caps
4 Extremely low oil pressure
5 Bent connecting rod

(n) Poor circulation. See Chapter 4

(o) Corrosion. See Chapter 4

(p) High fuel consumption. See Chapter 2

(q) Engine vibration

1 Loose generator bolts
2 Fan blades out of balance
3 Defective engine mountings

NOTES

CHAPTER 2

CARBURETTERS AND FUEL SYSTEM

The fuel pump is of the mechanical diaphragm type, operated from an eccentric on the camshaft. The general principle of working is shown on **FIG 2:1,** and is common to the two types fitted. The main difference between these is in the filter arrangement, the combined filter and fuel pump is shown in **FIG 2:2.**

The overhauling procedure to be described will be found to apply fully in most cases. However it should be born in mind that minor changes in manufacturing technique take place over a long period. This may affect certain small components (e.g. valves) to the extent that they are no longer readily removable by normal means. Should there be any doubt regarding the procedure in such cases, the complete assembly should be exchanged.

2:1 Pump mechanism

The pump is self-contained and mounted on the side of the crankcase, in which position the diaphragm operating-arm visible on **FIG 2:3,** on the pump engages a camshaft eccentric. The pump diaphragm is pulled downwards when the rocker arm is pushed upwards by the eccentric, and this movement fills the pump chamber with fuel. The return or pumping stroke is performed by a spring; thus the delivery pressure is determined solely by the spring, and the diaphragm stroke by the amount of

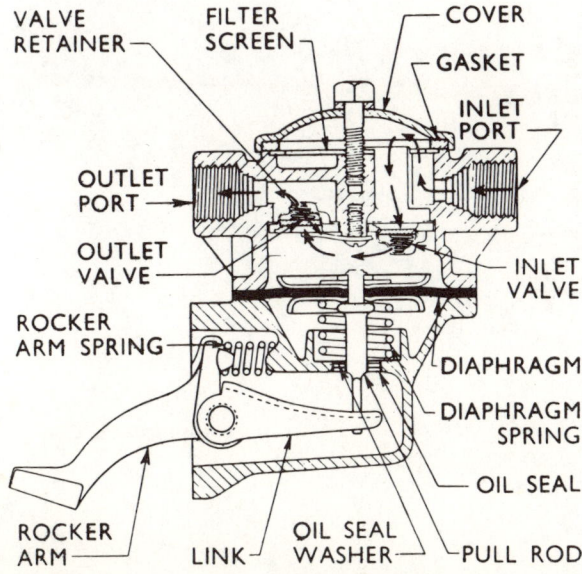

FIG 2:1   General arrangement of fuel pump

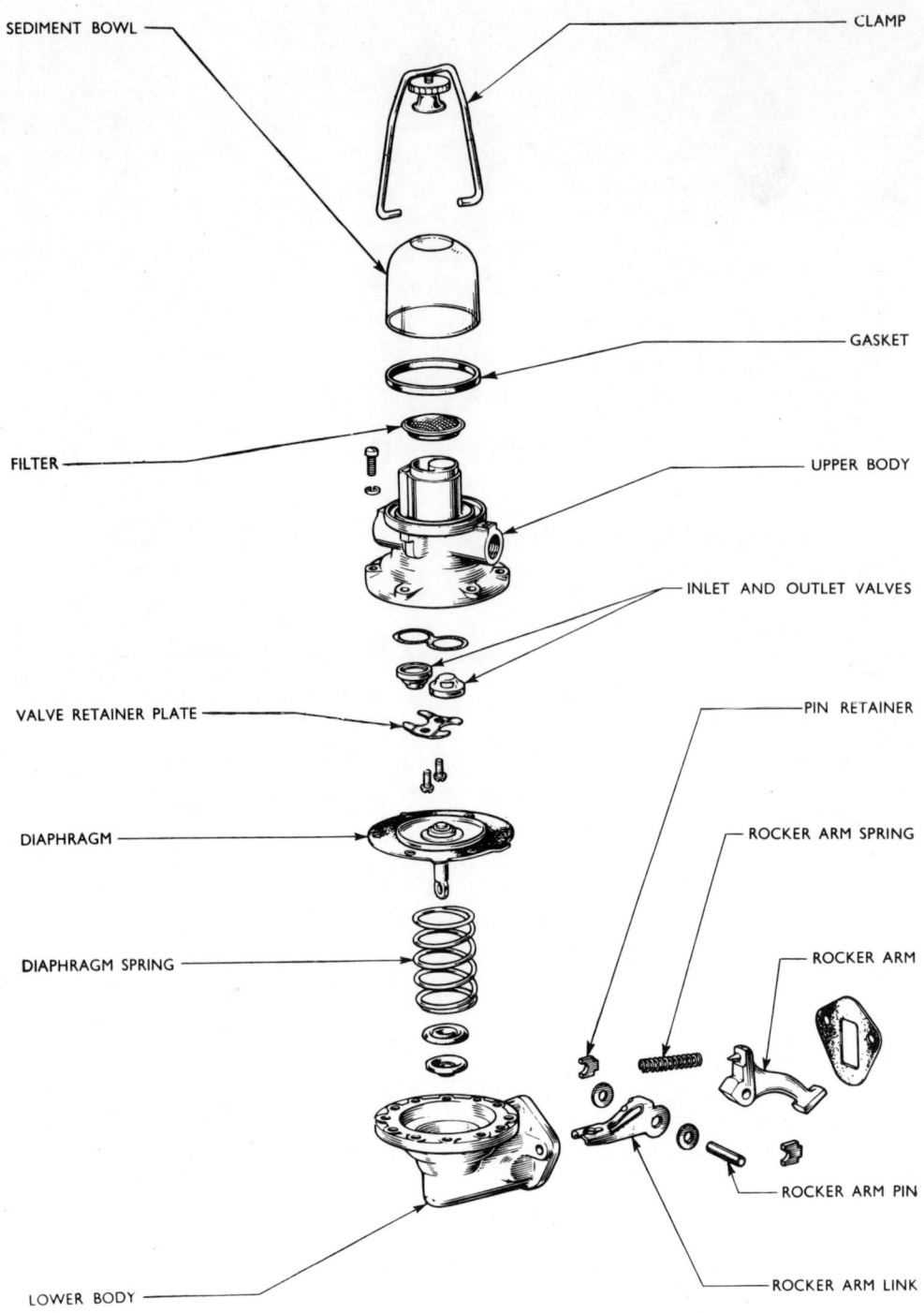

SEDIMENT BOWL

CLAMP

GASKET

FILTER

UPPER BODY

INLET AND OUTLET VALVES

VALVE RETAINER PLATE

PIN RETAINER

DIAPHRAGM

ROCKER ARM SPRING

DIAPHRAGM SPRING

ROCKER ARM

ROCKER ARM PIN

LOWER BODY

ROCKER ARM LINK

FIG 2:2 Components of fuel pump, larger type

FIG 2:3 Fuel pump removed from mounting flange

FIG 2:4 Small pump with cover removed, showing correct position of filter gauze

fuel in the pump chamber. If the latter is full the rocker arm reciprocates idly until fuel is used. In order to allow this, the arm is formed in two pieces united at the fulcrum. The part contacting the eccentric has an abutment which moves the second part coupled to the pullrod of the diaphragm. The eccentric arm is held in constant contact with the eccentric by a light compression spring to ensure quiet operation.

The fuel and delivery valves are of light spring-loaded plate type. Fuel is drawn in through a gauze filter screen, which in the case of the smaller pump is under a metal dome cover. The larger pump used on some engines has a transparent bowl over the screen.

Normal maintenance consists of removing the filter cover and gauze screen, and washing the latter in petrol about every 5000 miles if necessary. The metal reinforcing plate on the screen of the smaller pump seen on **FIG 2:4** should face upwards, while on the other type the screen is fitted so that its rim locates on the casting spigot. Before refitting the cover (or the transparent sediment bowl), these should also be cleaned, and a new gasket fitted if this is broken or has become hardened. It is most important that there is no leakage of air at this point, as any intake will reduce the pump suction effect, and in extreme cases will put the pump out of action.

2:2 Pump test

To test the pump, the delivery pipe is disconnected at the carburetter end, and its outlet led into a jar. When the engine is rotated by the starter, a good spurt of fuel should be obtained at each stroke of the pump (camshaft revolution). There should be no hesitancy in delivery or air bubbles present.

To test the suction it is necessary to use a vacuum gauge connected to the pump inlet union, in place of the pipe from the tank. The engine can then be run under power, on the carburetter contents, at idling speed. A vacuum reading of 8.5 inches of mercury should be obtained. The gauge should also take at least a minute to drop to zero, otherwise a faulty diaphragm must be suspected, or air-leaks elsewhere.

As the delivery pressure is dependent on the spring, it should not vary unless the diaphragm is faulty. leaks are of course generally obvious by the presence of petrol on the outside of the pump. If it is desired to take a pressure reading, a suitable gauge is connected to the delivery union. With the engine running as before (on the carburetter contents) the maximum pressure should be 2 lb and minimum 1.25 lb. Too low a pressure will starve the carburetter while if too high, flooding will be caused, leading to faulty mixture and highly erratic engine performance.

To overhaul the pump assuming it has been removed from the engine (Chapter 1) first remove the filter cover or sediment bowl, and the gauze screen. Then mark the upper and lower bodies at the diaphragm flange, adjacent to the smaller tab on the diaphragm, so that reassembly will be correct. Remove the screws and spring washers at the flange, and very carefully separate the joint. Ease the diaphragm away from its contact with the metal face, avoiding damage to the flexible material. The diaphragm pullrod is fixed permanently to the centre of the diaphragm, this item being supplied as a complete unit. The rod is freed from the rocker arm by turning the

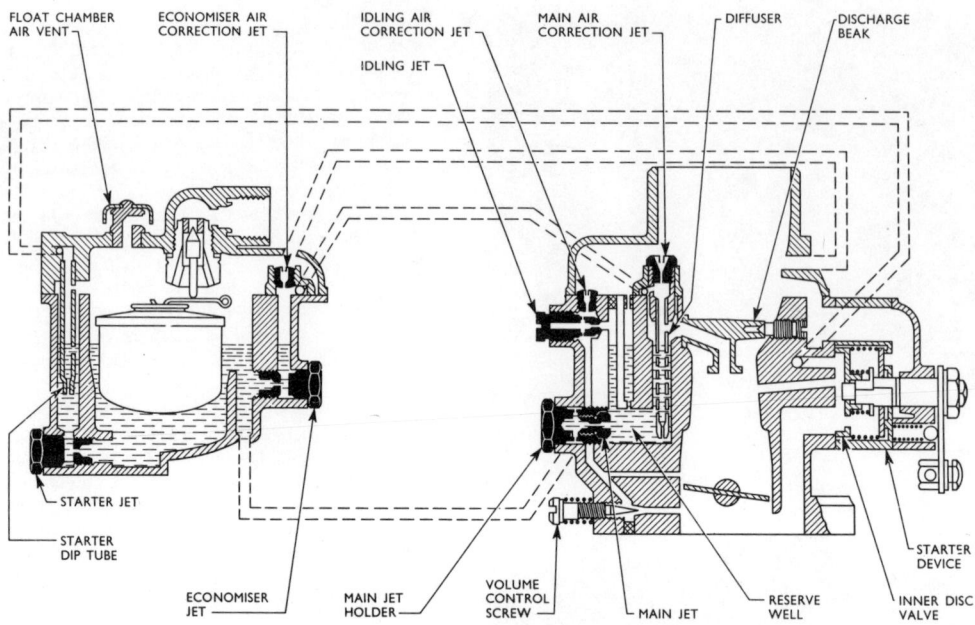

FLOAT CHAMBER AIR VENT — ECONOMISER AIR CORRECTION JET — IDLING AIR CORRECTION JET — IDLING JET — MAIN AIR CORRECTION JET — DIFFUSER — DISCHARGE BEAK

STARTER JET — STARTER DIP TUBE — ECONOMISER JET — MAIN JET HOLDER — VOLUME CONTROL SCREW — MAIN JET — RESERVE WELL — STARTER DEVICE — INNER DISC VALVE

FIG 2:5   Operational diagram of carburetter with progressive-starter device

diaphragm about a quarter-turn, in either direction relative to the lower body. After detaching, remove the spring, seal retainer and rubber seal.

2:3 Pump valves

The inlet and delivery valves are held in the top body by a plate secured by screws. They are in unit assemblies complete with their springs and seats, and can be taken out after removal of the two screws in the plate. Note that there is a figure-8 gasket interposed between the valves and body.

The rocker arm assembly in the lower body seldom requires attention, but if necessary the rocker arm fulcrum pin can be removed by reducing the peening over the two pin retainers, and withdrawing them. The pin is next taken out along with the arm and diaphragm link, return spring and washers.

Assuming that any defective components have been replaced, assembly of the lower body comprises re-alignment and assembly of the foregoing components. The rocker arm is positioned with its boss between the flanges of the diaphragm linkpiece, noting that the centre web of the latter and the spring seat on the rocker, are both uppermost. (This ensures the correct abutting action when pumping.) A thrust washer is now fitted next to the link on each side, and the whole inserted into the lower body casting, keeping the spring seat on the rocker uppermost. Put the compression spring into position, ensuring that it is located at its ends by the registers on the body and arm. Fit two new pin retainers into the body; make sure that they positively locate the pin in the casting, and then peen over the casting to secure them in position. If all is satisfactory the rocker arm will now operate against its spring; also when the diaphragm-end is held down (as when the carburetter is full) the other end of the arm assembly should be free to move up and down without

transmitting any motion. The diaphragm assembly must be examined very carefully for defects; if at all doubtful it must be replaced. To refit, the spring, oil seal washer and seal are first threaded over the pullrod. The end of the pullrod is next inserted into the end of the link, the grooves being engaged by turning the diaphragm through a quarter-turn so that the marks already made on the body align with the smaller tab on the diaphragm-edge. The upper body casting is now positioned over the diaphragm so that the mark on the flange aligns with that on the lower body. Insert the screws around the flange-edge to light finger tightness. Work the rocker arm by hand several times to allow the diaphragm to centralize itself. Finally, hold the arm fully 'up', so that the diaphragm is right down in the maximum-suction position, and tighten the flange screws very evenly.

It is quite unnecessary and wrong to use jointing compound on the diaphragm-edge to ensure a tight joint, but strict cleanliness must be observed both on the flange faces and the diaphragm itself.

The pump can next be held normally, and the valve assemblies refitted, first ensuring that the figure-8 gasket is in position. See that the valve assemblies are the correct way up, otherwise they will not function. The retainer plate is then refitted. The filter screen may now be replaced along with the cover or sediment bowl.

When refitting petrol pipes do not allow the flexible element to become twisted; hold the hexagon on the pipe with one spanner, while undoing or tightening the union nut with another one.

2:4 Carburetter with starter device

On all engines the carburetter is of the single-venturi downdraught type. Three variations are used, two with an accelerator pump and one without. The latter will be detailed first.

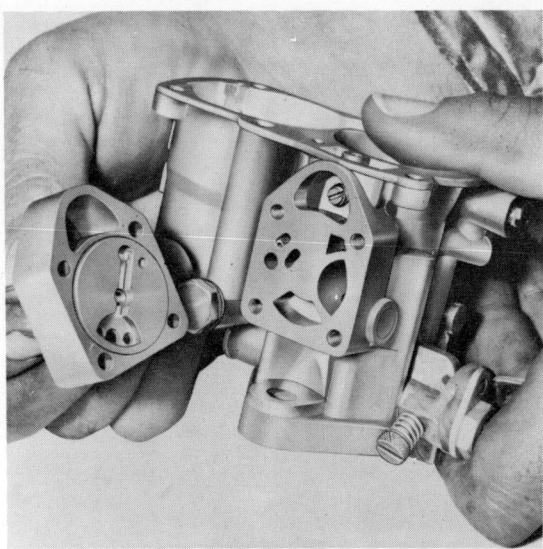

FIG 2:6   Starter device removed, showing disc valves

Reference to the operational diagram, **FIG 2:5**, shows that the type incorporates a two-stage progressive starter device, which weakens the mixture as the choke control is pushed to the off position. This device is mounted on the side of the carburetter body, and contains two disc valves of spring-loaded type. These valves are fitted on a spindle to which a lever is attached for operation by the choke control cable (see **FIG 2:6**). The outer valve disc is spring-loaded against the cover, in which are air-ports. The inner disc is formed with a machined slot, which connects the starter fuel supply drilling to the outlet port when the choke control is fully pulled out; this allows starting mixture to pass to the induction manifold.

2:5 Starting device operation

From the float chamber, fuel passes through the starter jet to the starter well. There is a dip-tube with air-bleed pressed into the float chamber cover and located in the starter jet well. The upper end of this tube is ducted by drillings in the carburetter body, to the fuel inlet port in the starter device. When the engine is spun by the starter motor, intake depression is communicated through the device outlet port, the slot in the valve disc, and the body drillings, to the top of the dip-tube. Thus, fuel is drawn up the dip-tube and emulsified by air drawn in via the air-bleed in the tube, and thence passes to the induction manifold by way of the body drillings and disc valve slot. When the engine starts, the manifold depression increases. This lifts the outer valve disc away from its seating against the light spring-loading, admitting additional air and thus weakening the mixture.

When the choke control is pushed to the intermediate position (which is definitely located by a spring-loaded ball) this rotates the disc valve spindle, to a position where the volume of mixture emerging from the dip-tube is considerably reduced. At the same time, the amount of air drawn past the outer disc is maximized. Air is also drawn through the starter air-bleed channel which again

reduces the volume of fuel drawn from the dip-tube. With the car being driven and the choke control in this position, the air speed through the choke tube, past the end of the starter air-bleed channel, will result in a depression in the channel, and draw additional mixture from the dip-tube. As the control is pushed further in, the valve discs are rotated and the mixture progressively weakened, until finally the fuel supply and starter air-ports are completely cut off.

2:6 Idling mixture

With the choke control fully in, starter device out of operation, and throttle in the idling position, the depression is concentrated on the idling discharge port and communicated, via the idling mixture volume control screw to the idling fuel and air correction jets. Petrol is supplied from the main jet to the reserve well, and is drawn through the idling jet from this well. The fuel thus metered is emulsified by air from the idling air correction jet, while extra air is drawn through the progression drilling. The amount of idling mixture supplied is controlled by the volume control screw, the mixture being further emulsified on discharge, by the air passing round the edge of the throttle valve-plate which is slightly open.

As the throttle is opened further, the passage of air creates a depression at the progression drilling, and mixture is supplied from here, in addition to that from the idling port.

2:7 Open-throttle operation

When the throttle is further opened, the air speed through the venturi increases and creates a depression around the main discharge beak. This is communicated to the main jet well and through the top drilling of the emulsion tube on the main air correction jet. Petrol is supplied through the main jet to the main and reserve wells, and depression on the beak draws from the former, the fuel being emulsified by air from the air correction jet, and through the lateral holes in the emulsion tube.

With increase of engine speed, and therefore air speed, the petrol level in the main jet well is lowered, which progressively uncovers the remaining holes in the emulsion tube. This increases the volume of air bled in, maintaining a correct and uniform mixture strength at all speeds.

2:8 Economy device

The economy device operation is controlled by the engine speed, which determines the air speed and depression at the main discharge beak. At high engine speeds the fuel from the main jet is supplemented by a discharge from the economizer jet, while at cruising and lower speeds the supply comes only from the former. Petrol is fed to the economizer jet well through the economizer jet. At the top of the jet well, and in the economizer body, are the air bleed and discharge ports. At high engine speeds, depression is communicated from the main jet well to the economizer discharge port, through the centre of the main jet diffuser. Thus, emulsified fuel is drawn from the economizer well to supplement the main jet discharge. With decrease of engine speed the economizer discharge is reduced until fuel is supplied only by the main jet.

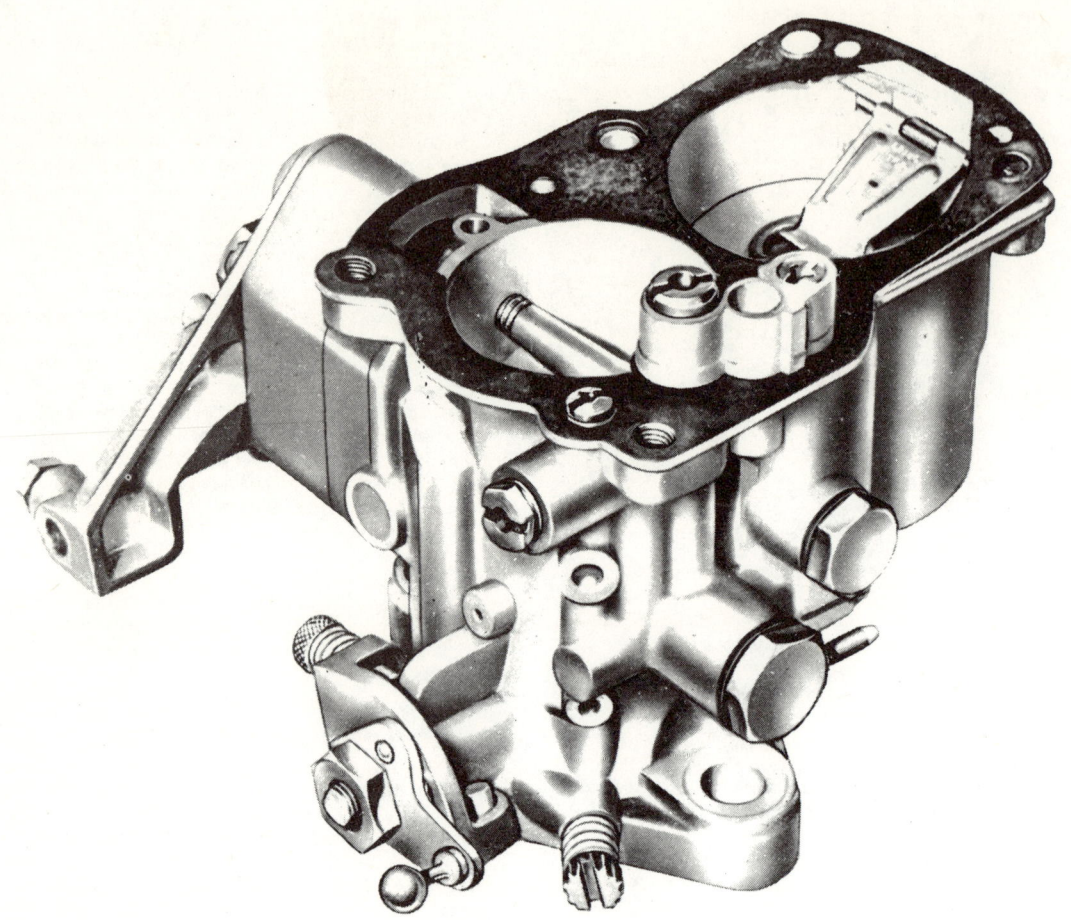

FIG 2:7 Carburetter with cover removed, showing float lever and jet positions

2:9 Dismantling

To remove the carburetter from the engine, first take off the air filter after unscrewing its clamp, and uncouple the petrol pipe and ignition control vacuum pipe. Detach the throttle control link from the lever ball joint, on to which it is spring-loaded, and disconnect the choke control cable and casing. After unscrewing the two flange nuts and lockwashers the carburetter and flange gasket can be lifted off.

When replacing, make sure that the flanges are perfectly clean, and fit a new gasket if the existing one is damaged in any way. Position the carburetter over the studs, and fit the washers and nuts, tightening the latter evenly and securely. When reconnecting the choke control, fit the outer casing of the cable so that there are three coils of the casing protruding through the attachment bracket. Check the operation, and if necessary adjust the length of the inner cable so as to leave a small gap between the control knob and the panel. This ensures that the starter device is fully out of action with the knob pushed in. The throttle link is coupled up by springing the

ball joint into position in the socket. Finally reconnect the fuel and vacuum pipes, and fit the air filter. If it is desired to dismantle the carburetter, first unscrew the four screws holding the float chamber cover, and remove the cover and gasket (see FIG 2:7). Detach the float by taking out the hinge-pin and arm. Take off the nut and flat washer from the end of the spindle of the starter device, pull the lever off the spindle, and extract the locking ball and spring. The starter device is then removed by taking out the four attaching screws. If access is required to the disc valves, remove the circlip which holds the inner cover to the shaft; the valves can then be detached as an assembly.

Unscrew the economizer and main jet air correction jets, from the body of the economizer, and lift off the body and diffuser tube assembly. Remove the gasket from the carburetter and economizer body. Take out the starter fuel jet, main jet holder (into which the main jet is screwed) idling fuel and idling air jets. Note that all the jets have fibre washers except the idling fuel jet.

The throttle plate and spindle can be removed after unscrewing the two screws holding the plate to the spindle.

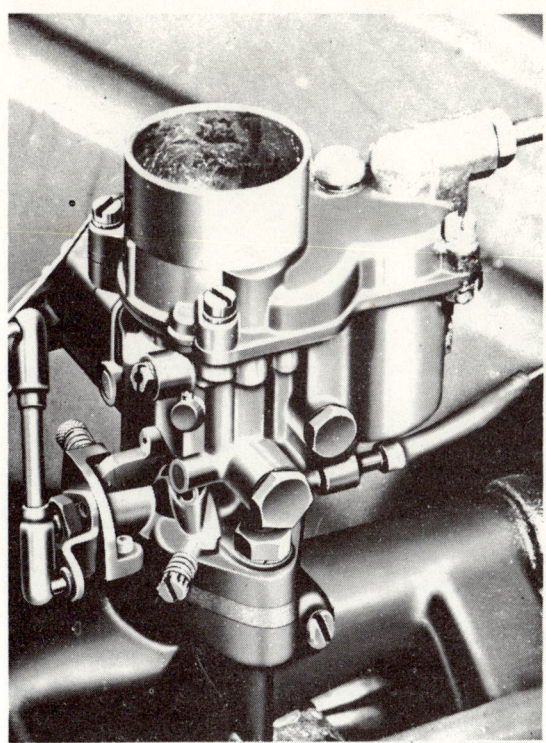

FIG 2:8 Carburetter mounted on engine, showing location of idling adjustment (left) and mixture volume control screws (bottom)

The carburetter is now completely dismantled, and should be thoroughly cleaned. Do not probe small passages or jets with wire, as this may alter critical dimensions; any blockages must be cleared by a compressed air blast, a tyre pump being perfectly adequate.

Defective parts must be replaced, but no alteration should be made to sized components such as jets, as these are selected to give the best all-round performance, including economy of fuel. Details are given in the Appendix. Gaskets and fibre washers should be renewed unless in perfect condition, which is unlikely after a long period of use.

2:10 Reassembly

If the throttle plate has been removed, this must be refitted first. Insert the spindle, and when assembling the plate note that the number 8 stamped thereon must face downwards, and towards the starter device when the throttle is closed. After tightening the two screws, lightly peen their ends over to ensure security. Replace the main jet in its holder, and fit the holder with its fibre washer, into the carburetter. Similarly, fit the starter and economizer fuel jets, and install the idling fuel and air correction jets. Note that the idling fuel jet is tapered on its inner end, and take care not to overtighten it. Replace the discharge beak, securing it with the taper-end clamp screw. Fit the gasket to the economizer body, assemble the body and diffuser tube, and fix in position with the single screw. Refit the economizer and main air correction

jets. Fit the disc valve assembly into the inner cover of the starter device, retain with the circlip, and replace the outer cover. Locate the ball and spring in the outer cover and set the disc valves with the slot in the inner disc vertical; then fit the operating lever. Check that, viewed from the front with the cable bracket to the right, the locking ball hole in the lever is to the left. If correct, replace the washer and nut to secure the lever. The starter device can then be assembled to the carburetter and fixed by the four screws.

Place the float in the float chamber noting that the cup washer is upwards, fit the lever with its curve at the end towards the float, and insert the hinge-pin. The cover may then be replaced, using a new gasket and tightening the four screws securely.

2:11 Adjustments

Incorrect operation is unlikely providing the carburetter is properly maintained. If adjustments are required, these are extremely simple.

The engine idling speed is adjusted by means of the slow-running screw at the throttle spindle. However, except in the case of very small adjustments to the idling rev/min, it is necessary to move this screw in conjunction with the second screw which controls the idling mixture volume as already described. These screws are shown on FIG 2:8. Note that both these screws have small coil springs under their heads; these must be in good condition otherwise the adjustment may alter due to vibration.

To obtain smooth idling, first warm up the engine to normal running temperature. Turn the slow-running screw on the throttle spindle clockwise (inwards) to speed up the engine slightly. Unscrew the volume control screw until the engine begins to run irregularly, or 'hunt', and then turn it clockwise very slowly to obtain smooth and even firing. At the same time, slow down the engine by turning the throttle screw anticlockwise. Do not attempt to obtain an unduly slow speed, otherwise the engine may stall at awkward moments; about 800 rev/min is quite slow enough. If 'hunting' recommences with this speed reduction, screw the volume control screw inwards by a very small amount, which should correct this. It should be emphasized that correct carburetter operation and adjustment is not to be expected unless the ignition and valve adjustments are properly set, and the air filter is clean.

2:12 Accelerator pump carburetter

The early type of carburetter, though similar in general operation to that already described, has a simple strangler-type choke valve instead of the starter device, and also incorporates an accelerator pump for giving a more rapid response to the throttle. An exploded view of the components is shown on FIG 2:9.

The operational description which follows can be further clarified by reference to the schematic diagram, FIG 2:10. The starting mixture is under control of the usual choke control cable which when pulled, closes a choke plate situated in the main air intake. At the same time, a connecting link opens the throttle by a small amount. This allows the induction pipe depression to be communicated to the main venturi area when the engine is spun by the starter motor. A suitably rich starting

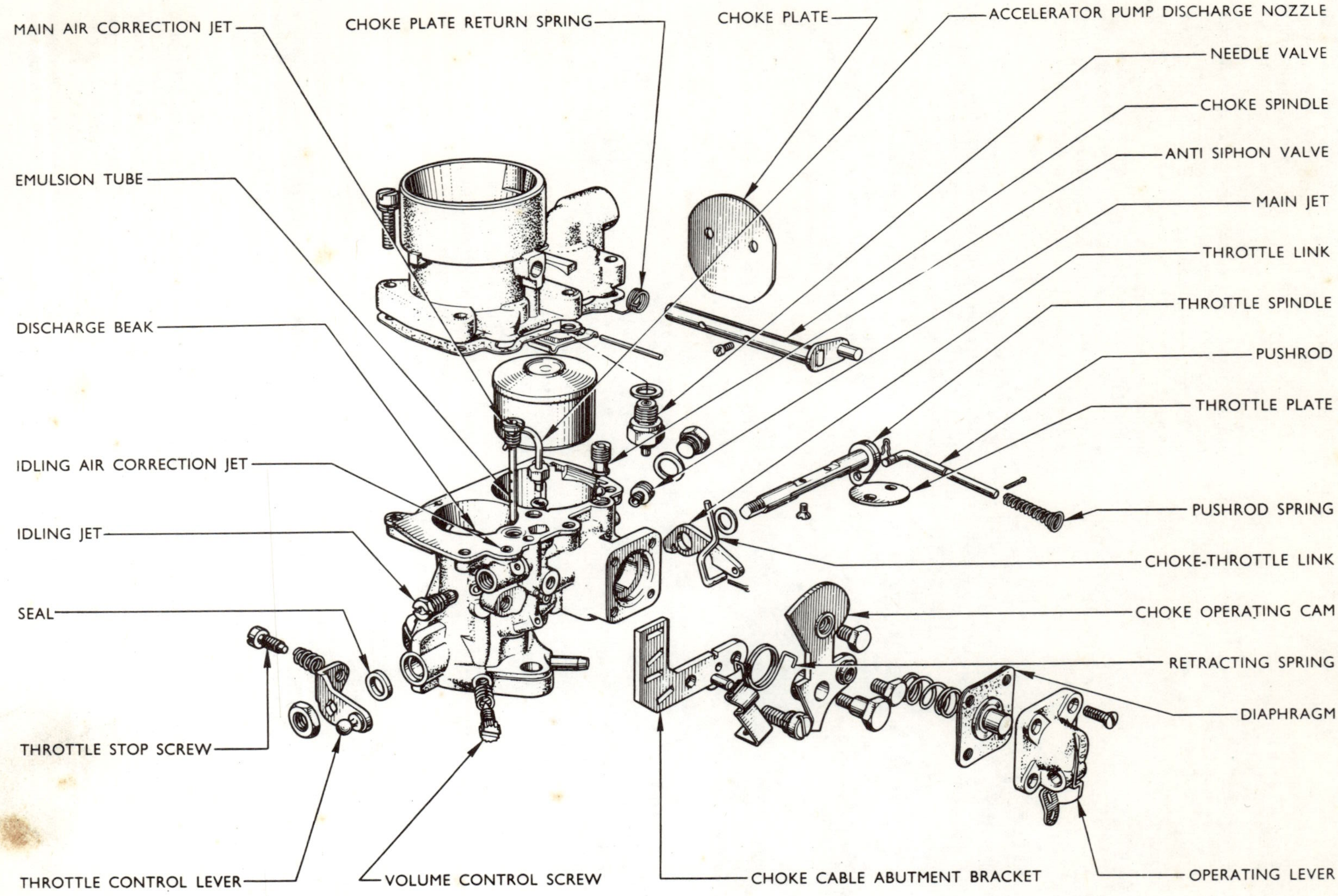

MAIN AIR CORRECTION JET

CHOKE PLATE RETURN SPRING

EMULSION TUBE

DISCHARGE BEAK

IDLING AIR CORRECTION JET

IDLING JET

SEAL

THROTTLE STOP SCREW

THROTTLE CONTROL LEVER

CHOKE PLATE

ACCELERATOR PUMP DISCHARGE NOZZLE

NEEDLE VALVE

CHOKE SPINDLE

ANTI SIPHON VALVE

MAIN JET

THROTTLE LINK

THROTTLE SPINDLE

PUSHROD

THROTTLE PLATE

PUSHROD SPRING

CHOKE-THROTTLE LINK

CHOKE OPERATING CAM

RETRACTING SPRING

DIAPHRAGM

OPERATING LEVER

CHOKE CABLE ABUTMENT BRACKET

VOLUME CONTROL SCREW

FIG 2:9   Components of accelerator-pump type carburetter

34

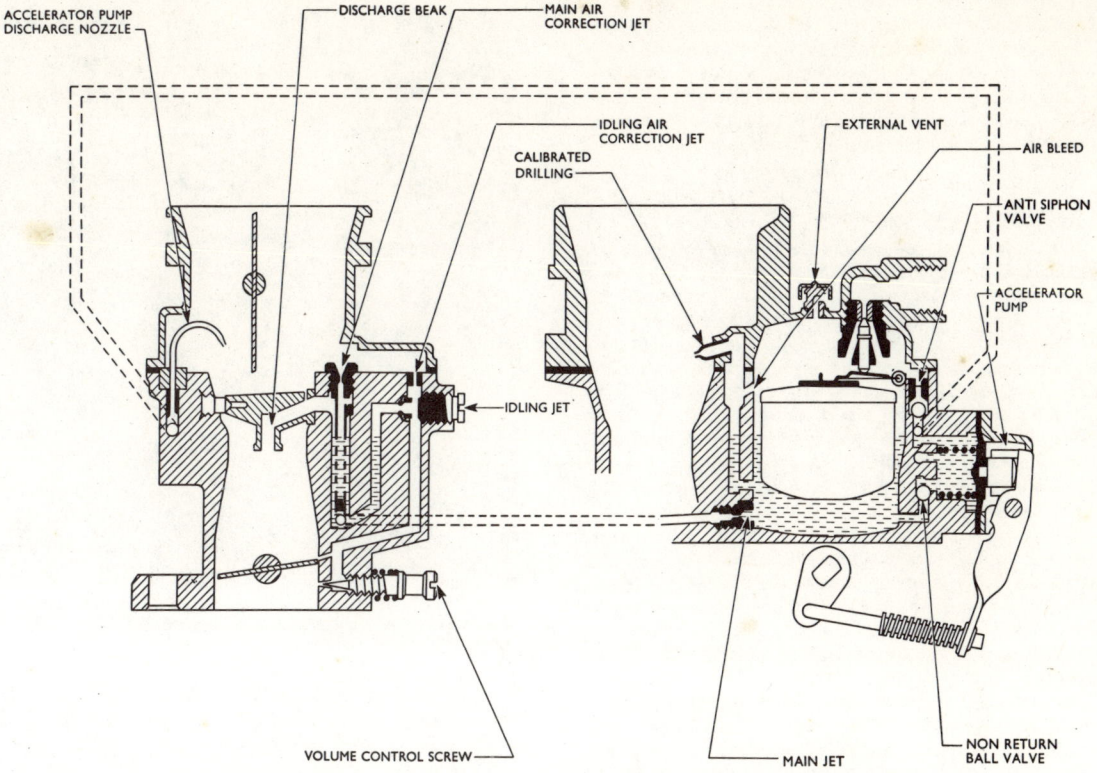

FIG 2:10 Operational diagram of accelerator-pump type carburetter

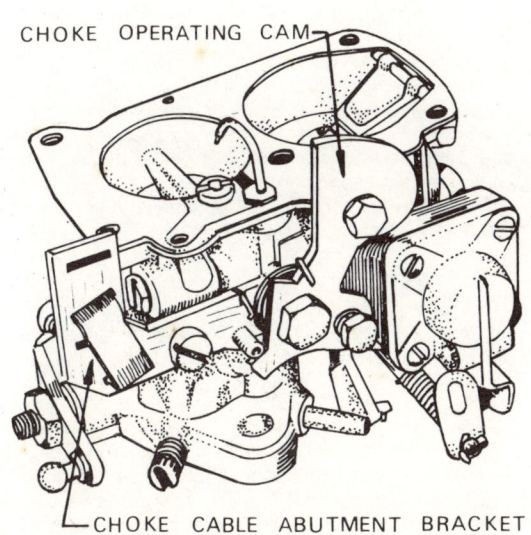

FIG 2:11 Carburetter with cover removed, showing pump and discharge nozzle and other details

mixture is thus discharged from the main spraying well, down the throughway and into the manifold. As soon as the engine fires, the increased depression causes the choke plate to open slightly, due to the latter being mounted on an offset spindle as shown on **FIG 2:10**. The mixture is thereby weakened and, in conjunction with the partly open throttle, provides a fast-idle setting which prevents the engine from stalling during the warm-up period. With increase of engine temperature, the choke control knob can be gradually pushed towards the fully-in position, and at normal working temperature it will of course be at the end of its travel, with the choke plate wide open and the air intake unobstructed.

The idling and main supply mixture is obtained in a similar manner to that described for the carburetter with starter device; the economy device is also similar.

2:13 Accelerator pump operation

The function of the accelerator pump is to provide smooth and rapid acceleration, and to prevent any hesitation on suddenly opening-up. To achieve this, the mixture is momentarily enriched by means of a diaphragm-type pump linked to the throttle spindle. The pump discharges a metered quantity of fuel into the main throughway of the carburetter when its diaphragm is displaced by throttle movement. A calibrated injector tube ensures correct placing of the fuel quantity into the main air-stream. This tube is clearly seen on **FIG 2:11**.

The pump is provided with ball valves, one of which prevents fuel from being fed back into the float chamber when on the injection stroke. The second valve assembly functions as a non-return to prevent air entering as the pump recharges, and also ensures that there is no overspill from the injector tube, which would possibly prejudice starting with the engine warm.

2:14 Removal and overhaul

The carburetter is removed in accordance with previous instructions. To dismantle, first take out the five screws and remove the float chamber cover and gasket. Lift off the float arm and hinge pin and remove the float. Remove the splitpin on the accelerator pump pushrod. Unscrew the four screws holding the pump to the carburetter body, and detach the pump body complete with its operating arm, diaphragm and return spring. The outer spring clip retaining the link from choke to throttle is next detached, followed by the screw holding the link to the choke operating arm. The link is then eased clear of the carburetter.

Take out the centre bolt holding the choke operating cam and spring, and unscrew the screw which retains the choke cable bracket; remove the bracket. Unscrew the idling jet, high-speed air correction jet, and emulsion tube assembly, and lift off the discharge nozzle of the pump. Unscrew the anti-siphon valve and take out the glass ball.

If it is desired to remove the discharge beak, the taper-ended screw which retains this is first unscrewed. However, removal of the beak is not normally necessary, and on replacing it, the taper-ended screw must be locked by means of a lead shot inserted through the vertical drilling immediately above the screw. This is done after the screw has been securely tightened.

Remove the main jet after unscrewing the bolt and flat washer. Withdraw the throttle spindle after taking out the two screws securing the throttle plate. This completes the dismantling operation. The parts must be inspected and dealt with as already described, it being necessary to check also the condition of the pump diaphragm and valves.

2:15 Reassembly

Fit the throttle spindle and attach the plate, noting that when in the closed position the number 8 stamped on the plate is facing downwards and away from the accelerator pump. After tightening the two screws, lightly peen over their ends for security.

Fit the main jet, blanking plug, and washer, also the idling and main air correction jets, emulsion tube assembly and accelerator pump discharge nozzle. Insert the glass ball and fit the anti-siphon valve. If the discharge beak has been removed, secure it firmly with the screw; the latter is then locked in position by a lead shot as already detailed.

The choke cable bracket is next fitted with its screw finger tight. Locate the choke operating arm and spring in their correct positions, using the hexagon-head bolt as a guide. Make sure that the inner end of the spring is in the slot in the bracket, and the outer end against the V-cut in the cam. Tighten both screws securely when all is correct.

FIG 2:12 Carburetter mounted on engine showing location of idling adjustment (top) and mixture volume control screws (lower)

The link from choke to throttle is next replaced; use a new spring clip if necessary. Refit the pushrod to the spindle link, again using a new spring clip if required. Fit the pushrod spring, attach the accelerator pump lever to the pushrod, and replace the splitpin.

The diaphragm and return spring assembly are next fitted into the pump housing, the unit offered up to the carburetter body, and the four screws inserted; tighten the latter evenly and securely. The action of the diaphragm should then be checked by working the lever. Replace the float in the float chamber, noting that the cup washer must be upwards, and fit the float lever with its curved end towards the float. The cover, with a new gasket, is then replaced and secured with its five screws. While this is being done, the choke plate must be held in the fully-open position, to give access to the screws.

The carburetter is refitted to the engine in accordance with previous details.

2:16 Adjustments

The slow-running is adjusted in a similar manner to that already described. The remaining adjustments concern the choke and the accelerator pump (see **FIG 2:12**).

There should be about .025 inch free play in the choke operating cable when the knob is pushed fully home, and this is achieved at the cable-end as in the case of the starter-device carburetter. When the choke plate is in the closed position for starting, the throttle should be opened to an extent which will allow the shank of a 1.1 mm (No. 57) drill to be inserted between the throttle plate edge and the carburetter throughway, at right angles to the spindle. This amount is equal to about three turns of the throttle-stop (slow-running) screw, from the point at which it abuts the fixed stop when the throttle is completely closed. If this method is used, it is first necessary to take out the screw and remove the coil spring. With the throttle opened to the degree stated, the choke to throttle link is then adjusted so that the cam is in the fully-closed position.

The accelerator pump stroke is normally that which is obtained when the pushrod is fitted into the outer elongated hole in the operating lever, with the splitpin through the outer hole in the pushrod. This setting injects an amount of fuel acceptable for operation in temperate conditions. However, for very cold climate the stroke can be reduced if necessary, by fitting the pushrod through the inner hole in the lever; the splitpin is then inserted into the inner hole in the pushrod. The Ford-manufactured carburetter fitted to the latest type cars is similar in construction and operation to the accelerator pump carburetter described. Slow-running adjustment is similar to previous descriptions but choke plate, accelerator pump and float level adjustments are shown on **FIGS 2:13, 2:14, 2:15, 2:16** and **2:17**. Removal, dismantling, reassembly and refitting are similar operations to those previously described.

2:17 General

If correctly adjusted and supplied with clean fuel, the carburetter is unlikely to give trouble. Should blockages occur, it is rarely necessary to dismantle the complete assembly, as most of the small orifices are accessible from outside. At very long intervals, however, it is advisable to give all parts a complete cleaning, particularly the float chamber in which sediment will collect. It has long been the fashion to blame the carburetter for obscure engine faults, but before making such assumptions it is essential that the other engine systems are checked for correct operation. This also applies when carrying out adjustments to the carburetter.

2:18 Air filter

Air filters may be of either the dry gauze, paper element, or oil bath type. The dry gauze type is clamped to the top of the carburetter, with its air inlet pipe pointing forward and left. The top cover is detachable by removing the centre screw, this exposing the gauze element which can be lifted out. The gauze is serviced by washing in petrol and allowing to dry; the cleaner body is also thoroughly cleaned. The element is then dipped in clean engine oil, the surplus shaken off, and the element refitted into the body, after which the top cover is replaced. This should be done every 5000 miles.

The paper element type of filter is dealt with in a similar manner, except that the element is discarded and replaced by a new one at the same mileage. In both types it is advisable to replace any sealing rings in the cover which appear unserviceable. The oil bath type is serviced by removing from the engine, taking care to keep it level as otherwise oil will be spilled. The hose clamp and centre wingnut will already have been removed, and the top cover and element can next be lifted from the body. The dirty oil is now poured out from the filter bowl, and both bowl, cover and element washed in petrol and allowed to dry. The body can then be refitted. Next refill the body with clean oil to the level indicated by the arrow inside. The cover and element are then replaced and the wingbolt and hose refitted.

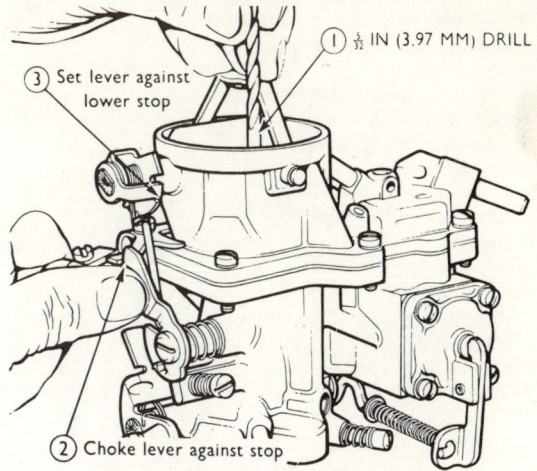

FIG 2:13 Choke adjustment. Set the controls as shown in 2, and 3, depress the choke plate and check as in 1. Bend the tab on the choke spindle to adjust

① $\frac{5}{32}$ IN (3.97 MM) DRILL

③ Set lever against lower stop

② Choke lever against stop

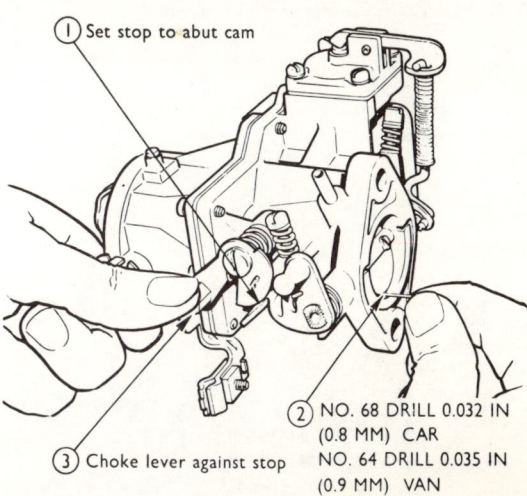

FIG 2:14 Fast-idle adjustment. Set the controls as shown in 1, and 3, and check clearance of throttle valve as shown at 2. Adjust the throttle lever tab to obtain the correct clearance

① Set stop to abut cam

② NO. 68 DRILL 0.032 IN (0.8 MM) CAR
NO. 64 DRILL 0.035 IN (0.9 MM) VAN

③ Choke lever against stop

2:19 Fault diagnosis

(a) Leakage or insufficient fuel delivered

1 Air vent in tank restricted
2 Petrol pipes blocked
3 Air leaks at pipe connections
4 Pump or carburetter filters blocked
5 Pump gaskets faulty
6 Pump diaphragm defective
7 Pump valves sticking or seating badly
8 Fuel vapourizing in pipe lines due to heat

(b) Excessive fuel consumption

1 Carburetter needs adjusting
2 Fuel leakage
3 Sticking controls or choke device
4 Dirty air cleaner
5 Excessive engine temperature
6 Brakes binding
7 Tyres under-inflated
8 Idling speed too high
9 Car overloaded

(c) Idling speed too high

1 Rich fuel mixture
2 Carburetter controls sticking
3 Slow-running screws incorrectly adjusted
4 Worn carburetter butterfly valve

(d) No fuel delivery

1 Float needle stuck
2 Vent in tank blocked
3 Pipe line obstructed
4 Pump diaphragm damaged
5 Inlet valve in pump stuck open
6 Bad air leak on suction side of pump

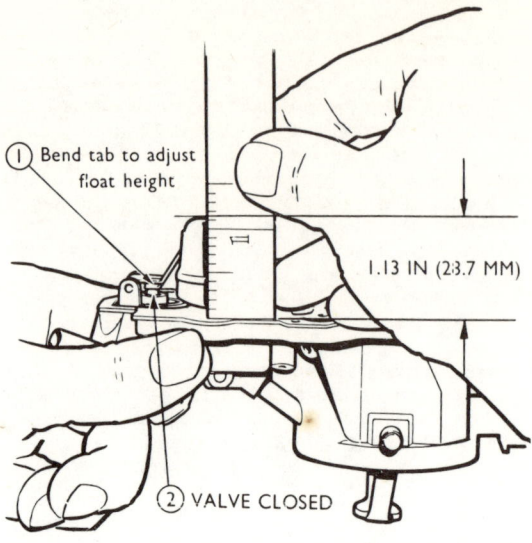

FIG 2:16 Minimum float height above float chamber cover face. Adjust as shown

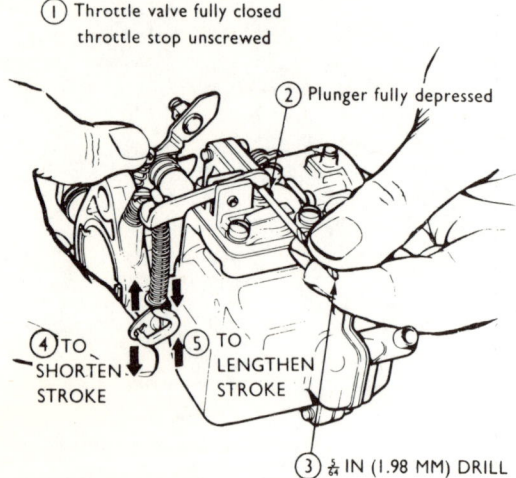

FIG 2:15 Accelerator pump stroke adjustment. With settings as shown in 1, and 2, check the clearance between the operating lever and the plunger, as shown at 3. Bend the gooseneck as shown by the arrows at 4, and 5, to adjust

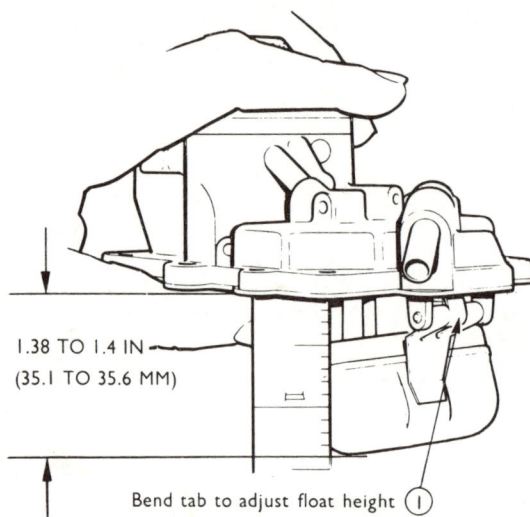

FIG 2:17 Maximum float height above float chamber cover face. Adjust as shown

CHAPTER 3

THE IGNITION SYSTEM

The ignition timing is controlled in the usual manner by a combination of engine speed and induction manifold pressure. A spring-loaded centrifugal governor advances the ignition as rev/min increases, while a diaphragm influenced by manifold pressure does likewise in conditions of low pressure, i.e. restricted throttle opening. The converse applies in both cases.

The governor mechanism turns the contact breaker cam in the direction of rotation as the governor weights fly outwards against spring tension. The vacuum mechanism has the diaphragm linked to the plate on which the breaker points are mounted, so that pull on the diaphragm under low pressure moves the plate in the opposite direction to that of the cam's rotation.

3 : 1 Automatic timing

The combination follows extremely closely the requirements of the engine in all conceivable conditions. When accelerating hard, hill climbing on a wide throttle and so on, the manifold pressure is high and the vacuum device retards the spark, while fast level-road operation with relatively low throttle opening gives a low absolute manifold pressure (high vacuum) and thus advances the

spark. The centrifugal mechanism also retards and advances under these respective conditions, so that little throttle and maximum revs gives maximum advance, and large throttle and minimum revs gives maximum retard.

The two controlling agencies are however very carefully graded to suit any particular engine type. The vacuum mechanism does not operate at idling speed because the throttle closes off the end of the vacuum pipe, the connection being suitably arranged for this in the carburetter throughway; the spark thus remains retarded for starting.

The centrifugal governor springs have different tensions so that the action of the weights is fully progressive, and in direct proportion to rev/min. The correct movement of the weights is aided by arranging them to follow a definite guided path as they move.

In view of the care taken to ensure suitability of the distributor unit for the engine, it is essential that the correct type is used. The details which follow refer to distributors of Lucas manufacture as shown on **FIGS 3 : 1** and **3 : 2,** these differing only in minor details. The distributor of Ford manufacture used on 1966 and later cars is described later in this chapter.

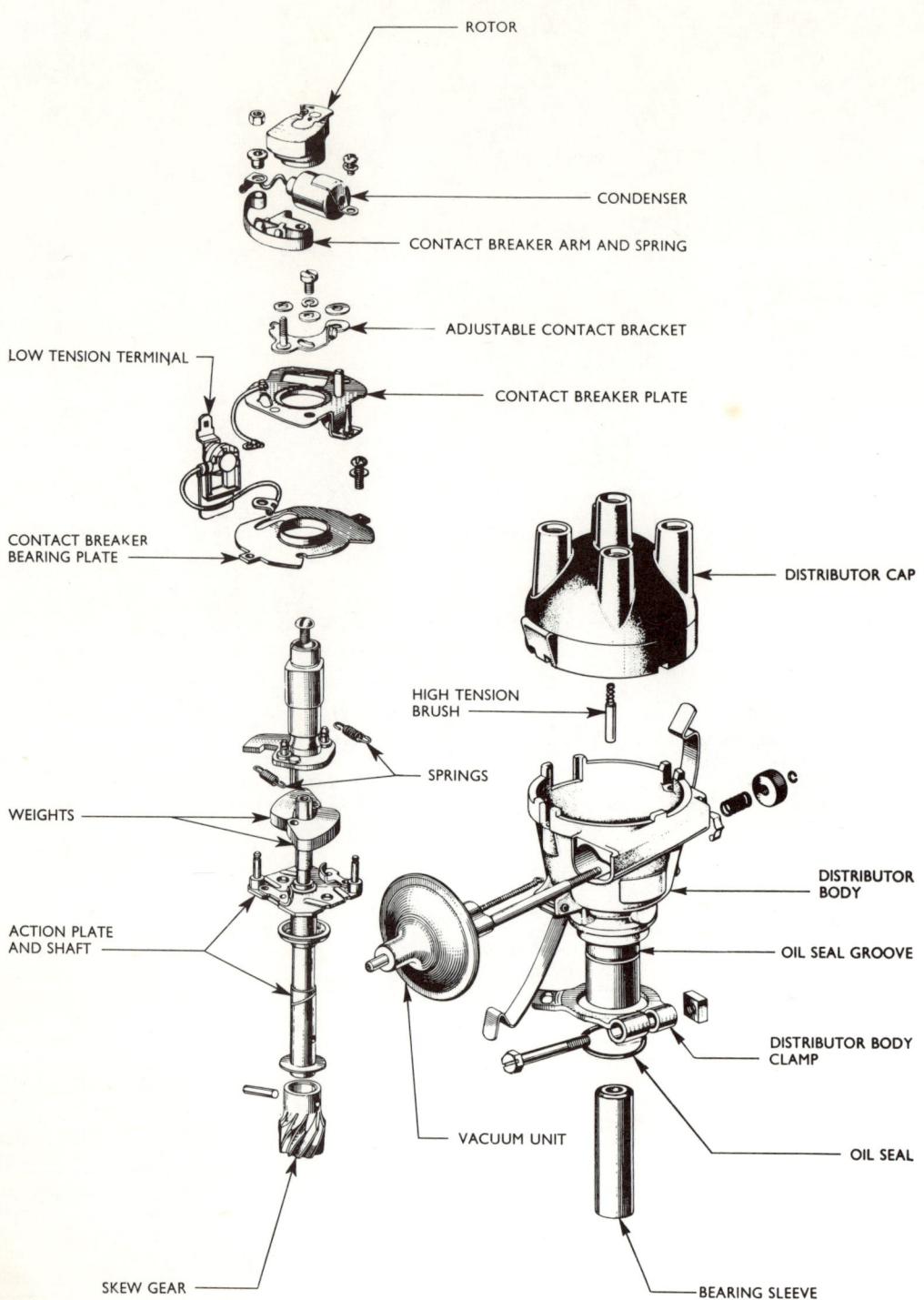

ROTOR

CONDENSER

CONTACT BREAKER ARM AND SPRING

ADJUSTABLE CONTACT BRACKET

LOW TENSION TERMINAL

CONTACT BREAKER PLATE

CONTACT BREAKER BEARING PLATE

DISTRIBUTOR CAP

HIGH TENSION BRUSH

WEIGHTS

SPRINGS

ACTION PLATE AND SHAFT

DISTRIBUTOR BODY

OIL SEAL GROOVE

DISTRIBUTOR BODY CLAMP

OIL SEAL

VACUUM UNIT

SKEW GEAR

BEARING SLEEVE

FIG 3:1   Components of Lucas distributor, first type

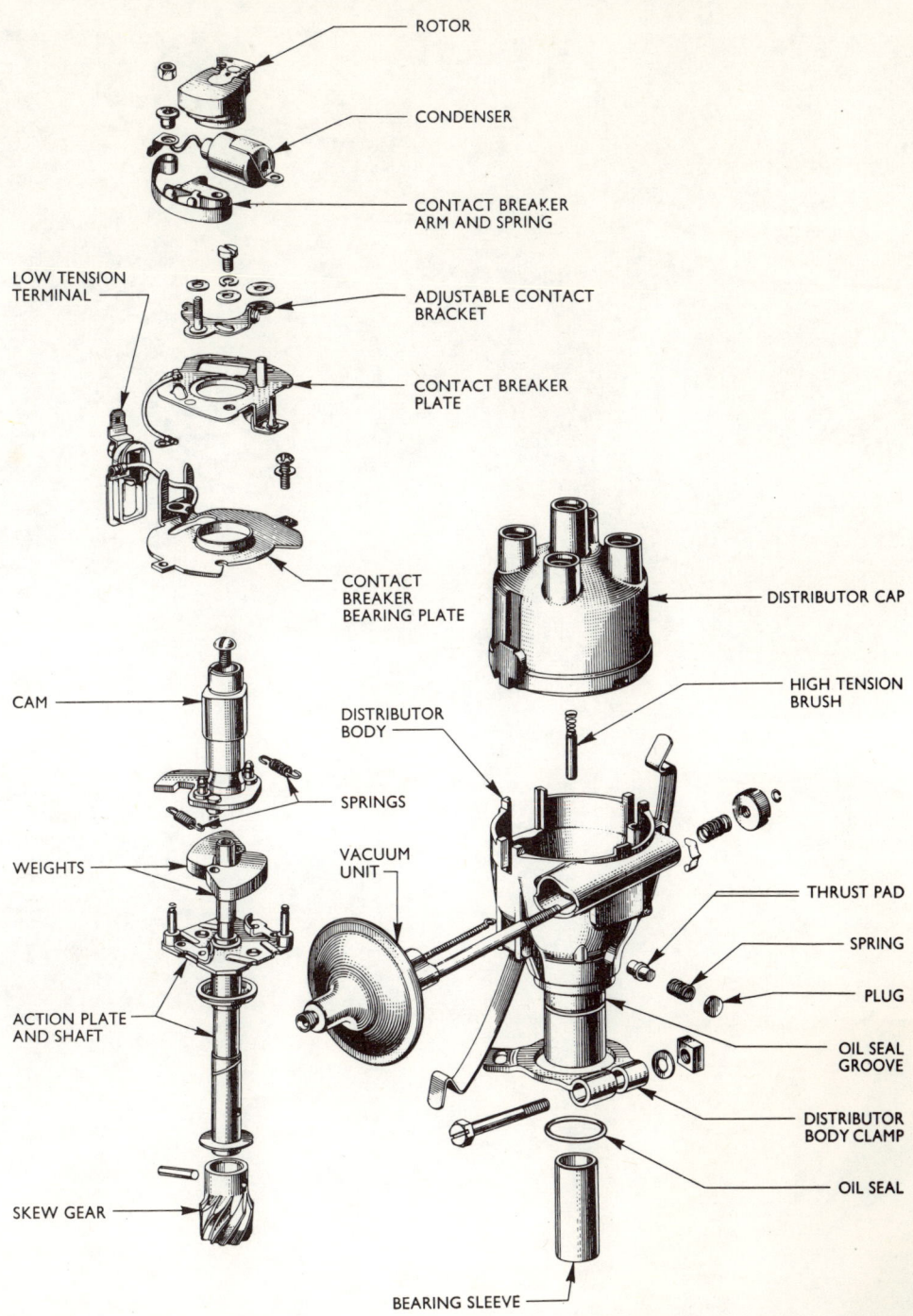

ROTOR

CONDENSER

CONTACT BREAKER
ARM AND SPRING

LOW TENSION
TERMINAL

ADJUSTABLE CONTACT
BRACKET

CONTACT BREAKER
PLATE

CONTACT
BREAKER
BEARING PLATE

DISTRIBUTOR CAP

CAM

DISTRIBUTOR
BODY

HIGH TENSION
BRUSH

SPRINGS

WEIGHTS

VACUUM
UNIT

THRUST PAD

SPRING

PLUG

ACTION PLATE
AND SHAFT

OIL SEAL
GROOVE

DISTRIBUTOR
BODY CLAMP

SKEW GEAR

OIL SEAL

BEARING SLEEVE

FIG 3:2   Components of Lucas distributor, second type

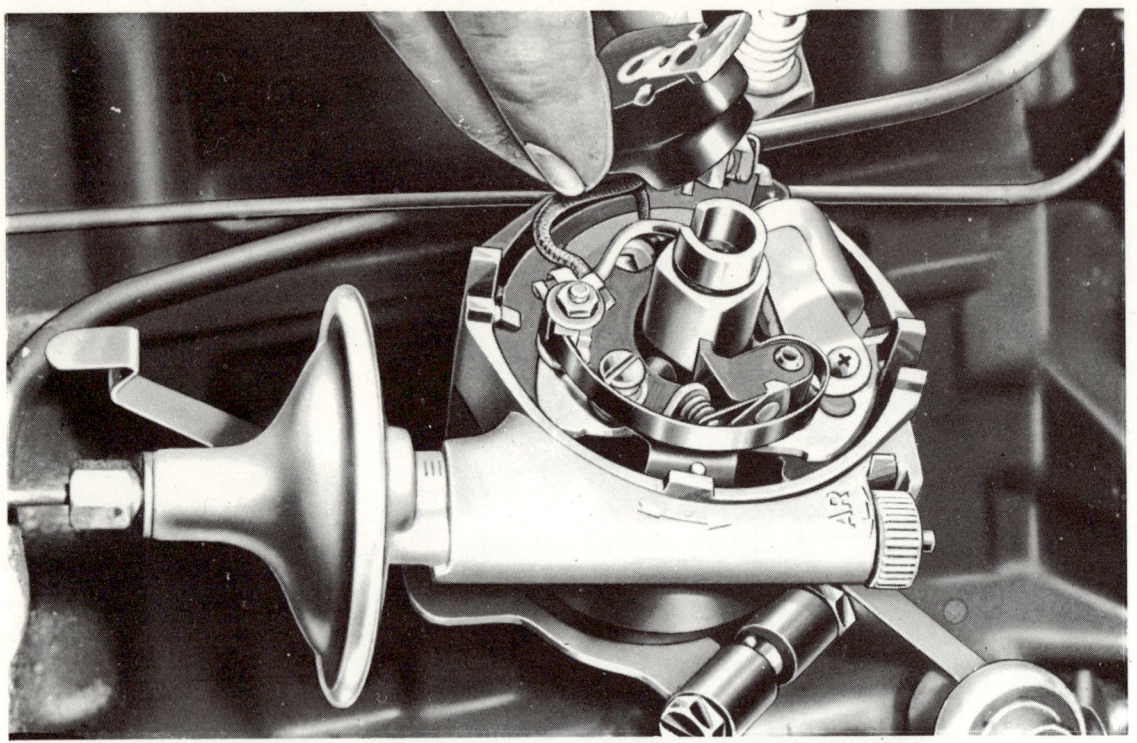

FIG 3:3 Position of cam-lobe and heel, with contact points fully open

FIG 3:4 Correct positioning of contact points for gap gauging

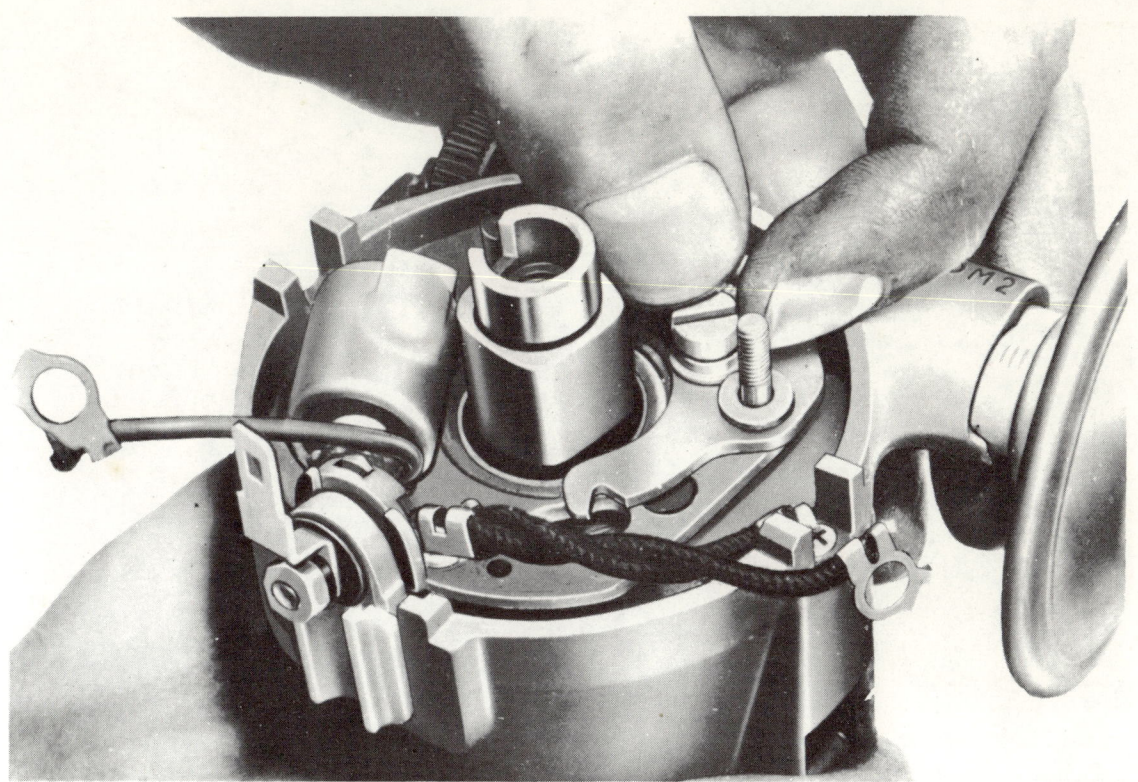

FIG 3 : 5   Removal of fixed contact point

3 : 2 Maintenance, Lucas distributor

Normal maintenance consists of lubricating the cam with petroleum jelly, and the spindle, governor weights, and moving contact arm pivot with engine oil, every 5000 miles. The cam spindle is oiled by removing the distributor rotor and applying two drops of oil to the spindle centre (there being an oil passage around the bolt head). The weights can be oiled through the openings in the breaker base plate. It is essential not to overdo lubrication, particularly of the cam and breaker arm pivot, as an excess will encourage electrical trouble.

To adjust the contact breaker points, the distributor cap and rotor arm are first removed. Then the engine must be turned until the fibre heel of the moving contact is resting on the tip of one of the cam lobes; this position is clarified on **FIG 3 : 3**. The single locking screw which holds the adjustable bracket of the other contact is now slackened. The bracket can be moved by means of the slot in its end (the bracket will swing about the moving contact pivot) to obtain the correct gap between the points, which should be .014 to .016 inch. It is essential that the points are correctly aligned, and meet face-on as seen on **FIG 3 : 4,** and the adjustable contact bracket may be bent slightly to assist this. Having set the gap, tighten the locking screw, and recheck to make sure nothing has moved. When refitting the rotor arm see that the moulded key engages the slot in the top of the cam, and that its lower face abuts firmly on to the register. The distributor cap can then be replaced.

Contact breaker points give no trouble over long periods and do not require constant dressing; they can however be given attention with a fine emery stone if considered advisable. To remove for this purpose, the distributor rotor is taken off as before, and the moving contact arm can then be detached, after unscrewing the terminal nut and removing the nylon bush and condenser leads. The end of the spring can then be pulled off the terminal post, simultaneously with removing the fibre rocker from its pivot. Note the fibre washers on the terminal and pivot posts.

The detachable contact will come clear after taking out its adjusting screw completely, as shown on **FIG 3 : 5**. If the contacts are pitted or badly worn they must be renewed as a matched set.

Replacement is largely a reversal of the above procedure. The locking screw in the adjustable contact plate should be fully tightened until the points have been adjusted. The pivot post for the moving contact must be lightly lubricated before the arm is fitted; note also that the fibre washers are in position before putting the arm on its pivot, and the spring-end on the terminal post.

The low-tension and condenser leads are next fitted to the terminal post above the spring-end, the nut replaced, and securely tightened.

3 : 3 Dismantling

When difficult starting is experienced from an ignition defect and the contact breaker points show signs of

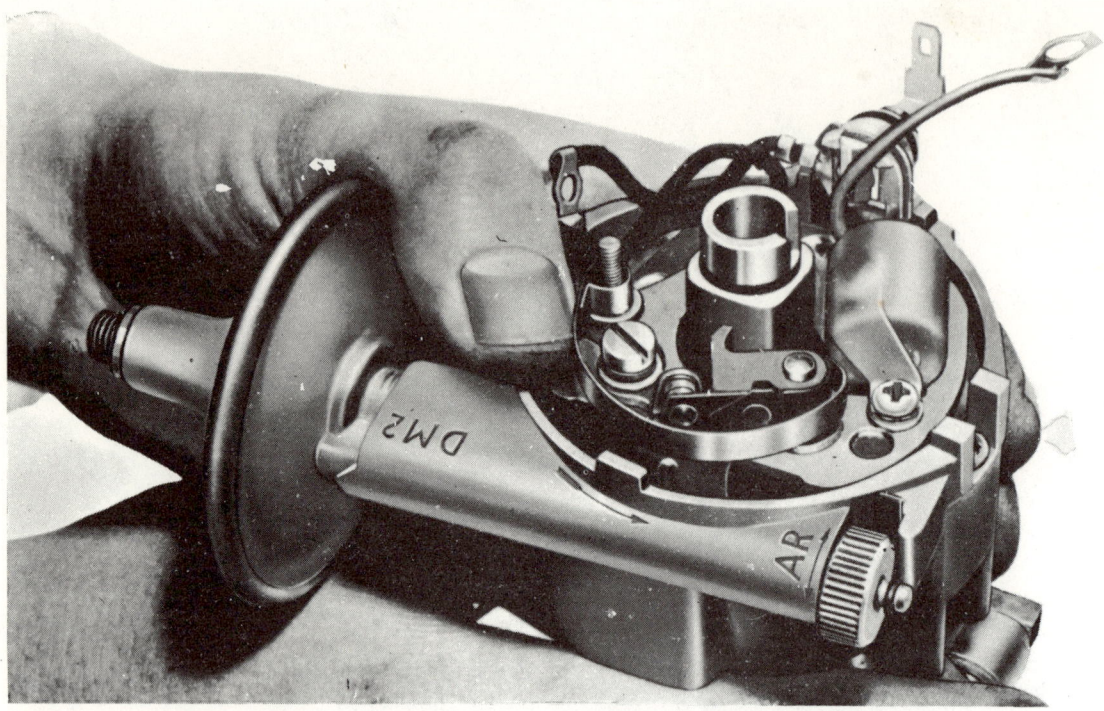

FIG 3:6 Condenser location, showing single attachment screw

excessive burning, the condenser is likely to be at fault; the burning of points is however the best guide, and condensers need never be replaced unnecessarily through faulty diagnosis. Electrical test equipment is of course available, but probably most owners will have to look for the signs aforementioned. The condenser capacity is .18 to .22 Mf.

The condenser is removed by taking its lead off the terminal post as already described, and then removing the single screw holding it to the breaker base plate, which can be seen on **FIG 3 : 6.** As the condenser has a definite location on the plate, it cannot be refitted wrongly, but make sure that its lead is not trapped, and with no possibility of short-circuiting.

If it is desired to dismantle the complete distributor unit, this must be removed from the engine, having first disconnected the lead from the coil, the primary wire to the contact breaker terminal and the vacuum pipe from the manifold. The clamp bolt is then slackened, and the assembly withdrawn. The contact breaker points are removed as already described, also the condenser. The tension spring from the vacuum unit is next unhooked from its pin on the plate. Now take out the two screws holding the plate to the body, noting that one of the screws also secures the earth lead. Remove the low tension terminal at the edge of the plate by sliding it out of its location bracket along with the nylon block and short lead. The plate can then be lifted off. It will be noted that the plate also combines with it, the bottom bearing plate on which it rotates for automatic ignition timing. The two portions can be separated by turning the top plate fully anti-clockwise, until the peg enters the opening at the end of the slot in the lower plate as on **FIG 3 : 7.** If the

spring clip is then disengaged, the two plates will come apart.

The centrifugal governor is now exposed. The weight springs can be unhooked from their pegs on the cam plate, and the screw removed in the top of the shaft above the cam; the cam can then be lifted clear of the weights.

The springs are unhooked from the pegs on the action plate, and the weights removed.

If excessive end float is apparent in the main shaft, or other wear in this part, it is necessary to relieve the end of the pin securing the skew gear at the bottom end, and drive out the pin with a thin punch; the gear and its washer can then be taken off. The shaft will pull out of the bearings along with the action plate. There is a spacing washer below the latter.

The vacuum unit is detached by removing the circlip holding the advance adjustment nut at the screwed end of the rod, and taking off the milled nut; the unit is then pulled out of the body. Make sure that the linking spring and milled nut spring do not get lost, as they may fly out. The diaphragm unit is sealed, and must not be taken apart. There is a thrust pad bearing against the upper journal of the main shaft, and if this is worn it can be removed by drilling out its cap and removing the spring and pad.

3 : 4 Reassembly

To reassemble all the parts after checking for wear and cleaning, the thrust pad (if removed) is first replaced, the spring being located on the pad and the whole inserted into the body. A new retaining cap is necessary, this being lightly tapped in the centre so as to hold it in the body.

The spacing washer is now put on the shaft under the action plate, and the shaft refitted. The thrust washer is placed on the lower end, followed by the gear, and a new retaining pin fitted, using a punch. If a new thrust washer has been fitted, rotation of the assembled shaft through a few revolutions (by hand) will remove the three 'artificial' protrusions on the washer and provide the correct end-play.

If the shaft is new, it will have to be drilled for the skew gear pin, using the holes in the gear as a guide for a No. 16 (.177 inch or 4.5 mm) drill. With a new thrust washer also fitted, the axial location of the gear on the shaft will of course be just right, as the end float is corrected afterwards as above. Next fit the governor weight springs to the pegs on the action plate, and also the weights, with their flat sides abutting the cam ramps and the cutaways nearest to the shaft. Refit the cam, ensuring that it can turn freely; the pegs on the cam base are then engaged in the holes in the weights, and the top screw refitted. Next the other ends of the springs are hooked over the pegs in the cam base. Move the cam with the shaft held rigidly to test the action, noting that all the parts move freely, and lightly oil all components of the motion.

3 : 5 Vacuum unit

The vacuum unit can be refitted after checking its linkage for wear. The adjustment nut, spring, circlip and linking spring are replaced as they come off, the nut being turned until the fourth line on the scale (on the shank between the diaphragm housing and the main body) is in line with the edge of the latter.

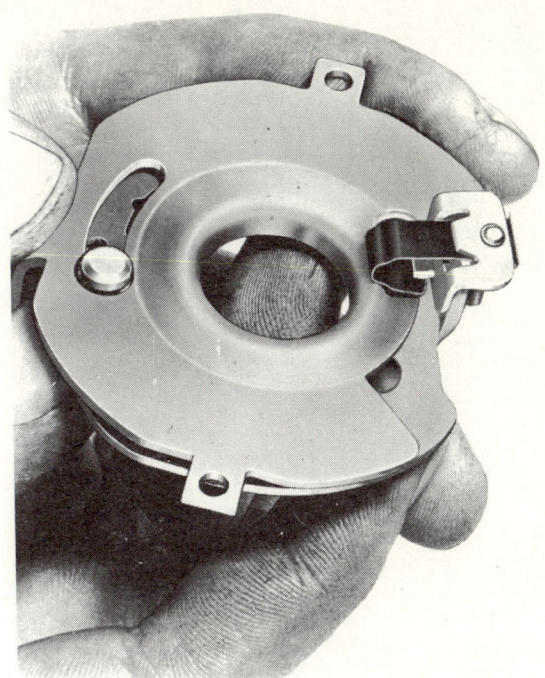

FIG 3 : 7 Method of holding and separating fixed and moving base plate portions

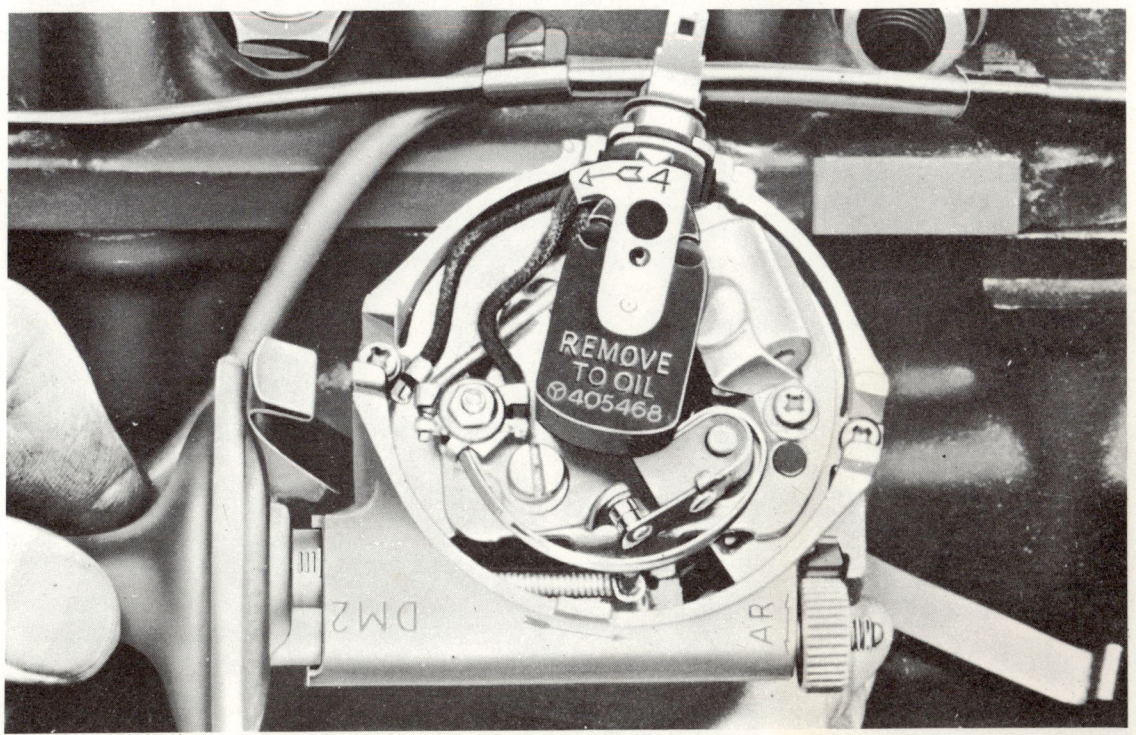

FIG 3 : 8 Vernier adjustment scale of vacuum mechanism

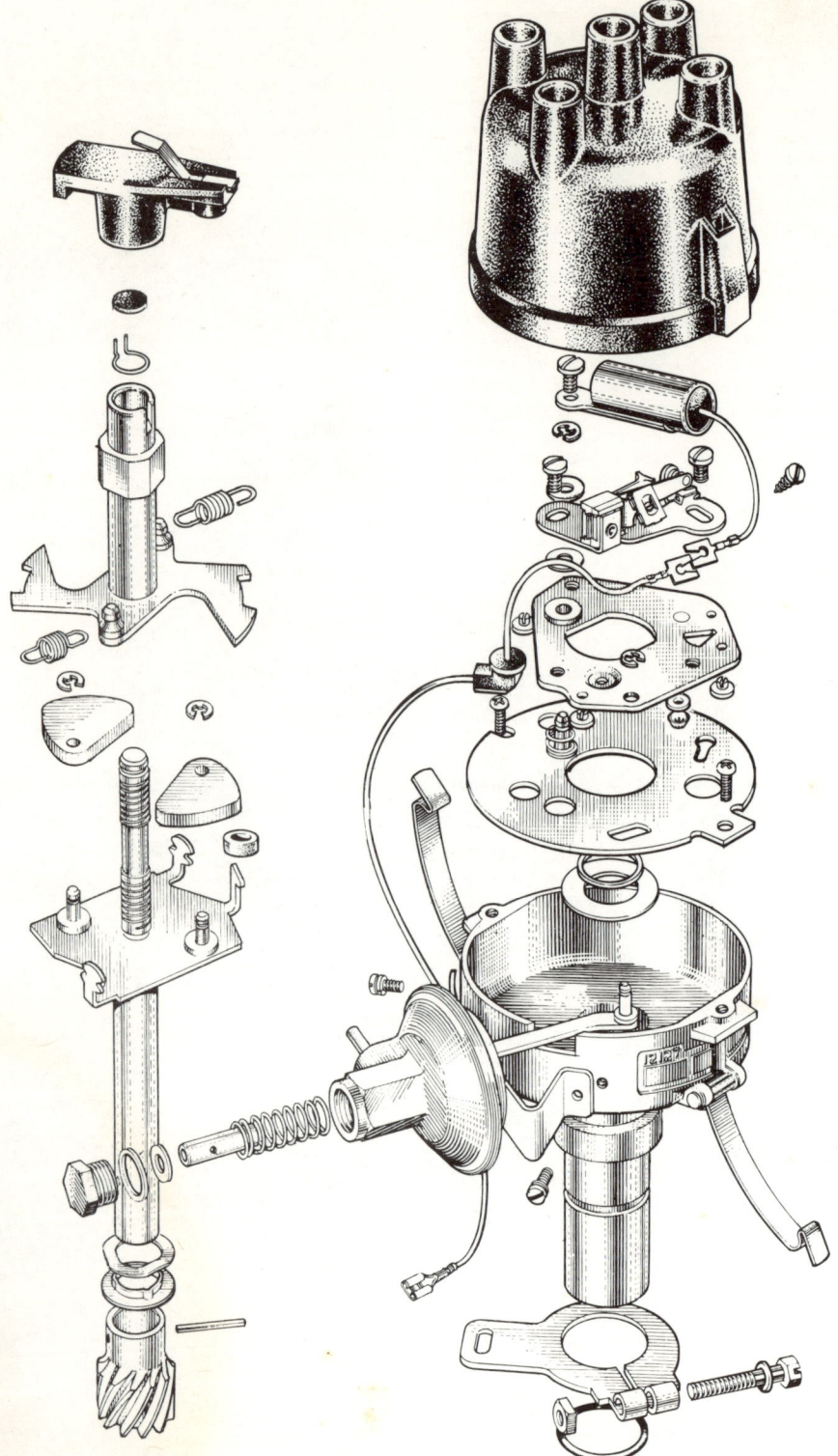

FIG 3:9   Components of distributor of Ford manufacture

The two parts of the plate assembly can be united, after checking that the moving plate is a good fit without looseness, and that the pivot of the moving contact arm is firm and unworn. The spring clip is sprung over the slot edge in the lower plate, the peg of the top plate inserted in the slot in the lower plate, and a slight twist given clockwise relatively to the plates.

The plate assembly can now be put on to the body, and the end of the linking spring of the vacuum unit secured to its post on the lug of the breaker plate. Refit the two holding screws at the body edge, noting that one of these (adjacent to the vacuum unit) also takes one end of the earth lead to the contact breaker.

The remaining items are then dealt with as already detailed.

If it is desired to check the tension of the contact breaker spring, this is done by arranging the points in the closed position by rotating the cam, and using a pull-scale hooked over the breaker arm adjacent to the contact. With a reading taken just as the points are pulled apart, the pull should be between 18 and 24 ounces. The spring can be bent, within reason, to decrease or increase the tension.

3:6 Retiming

The distributor is placed on the engine, and retimed as indicated in Chapter 1. However it will be useful to give more details of the procedure for obtaining precision of timing in relation to the markings on the distributor scale, both with and without the use of a 'timing light'.

Assuming that the distributor is correctly set for firing TDC on No. 1 cylinder, this should represent the initial timing before TDC at static advance. Refer carefully to **FIG 3 : 8,** noting that the fourth line from the diaphragm housing must be in line with the distributor body to give this position, as shown on **FIG 3 : 8.** Each division on the vernier scale represents 4 crankshaft degrees, and for conditions such as the sustained and unavoidable use of inferior fuel, the timing must be retarded; for high altitudes it may require advancing appreciably.

Next note that the contact breaker points are just opening when the rotor is adjacent to No. 1 contact in the distributor cap, the rotation being anticlockwise. If the clamp bolt has to be slackened to enable the unit to be turned to correct this, remember to retighten the bolt. The car is then taken on the road, run up to normal operating temperature, and accelerated hard on a wide throttle from 20-40 mile/hr. If there is a lot of pinking, retard the ignition by turning the distributor body anticlockwise until there is just a shade of pinking under the same conditions.

If a timing light is used, its two leads are connected to six volts of the battery, the positive and negative ends being indicated by red and black connecting clips. There is a third lead which must be connected to the low-tension terminal of the distributor. The notch on the pulley must be clearly identifiable, and if necessary it can be marked with paint for this purpose. Then arrange for the light to shine on the indicator marks on the timing cover, and on the pulley rim adjacent to these.

Disconnect the vacuum pipe from the manifold, and idle the engine at about 600 rev/min. The light will now operate in a 'stroboscopic effect', enabling the notches on the pulley and their relative positions to the stationary indicating marks, to be seen. If the notch seems to be above the marks, the ignition is too far advanced, and the body should be turned anticlockwise slightly. If below the indicator marks, the body needs turning the opposite way.

The vacuum pipe is then reconnected. If the engine speed is now varied by operating the throttle, the action of the centrifugal governor can be checked. As the speed increases, the notch should move away upwards from the indicator marks, and on reducing speed it should move down and into line with the indicator again. If the position is jumpy, and not steady in movement under these conditions, the governor is evidently sticking in some way, or the springs are faulty. Slight adjustments may subsequently be required to suit the particular types of fuel used.

The Ford manufactured distributor differs considerably in construction from the description already given, but the same general principles should be adhered to when dismantling, particularly as regards care in handling small parts, and cleanliness. The unit is shown in detail on **FIG 3 : 9.**

3:7 Maintenance, Ford distributor

The cam, pivot points of the governor weights, and cam spindle, should be lubricated with an approved lithium-base grease, only a smear being necessary on the cam. At 5000 mile intervals the rotor should be taken off and engine oil applied to the wick positioned in the end of the spindle. It is important not to overdo lubrication, as an excess will encourage electrical faults.

The contact breaker is renewed as an assembly when the points are no longer serviceable. To do this the distributor cover and rotor arm are first removed. The self-tapping screw holding the condenser and lead, and the two screws securing the contact breaker, are then taken out, releasing the complete assembly. When refitting, the breaker plate screws should first be inserted and tightened until they are just nipping. Turn the engine until the heel of the moving contact is resting on the tip of a cam lobe. A screwdriver blade is now inserted into the V-notch in the breaker plate, and manipulated until the correct gap of .025 inch measured by feeler gauge, is obtained between the points. The screws holding the plate are then securely tightened, and the gap rechecked. Refit the condenser and secure with the self-tapping screw. This procedure is followed whenever it is necessary to adjust the gap, but it should be emphasized that there is only minor variation over very long intervals, it being appreciated that the gap of .025 inch is considerably larger than has been usual.

When difficult starting is experienced from an ignition defect, and there is excessive burning of the points, the condenser is likely to be at fault. The best guide is the condition of the points, and previous remarks should be noted.

3:8 Dismantling

If it is desired to dismantle and overhaul the complete distributor unit, it must first be removed from the engine as described in Chapter 1. Remove the distributor cover and rotor, and the screws securing the breaker plate assembly and the vacuum unit, to the body. These parts can be lifted off as an assembly. To remove the governor

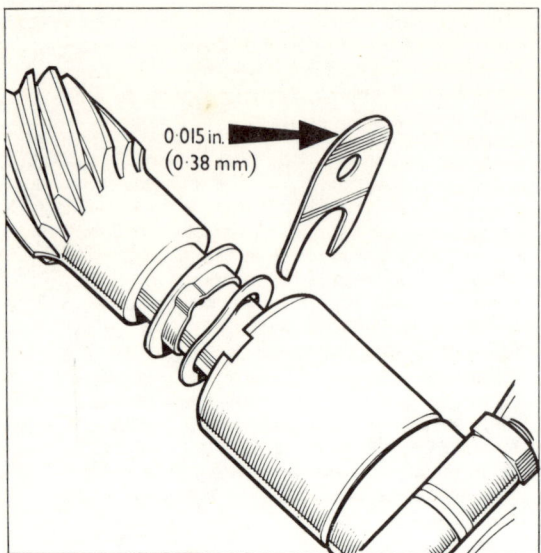

FIG 3 : 10 Use of gauge plate for obtaining correct preload on distributor shaft

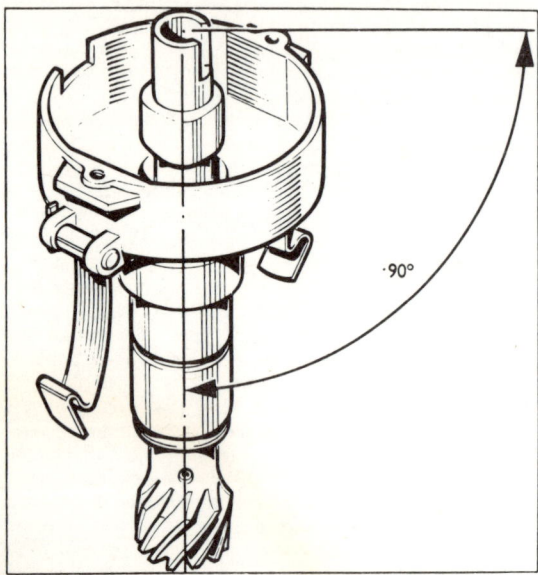

FIG 3 : 11 Position of pinhole for drive gear, relative to rotor arm slot at top of shaft

weights, the clips should be prised off. Note carefully which of the governor springs fits on its particular post, marking the parts if necessary, and unclip the springs. The felt pad is next removed from the top of the spindle; this will expose a circlip which is expanded and removed. The cam spindle can then be detached from the main shaft. To withdraw the shaft, drive out the pin retaining the skew gear, and pull the latter off the shaft. The shaft and action plate can then be taken out from above, noting that there are thrust washers below the action plate.

The spring, stop and shims are removed from the vacuum unit by unscrewing the bolt on its end. Finally, separate the contact breaker and bearing plates by detaching the circlip on the pivot post.

3 : 9 Reassembly

All parts must be checked before reassembling, and replaced if necessary. If wear is general throughout the unit, it is probably the best policy to replace it with an exchange distributor assembly. In any case, all parts must be carefully inspected before reassembling. When this has been done, check that the three nylon bearing faces are properly located in their holes in the contact breaker plate. Fit the bearing plate thereto, place a flat washer followed by a wave washer on the pivot post, and replace the circlip. Fit the vacuum spring, stop and shims to the vacuum unit, and secure them by the bolt, which has a sealing washer, on the shaft below the action plate, fit the thrust washers, and then insert the shaft into the distributor body. At the lower end of the shaft, fit the wave washer and thrust washer. Finally fit the gearwheel and secure it with a new tension pin. If the shaft and gear are to be renewed, the shaft will have to be drilled for the pin hole (the new gear is supplied ready drilled with a pilot hole). The procedure in this case is to make a .015 inch thick gauge plate, and to insert this along with new wave and thrust washers, at the shaft-end, as shown on **FIG 3 : 10**.

Position the gear with the hole at 90 deg. to the rotor arm slot, with zero advance on the governor mechanism. This position is shown on **FIG 3 : 11**. By means of a suitable clamp, press the gear on to the shaft sufficiently to flatten the spring washer and remove all end play; do not use too much force as it is quite unnecessary. With the gear held thus, and the assembly suitably supported, a .125 inch hole is drilled through the shaft and gear, with the gear pilot hole as a guide. If the existing gear is in good enough condition to be replaced on a new shaft, the pin hole should be drilled at right angles to the original hole. A new pin must be used to secure the gear. The clamp is then removed and the .015 inch shim taken out, leaving the correct running clearance.

The cam and spindle assembly is refitted to the top of the shaft, and secured by the circlip. The lubricating wick is then replaced in the top of the spindle. Before fitting the shaft to the body, and the cam spindle to the shaft, the parts should be lightly oiled.

The centrifugal advance mechanism can next be reassembled by refitting the springs to their respective posts as previously identified; the primary spring has a larger diameter and must be replaced on the post from which it was removed. The governor weights are fitted with their flat edges adjacent to the spindle, and retained by the spring clips. The contact breaker plate and vacuum unit assembly are next fitted and secured by means of their screws. Finally adjust the contact points as already described.

3 : 10 Timing, Ford distributor

Operation of the automatic advance mechanism can be checked as already described, but unless the necessary standards of accuracy can be obtained, it is preferable for this to be done by a Ford distributor with the approved testing equipment. When the distributor has been replaced on the engine as already described, the timing should be accurately adjusted. This is done by taking off the distributor cover and slackening the clamp bolt. The body is then turned clockwise until the contact points are just opening with the rotor arm adjacent to the contact for No. 1 cylinder, and the crankshaft pulley arrow aligned with the timing mark as previously detailed, for the static advance required. When this is correct, tighten the clamp bolt and replace the cover. The final setting is then obtained by road-testing as described for the Lucas distributor, but as there is no vernier adjustment on the Ford unit it is necessary to slacken the clamp bolt and to turn the complete body.

Assuming that considerable pinking is experienced when accelerating in top gear from about 20-40 mile/hr, the distributor must be turned in the direction of rotor shaft rotation, until there is a bare trace of pinking. Only a little movement should be made at a time, and the clamp screw properly tightened between adjustments. Fuel of the correct octane rating must be used, there being no advantage in using a higher rating than this, nor in attempting to run with an over-advanced setting.

3:11 Spark plugs

With an engine in good condition, the standard spark plugs have a perfectly adequate heat range to cater for all eventualities. Thus, plug trouble must not be put down to the use of an unsuitable grade, nor attempts made to cure it by haphazard substitution. Other causes should first be looked for, such as mixture derangement, excessive lubricant in the combustion chamber, or too great a working temperature due to defective water circulation, faulty ignition timing, preignition and so on.

The standard spark plug is the Autolite type AG32, 14 mm, but as research into plug operation is continuous, and improvements are made regularly, it is advisable to ensure that the current recommendations are always in use so as to obtain maximum performance, as well as economy. The latest types are likely to operate without trouble for considerably greater mileages than was the case in the quite recent past.

3:12 Fault diagnosis

(a) Engine will not fire

1 Battery discharged
2 Distributor points dirty, pitted or out of alignment
3 Distributor cap dirty, cracked or 'tracking'
4 Carbon brush inside distributor cap not in contact with rotor
5 Faulty cable or loose connection in low-tension circuit
6 Distributor rotor arm cracked
7 Faulty coil
8 Broken contact breaker spring
9 Contact points stuck open

(b) Engine misfires

1 Check 2, 3, 5 and 7 in (a)
2 Weak contact spring
3 High-tension plug and coil leads cracked or perished
4 Spark plug loose
5 Spark plug insulation cracked
6 Spark plug gap incorrect
7 Ignition timing too far advanced

NOTES

CHAPTER 4

THE COOLING SYSTEM

The cooling water circulation is by thermo-syphon, assisted by a belt-driven pump which is attached to the front of the cylinder block. The flow of water is from the radiator base to the pump intake, thence into the block and up around the cylinder head, combustion chambers and valve seats, emerging by way of an outlet containing a thermostat unit and back to the top of the radiator. The radiator core has its airflow augmented by a fan mounted on the pump shaft. When cold, the thermostat is closed, but a bypass tube is incorporated in the cylinder head and thus assists in rapid warming-up of the engine. When the thermostat is opened fully, the whole of the flow passes through the radiator.

4 : 1 Maintenance

Little maintenance is called for on the cooling system, apart from periodic checking of the belt tension and the water level in the radiator. The belt adjustment is shown on **FIG 4 : 1**, and this is correct when the belt can be moved sideways for .5 inch at a point midway between the pump and generator pulleys. Tighten the generator bracket bolts securely to make sure that the adjustment does not shift.

When checking the water level, the filler cap must never be removed quickly if the engine is hot, as the water is obviously under pressure. The filler cap must first be turned slightly to loosen it, without disengaging it from the filler neck; this will allow the pressure to be relieved, and the cap may then be removed. Topping-up is only necessary to a level coincident with the bottom of the filler neck. If plain water is used, the effect of dilution of the antifreeze solution must be taken into account. Long-life antifreeze is normally used, which only requires renewal at intervals of 40,000 miles. Defective circulation is most unlikely so long as clean, soft water, plus an approved antifreeze is used. However, if it is desired to flush the system, the drain plugs situated at the base of the radiator and on the cylinder block should be opened and the filler cap removed to prevent airlocks. If there are signs of foreign matter around the drain plugs, the holes should be skewered to ensure a clean outlet. The engine should be allowed to cool down before draining.

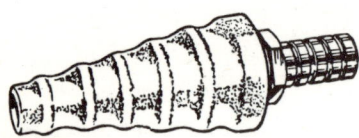

FIG 4:1   View of slotted adjustment bracket for driving belt

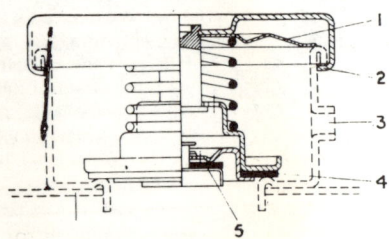

FIG 4:2   Hosepipe adaptor used when reverse-flushing radiator

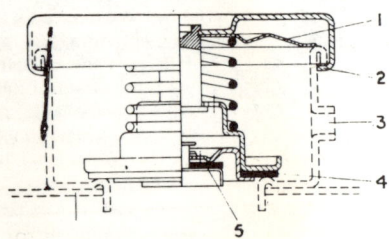

FIG 4:3   Section of radiator filler cap

Key to Fig 4:3   1 Friction plate   2 Retaining lugs
3 Overflow pipe connection   4 Pressure valve
5 Vacuum valve

4:2 Flushing

To flush through the system, this can be done by allowing fresh water from a hosepipe to flow into the filler neck for a period of 15 minutes or so with the drain plugs removed. When the radiator is seriously choked, it is often possible to clear the obstructive matter by removing the bottom hose connection, and forcing water from the hosepipe into the bottom stub, using a suitable adaptor on the hosepipe so as to obtain adequate pressure (see **FIG 4:2**). Provision must of course be made for dealing with the waste water emerging from the filler neck, to ensure that it does not flood over the engine. This reversal of the normal flow will often dislodge a lot of foreign matter without more drastic measures. When refilling the system, make sure that the drain plugs are properly positioned and tightened, and that the heater water valve is open to prevent an airlock in the heater. It is advisable to fill the system slowly, so as to allow air-bubbles to escape. It is preferable to use soft water at all times, but if the water available tends to hardness, it may be necessary to flush the system at intervals to prevent the build-up of deposits. The temperature gauge is obviously an excellent guide to the state of water circulation, and if an unduly high temperature is shown, the system must be investigated. There is no objection to reusing a long-life antifreeze solution, if this has been drained in advance of the stipulated period, so long as it is strained through a suitable filter before it is put back into circulation.

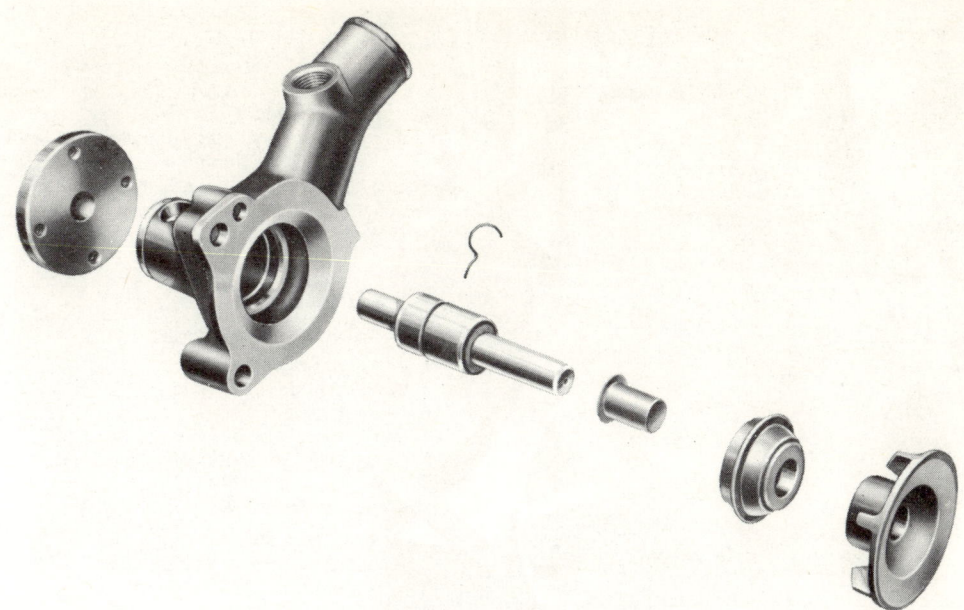

FIG 4 : 4   Water pump shown dismantled

4 : 3 Filler cap

In order to retain pressure in the system but at the same time allowing air to enter as the engine cools, the filler cap is spring-loaded to provide both a pressure and a vacuum seal as shown on **FIG 4 : 3**. The loading is such that an internal pressure of 4-7 lb/sq in. is maintained in the system. Service stations are provided with a gauge for testing the filler cap seal, the device registering the pressure which the cap is capable of holding for a period of about 10 secs. The cap must be replaced if found defective.

4 : 4 Thermostat

The thermostat may be removed after draining the system, by taking off the water outlet casting and gasket, and lifting out the thermostat unit from its recess in the cylinder head. If it is desired to test for correct operation, the thermostat should be immersed in water having a thermometer therein to register the temperature. On heating the water, the valve should commence opening at a temperature of 80°C. Replacement of the thermostat in the housing is a reversal of removal; make sure that it is located properly in the recess, and that the gasket is in good condition when the water outlet is replaced. Tighten the securing nuts evenly.

4 : 5 Radiator

The radiator is removed, after draining, by taking off the hose attachments and undoing the securing nuts and bolts. The radiator can be cleaned externally by means of a brush and high-pressure airblast, but at all times when off the car, take care that the matrix is not damaged. When replacing, ensure that any packing pieces which may be present are replaced in their correct positions. It is not necessary to take off the radiator in order to remove the water pump.

4 : 6 Water pump

The water pump can be taken off the engine after first draining the cooling system, detaching the bottom hose from the pump, and removing the heater hose if fitted. The generator clamp bolts, and the bolt on the belt-adjusting link, are then slackened, this enabling the generator to be swung towards the engine so as to slacken the belt, which can be removed.

Remove the bolts holding the fan and pulley to the hub, and detach the fan and pulley. After taking out the securing bolts to the cylinder block, the complete pump can be removed.

A defective pump may be exchanged as a unit, but overhaul is quite feasible by making use of the repair kit available. This contains a sealed double ballbearing assembly integral with the shaft, and is not dismantled; there is also a slinger unit, seal, retainer clip and gasket. Special tools are required for dismantling and reassembly to avoid damage, these being numbered CPT.8000 and P.8000–4, the latter being an adaptor set. The dismantled pump is shown on **FIG 4 : 4**.

To dismantle the pump, the bearing retainer clip is first extracted from the slot in the housing. Next press the pulley hub from the shaft using the tool CPT.8000 along with its split ring and centre screw adaptor; the latter applies pressure to the shaft centre as shown on **FIG 4 : 5**. Using the same tool, press out the shaft along with the impeller, seal, slinger and bearing assembly. In this case the ring and thrust block adaptors are employed with the tool. The impeller can next be pressed off the shaft using the same adaptors as for the hub; take care that the impeller vanes do not foul the slots. The pump seal is then removed from the shaft and the slinger bush split with a chisel and detached. This completes the dismantling operation; all parts to be retained must be cleaned thoroughly.

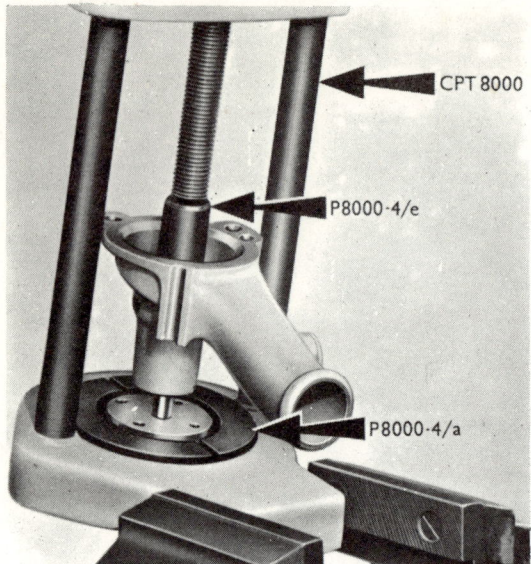

CPT 8000

P8000·4/e

P8000·4/a

FIG 4 : 5   Use of Ford tool for dismantling pump

4 : 7 Pump reassembly

To reassemble with the new parts, first press the new shaft and bearing assembly into the housing, with the short end of the shaft to the front of the housing, until the groove in the shaft lines up with the groove in the housing. The same tool and adaptors are used as for removal, i.e. ring and thrust block adaptors. Next fit the retaining clip into its groove. Replace the hub by using the tool plus split ring and thrust block adaptors; the shaft-end must be left flush with the hub. The new slinger bush is next fitted on to the rear of the shaft, flanged-end, leading. The driver adaptor is used for the purpose. Fit the new seal to the bush, carbon face to the impeller. The impeller is then pressed on using the centre screw and split ring adaptors. The positioning of the impeller on the shaft must be such that there is a clearance of .030 inch between the impeller vanes and the face of the housing.

This completes reassembly, and the pump must then be checked for free rotation. Thoroughly clean the joint face before replacing on the engine, and tighten the holding bolts evenly. Bolt the pulley and fan to the hub and replace the belt. Tighten the latter to give the required amount of free movement, and then tighten the generator pivot and adjusting link bolts. Refit the water hoses, refill the system and check for leaks.

4 : 8 Fault diagnosis

(a) Internal water leakage

1 Cracked cylinder wall
2 Loose cylinder head nuts
3 Cracked cylinder head
4 Faulty head gasket
5 Cracked tappet chest wall

(b) Poor circulation

1 Radiator core blocked
2 Engine water passages restricted
3 Low water level
4 Loose fan belt
5 Defective thermostat
6 Perished or collapsed radiator hoses

(c) Corrosion

1 Impurities in the water
2 Infrequent draining and flushing

(d) Overheating

1 Check (b)
2 Sludge in crankcase
3 Faulty ignition timing
4 Low oil level in sump
5 Tight engine
6 Choked exhaust system
7 Binding brakes
8 Slipping clutch
9 Incorrect valve timing
10 Retarded ignition
11 Mixture too weak

CHAPTER 5

THE CLUTCH

The clutch is of the single dry-plate type, the driven plate incorporating a spring-cushioned hub and linings flexibly mounted to ensure smooth take-up. The construction is as normal practice, with the plate free to slide on splines on the gearbox input shaft, this shaft locating in a spigot bearing at the flywheel centre. The pressure unit comprising cover, springs, release levers and pressure plate, is obtainable and serviced as an assembly; no useful purpose is gained by dismantling it, since special gauges, etc., are required to ensure correct setting-up. The rear face of the flywheel forms the opposite contact surface relative to the pressure plate, the driven plate being sandwiched between them.

5 : 1 Operation

The release mechanism comprises a hydraulic master cylinder operated by a suspended pedal, the cylinder being flexibly piped to an operating cylinder mounted on the clutch housing. This non-mechanical connection ensures that engine movement is not felt at the pedal. The operating cylinder piston operates a pushrod, acting on the end of the clutch release arm which pivots on a fulcrum inside the housing; this is shown in the next chapter, **FIG 6 : 2**. The release arm carries the release bearing which on actuation presses on the clutch release levers at the pressure unit, to withdraw the pressure plate and thus free the driven plate. The only maintenance normally required is to keep the fluid reservoir topped up to the correct level which can be seen on **FIG 5 : 1**, and to ensure that the adjustment on the operating cylinder gives the necessary free movement. When the pedal is moved through the whole of its return travel, there should be $\frac{1}{16}$ inch clearance between the operating cylinder pushrod and the release arm. This is adjusted by releasing the tension spring on the release arm, slackening the locknut, and while holding the pushrod at its 'flats' (machined for the purpose) turning the adjusting nut until the clearance is obtained between the nut and the release arm end. The locknut is then tightened, clearance rechecked, and the spring refitted.

The fluid level should be kept within about $\frac{1}{2}$ inch of the top face of the reservoir, which is integral with the body of the hydraulic cylinder. Take care not to allow dirt to enter with the fluid, and always ensure that the air vent in the filler cap is clear, and the cap firmly in place.

5 : 2 Maintenance

The system should not require bleeding unless components have been dismantled. However, a bleed valve is provided for this purpose on the operating cylinder at the end remote from the pushrod, and this is opened by turning it anticlockwise; the valve can be seen below the fluid pipe on **FIG 5 : 2**. To exclude all air from the system, a tube is first attached to the valve and led into a receptacle containing fluid. The valve is then opened, the reservoir filled, and the pedal operated several times in slow motion so that fluid is pumped right through from the reservoir to the jar. When the fluid entering the jar is seen to be free from air bubbles the bleed valve can be closed and the tube and jar removed. Fresh fluid should of course be used at all times for topping-up the reservoir.

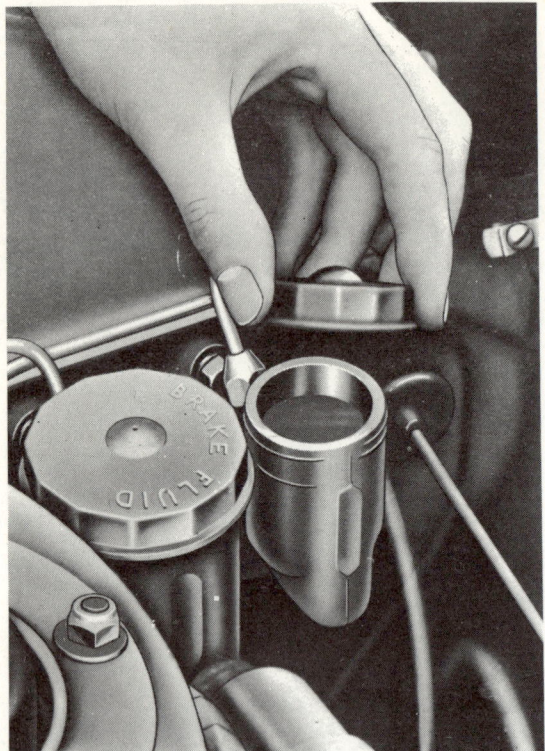

FIG 5:1 Clutch master cylinder, showing correct level of fluid

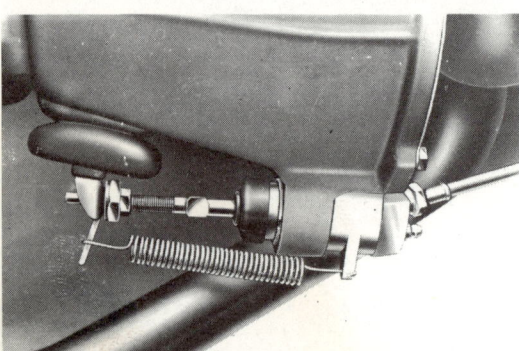

FIG 5:2 Clutch actuating cylinder, showing positions of bleed valve and pipe union

The hydraulic master cylinder is mounted on the engine side of the bulkhead, the same attachment bolts being used to secure the bracket for the pendant clutch and brake pedals on the opposite side of the bulkhead. The cylinder is open at one end (except for a rubber boot cover) where the piston and pushrod assembly is entered. At the opposite (blank) end of the cylinder are the integral fluid reservoir, and the union for fluid delivery to the clutch operating cylinder.

The piston has a spigot at its front end to receive a valve stem, and also carries the retainer for a compression spring which serves to return the piston to the start of the stroke after pedal operation. This spring is held by a spacer at its front end. At the front end of the valve stem is a seal-type valve. When the piston is fully returned, i.e. with the spring free, a port from the reservoir to the cylinder is open, and fluid can enter the cylinder. On pedal depression, the piston moves down the cylinder, this also pushing forward the valve stem and valve. The spacer then contacts the cylinder end, and the 'bent' shim between the valve stem flange and spacer pushes the valve firmly into contact with the reservoir port at the end of the cylinder. This prevents fluid from being forced back into the latter, and it is thus expelled from the delivery union under pressure to the operating cylinder; the pressure build-up also helps to keep the valve firmly seated. On releasing the pedal, the compression spring returns the piston to the open end of the cylinder. Since at the same time the clutch operating cylinder is also retracting, the fluid is returned to the master cylinder. At the end of the travel, the valve spacer and valve are disengaged from the port, so that if necessary fluid can pass into the cylinder. It will be appreciated that in use, and assuming the system is in good condition and leakproof, no fluid is actually consumed; the reservoir simply serves to preserve a pressure balance and prevent leakage of air, and airlocks by forming a hydraulic seal.

The rubber boot fitted over the main pushrod at the open end of the cylinder prevents the entry of dirt and moisture. At the same time the open-ended construction makes dismantling a simple matter should components require replacement due to leakage and loss of pressure.

5:3 Main cylinder

The main pushrod is first disconnected from the pedal by removing the nut and taking out the concentric bolt. Have a suitable blanking plug ready for insertion in the delivery union of the cylinder; unscrew the union nut, detach the pipe, and fit the blanking plug to prevent dirt entering. Take off the master cylinder after undoing the nuts securing it to the screws which pass through the bulkhead from the pedal bracket. Then empty the fluid from the reservoir.

Remove the rubber boot at the cylinder open end, take out the circlip from the groove in the bore, remove the pushrod and then the piston and valve assembly. The piston is next detached from the valve assembly. Prise up the tab which holds the spring retainer in position on the front end of the piston (and which fits under a shoulder on the front of the piston) by using a screwdriver as shown on **FIG 5:3**. Then remove the retainer, spring, and valve assembly from the piston.

The valve assembly is dismantled by compressing the spring and moving the stem to one side in the retainer, this action releasing it through the keyhole slot in the retainer end. The valve seal and also the piston seal can then be removed if defective.

All parts should be cleaned, using no liquid other than brake fluid at any time; this is most important. Inspect all parts carefully for damage or wear; in particular, note the condition of the lip on the piston seal, but do not distort the seal when examining. To reassemble the master cylinder, first replace the piston seal, with its lip facing down the cylinder, in the direction of pressure. Also fit the valve seal, lip outwards and away from the spring. Next the bent shim, spacer (legs over the valve seal) and spring are fitted in that order over the stem. Make sure that the valve stem flange is contacted by the convex face of the shim. The retainer can then be fitted in the end of the spring. Compress the spring, fit the valve stem into the keyhole slot, and locate.

Now insert the piston front end into the retainer, securing it by fitting the retainer tab under the piston front shoulder.

After dipping in hydraulic fluid, the assembly can be inserted in the cylinder; use great care to ensure that the lip of the piston is not damaged on entry, and ease it gently into the bore. Fit the main pushrod and rubber boot. This completes the assembly.

The master cylinder can then be replaced on the bulkhead, tightening the nuts securely. Reconnect the fluid pipe, ensuring a tight joint, but do not overtighten as this will damage the threads in the casting. The pushrod is then attached to the pedal by fitting the concentric bolt, first through the rod-end and then the pedal hole. The reservoir must then be filled and the system bled as already described.

5 : 4 Operating cylinder

The clutch operating cylinder is located in a circular-bore boss on the clutch housing, lefthand side, and is retained by a circlip. The cylinder is removed by taking off the circlip and disconnecting the return spring from the cylinder-end anchorage. Detach the pipeline (with a blanking plug handy to insert in the union hole as soon as the pipe is removed). Take off the pushrod and rubber boot from the cylinder, and slide out the cylinder from its location.

The piston and its seal can be removed by tapping the cylinder lightly with a wooden mallet or on a block, until the parts emerge. The bleed valve at the blank end of the cylinder is unscrewed and removed along with its ball. The piston seal can then be pulled off its spigot on the front end of the piston. Reference to **FIG 5 : 4** will help to clarify the position of these parts.

All parts must be cleaned, using no liquid but brake fluid. The piston seal should be examined for damage or wear and renewed if necessary. To reassemble the cylinder, first fit the seal on the piston spigot with the lip facing the blank end of the cylinder in the direction of pressure. Dip the piston and seal in hydraulic fluid and carefully insert in the cylinder, taking the same precautions as detailed for the master cylinder. Then replace the bleed valve, with its ball, but do not tighten as the system has to be bled.

Slide the cylinder into its boss from the front, and fit the circlip making sure that the latter is in good condition and firmly in its groove. Fit the boot over the open end of the cylinder, and insert the pushrod. The fluid pipe can now be reconnected, taking care not to overtighten and damage the threads. The free movement is then adjusted, and the system bled as already detailed.

5 : 5 Clutch dismantling

To obtain access to the clutch and its release bearing, etc., it is necessary to part the housing flange, as described in Chapters 1 and 6. The clutch release mechanism is located in the gearbox part of the housing, as shown on **FIG 5 : 5**.

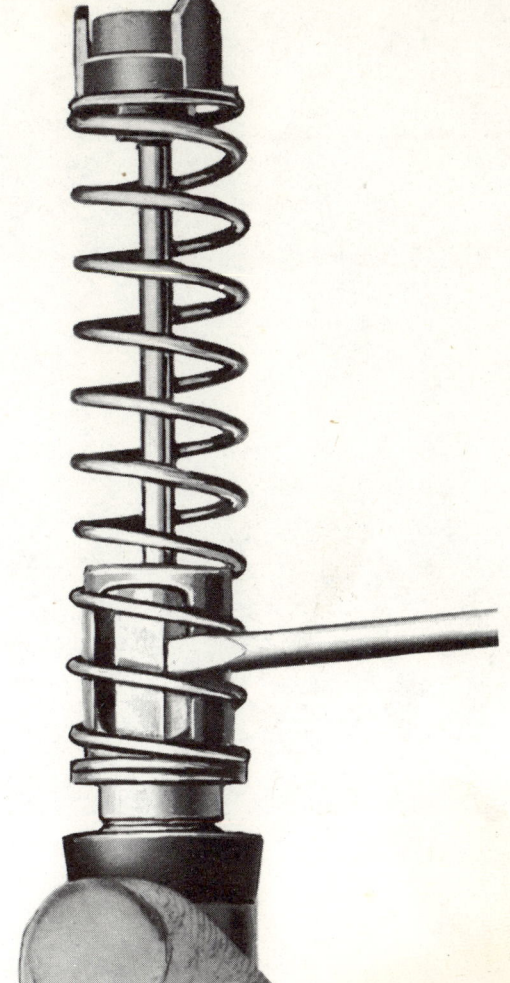

FIG 5 : 3 Method of detaching spring retainer from front end of master piston

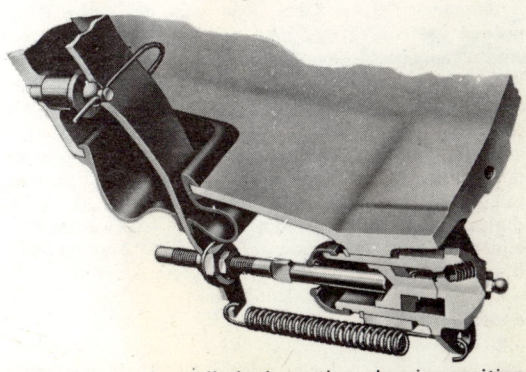

FIG 5 : 4 Actuating cylinder in section, showing position of components

FIG 5:5 Interior of gearbox portion of clutch housing, showing clutch release mechanism

The splined centre of the clutch driven plate can be seen on **FIG 5:6,** and access to the plate is obtained after removing the pressure unit from the flywheel, following the procedure as in the chapters mentioned above. The driven plate should be carefully examined to ensure that it is not unduly worn and that the linings are secure and do not show suspicious signs of discolouration. If defective, the complete plate must be replaced. In normal use the linings take on a polish, giving very smooth engagement with adequate transmitting capacity, if the spring pressure is sufficient. This polish is easy to see, but does not affect the colour of the linings, which together with the natural grain of the material can be seen quite clearly through the glaze. Darkening of the surface denotes that small quantities of oil have been present, but have been burnt off as a result of heat generated during starting. A momentary defect of this kind has little effect on performance, and in fact is more likely to make the clutch fierce when engaging than to cause slip.

Larger quantities of oil not only give a much darker appearance to the linings but will only burn off in part and leave a definite deposit on the surface. This then becomes glazed, but unlike the 'natural' polish gives a coating to the face which will spoil the frictional grip.

To some extent also it causes the plate to stick on engagement, so that the clutch will not free properly when the pedal is depressed but will at the same time slip when driving; this state of affairs can cause a lot of confusion.

The more oil present the worse the effects, so that any discoloration of the linings must be suspect, and other evidence looked for of oil coming from somewhere in quantity.

5:6 Pressure unit

The pressure unit should be left alone apart from examining the face of the pressure plate for signs of scoring, overheating or distortion. If weakening of the clutch springs or uneven withdrawal (due to inaccurate setting of the levers) is suspected, the unit should be examined by an agent equipped with the necessary gauges, and a replacement fitted if advised.

The gearbox input shaft locates in a sintered bush at the flywheel centre. In order to facilitate uniting the engine and gearbox after refitting the clutch, a lining-up tool should be used to centralize the components, as described in Chapter 1 and shown in **FIG 1:8.** The clutch release mechanism can be dismantled from the gearbox part of the housing if necessary. The return spring is first taken off the lever which engages the operating cylinder pushrod on the outside of the housing, and the rubber gaiter over the lever removed. The release arm pivots on a fulcrum pin inside the housing, which can be seen on **FIG 5:5,** and is retained by a spring clip. It can be taken off after removing this clip. The release bearing link can then be slid from the assembly of bearing and arm, and the two bearing locating springs detached from the arm. The release bearing is a light press-fit on its hub, and the assembly is held with the bearing downward and tapped sharply on a wooden block to detach the bearing. **FIG 5:7** shows the detached assembly.

When fitting a new bearing, its thrust face must be away from the hub, and the latter pressed squarely into position so that it enters the bore properly and seats firmly. The assembly of hub and bearing is replaced by refitting the bearing link between the arm and bearing, taking care to locate the link in the grooves. Assemble the bearing locating springs; the ends of the springs having almost complete coils are fitted to the bearing, and the opposite ends to the arm. The arm is now passed through the housing, and the bearing hub bore located on the bearing retainer of the gearbox input shaft, after first inspecting the retainer exterior to ensure that there are no burrs or scores to prejudice movement, and lightly applying a little high-melting point grease to its surface.

The release arm can then be located on the fulcrum pin, and the spring clip refitted. The ends of the clip are inserted first into the holes in the arm and then the centre loop engaged under the pin head.

The gaiter can now be refitted and the return spring stretched and hooked to the end of the arm.

5:7 Pedal mechanism

The clutch pedal is of the suspended or pendant type, and is mounted along with the brake pedal on a bracket attached to the engine bulkhead by four bolts and nuts which also secure, on the opposite side, the two hydraulic

FIG 5:6 View of clutch, showing operating fingers and splined centre of driven plate

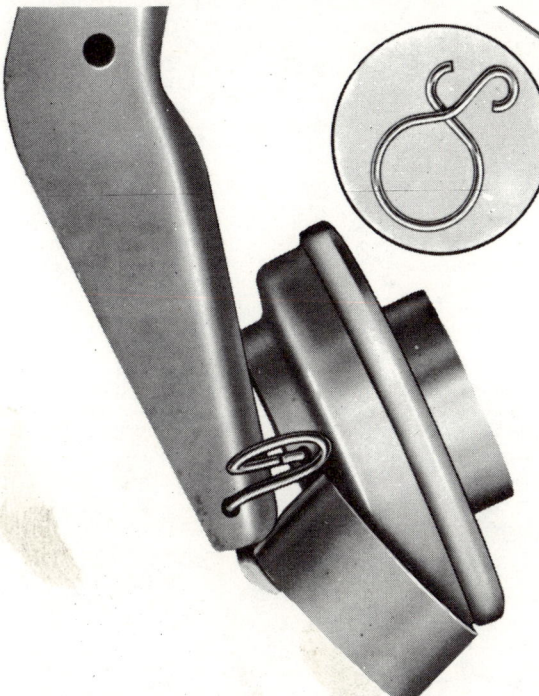

FIG 5:7 Clutch release thrust bearing shown detached

master cylinders. On early cars, there is an adjustment on each pedal by which the height can be varied, the master cylinder pushrods being attached to the pedals by eccentric adjuster bolts which on being rotated will vary the effective length of the pushrod. The concentric bolts used on later cars do not allow of this adjustment, but overhauling details are not affected.

The two pedals are mounted on a common shaft, headed at one end and having a circlip at the other.

To remove the assembly, first disconnect the return

springs, and also the stoplight switch connections (if a mechanical switch is fitted). Take off the accelerator pedal by removing its clamp bolt, and uncouple the throttle linkage at the carburetter. The linkage can then be moved out of engagement with the bush in the bracket.

Take out the four bolts securing the bracket, after unscrewing the nuts; also remove the bolt from each side of the bracket assembly upper face. The complete bracket with pedals can then be worked downwards and removed from the car. The pedal spindle is pulled out after detaching the circlip from one end. Note that there is a sintered bronze washer located between the bosses of the two pedals, and that both pedal pivots have bronze bushes. If the spindle is worn it should be replaced. If the bushes are unserviceable, have new ones fitted by a Ford agent who will also match them to the spindle. Check the condition of the plastic washers in the pushrod eyes, and ensure that their bolts are unworn; renew the parts if necessary.

5:8 Refitting pedals

Apply lubricant to the pedal bushes, position the pedals in the bracket and place the sintered washer between the pedal bosses. Slide the spindle home and secure with a new end-circlip. Refit the return springs, and position the assembly as when removed, fitting the two upper bolts, washers and nuts. Tighten the latter finger tight only, and ensure that the pushrods are properly located in their master cylinders.

The accelerator pedal linkage is next located in the bush on the pedal bracket. Recouple the linkage to the carburetter and engine bulkhead, and fit the accelerator pedal and return spring; tighten the clamp bolt. Fit the remaining two fixing bolts, with their nuts and lock-washers. The four nuts securing the bracket and master cylinders should now be tightened firmly and evenly; also fit the two bolts to each side of the upper face of the bracket and tighten. Reconnect the stoplight wiring (mechanical switch only). This completes the assembly.

5:9 Fault diagnosis

(a) Drag or spin

1 Oil or grease on driven plate linings
2 Bent engine backplate
3 Misalignment between the engine and the gearbox first motion shaft
4 Fluid leaks at master cylinder, slave cylinder or pipe line
5 Driven plate hub binding on first motion shaft splines
6 Binding of first motion shaft spigot bearings
7 Distorted clutch plate
8 Warped or damaged pressure plate or clutch cover
9 Broken driven plate linings
10 Dirt or foreign matter in clutch
11 Air in the clutch hydraulic system

(b) Fierceness or snatch

1 Check 1, 2, 3 and 4 in (a)
2 Worn clutch linings

(c) Slip

1 Check 1, 2 and 3 in (a)
2 Check 2 in (b)
3 Weak pressure springs
4 Seized piston in clutch slave cylinder

(d) Judder

1 Check 1, 2 and 3 in (a)
2 Pressure plate not parallel with flywheel face
3 Contact area of driven plate linings not evenly distri-
  buted
4 Bent first motion shaft
5 Buckled driven plate
6 Faulty engine or gearbox rubber mountings
7 Worn suspension shackles
8 Weak rear springs
9 Loose propeller shaft bolts
10 Loose rear spring clips

(e) Rattle

1 Check 3 in (c)
2 Broken springs in driven plate
3 Worn release mechanism
4 Excessive backlash in transmission
5 Wear in transmission bearings

(f) Tick or knock

1 Worn first motion shaft spigot or bearing
2 Badly worn splines in driven plate hub
3 Pressure plate out of line
4 Faulty pinion drive on starter motor
5 Loose flywheel

(g) Driven plate fracture

1 Check 2 and 3 in (a)
2 Drag and distortion due to hanging gearbox in plate hub

CHAPTER 6

THE GEARBOX

6 : 1 Removal   6 : 2 Inspection   6 : 3 Fault diagnosis

The gearbox is of the normal constant-mesh type with four forward speeds and reverse. On 1000 cc cars, the upper three ratios are provided with synchromesh mechanism, while the 1200 cc models have all four ratios so equipped. No adaptation is however feasible as between internal components for conversion purposes. **FIG 6 : 1** shows the general construction in section, while the components are detailed on **FIGS 6 : 2** and **6 : 3**.

Trouble inside the gearbox is unlikely so long as the car is handled intelligently, but in any case dismantling is an involved operation requiring the use of special equipment. In the event of trouble therefore specialist advice should be sought.

The gear control is by a lever mounted on the box rear. The method of ratio selection is quite conventional, all wheels in constant mesh being of the single helical-type to encourage quiet operation. Normal maintenance consists of periodic checking of the oil level and changing of the oil at the stipulated intervals. The filler and drain plugs are positioned as shown on **FIG 6 : 4.** Should the gearbox require attention, it may be replaced by a serviced unit to save overhaul time. In any case, the work of removal and replacement will effect an economy in such cases, and this will now be described.

6 : 1 Removal

For gearbox overhaul (or access to the clutch) the unit can be removed leaving the engine in the frame. The procedure is first to drain off the oil, then disconnect the battery and the cable from the starter motor. The starter motor is removed and also the bolts securing the clutch housing to the engine block (Chapter 1).

The return spring of the clutch arm is next removed, along with the rubber boot covering the arm, the clutch operating cylinder, and the pushrod. Chapter 5 gives details for these operations.

Free the speedometer cable retainer from the extension at the box rear by undoing its bolt, and withdraw the cable. The earthing strap should also be disconnected from its bracket and the exhaust pipe uncoupled from the engine manifold. Now mark the rear drive coupling and flange to ensure that the parts are reassembled in the same relative positions. Take out the four self-locking nuts and their bolts from the rear coupling, and gently tap the flange, which will free the joint. The end of the shaft is then lowered and slid back until the front end clears the splines on the gearbox output shaft.

The gearlever is now put in neutral, and its gaiter removed by taking out the four self-tapping screws.

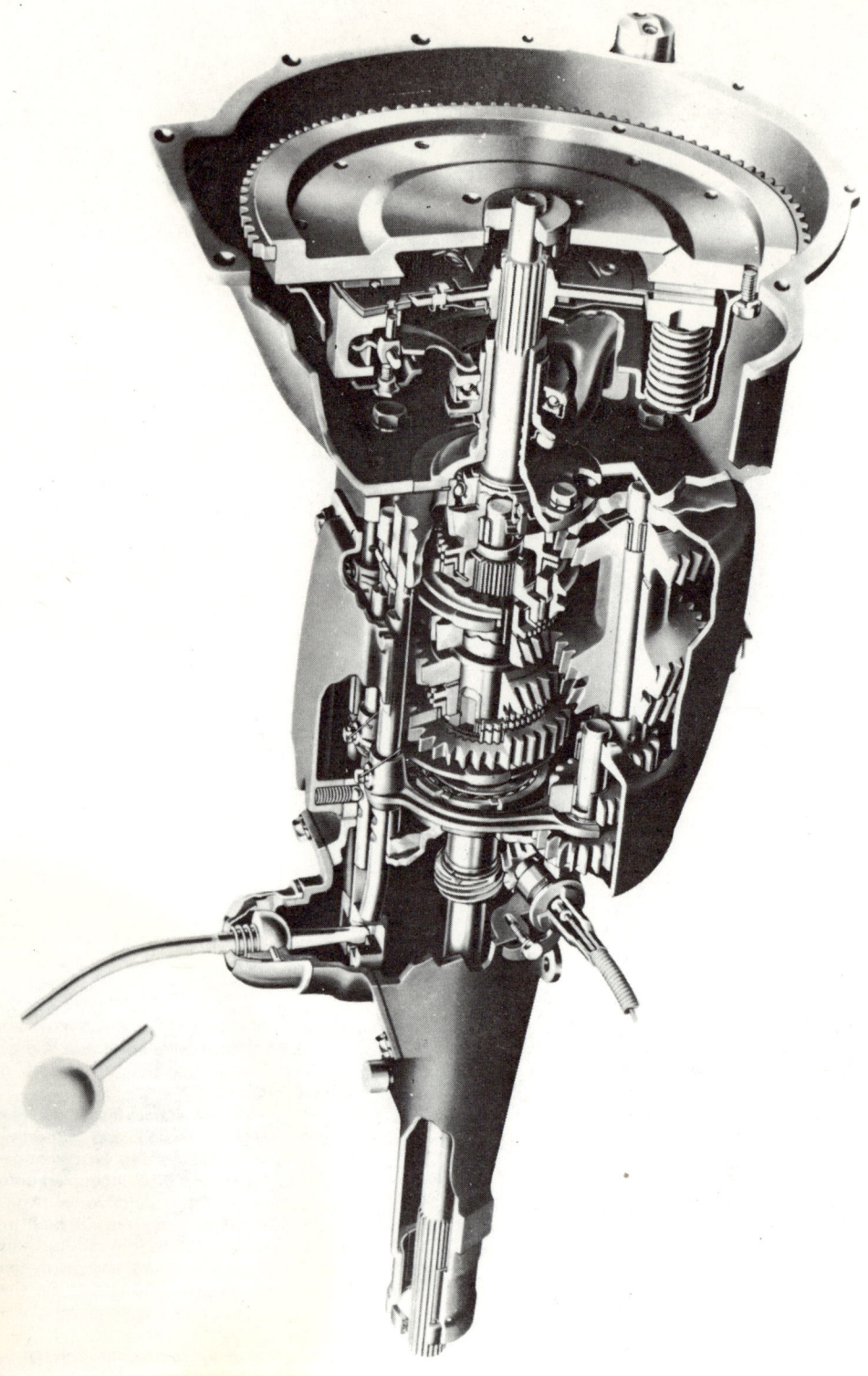

FIG 6 : 1   Part-section of gearbox, showing general arrangement

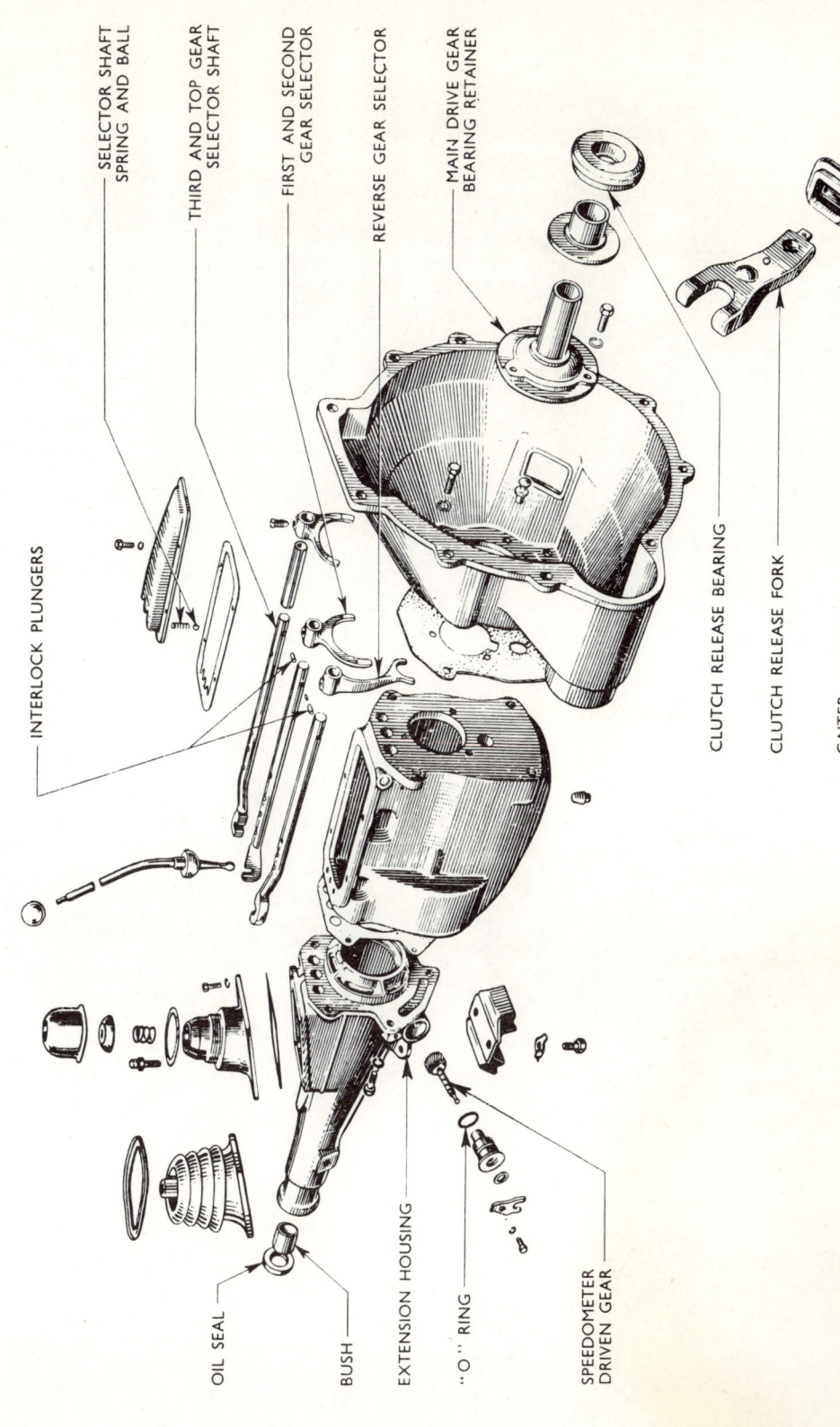

SELECTOR SHAFT
SPRING AND BALL

THIRD AND TOP GEAR
SELECTOR SHAFT

FIRST AND SECOND
GEAR SELECTOR

REVERSE GEAR SELECTOR

MAIN DRIVE GEAR
BEARING RETAINER

INTERLOCK PLUNGERS

CLUTCH RELEASE BEARING

CLUTCH RELEASE FORK

GAITER

OIL SEAL

BUSH

EXTENSION HOUSING

"O" RING

SPEEDOMETER
DRIVEN GEAR

FIG 6:2   Gearbox casing and components

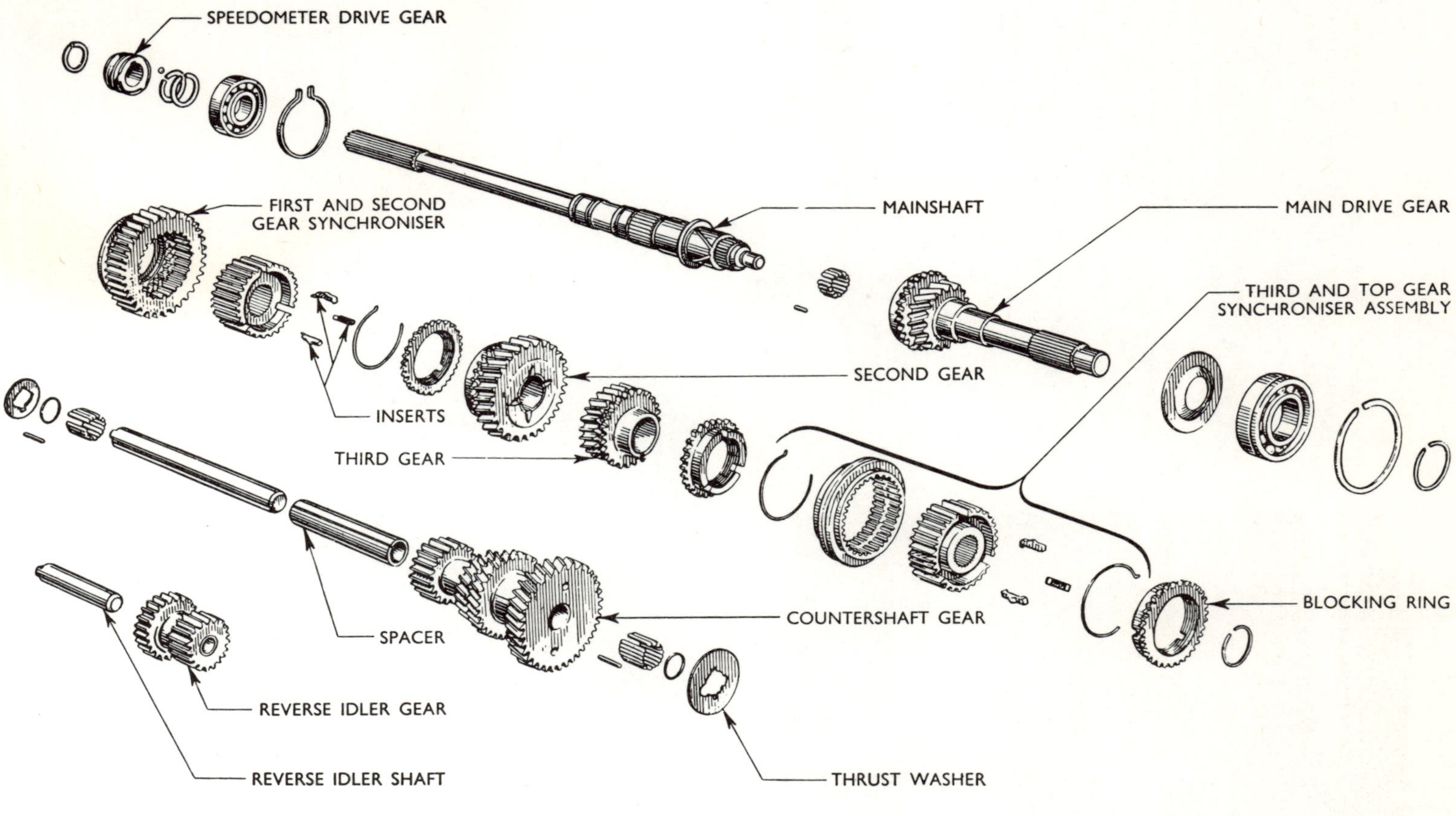

SPEEDOMETER DRIVE GEAR

FIRST AND SECOND GEAR SYNCHRONISER

MAINSHAFT

MAIN DRIVE GEAR

THIRD AND TOP GEAR SYNCHRONISER ASSEMBLY

SECOND GEAR

INSERTS

THIRD GEAR

COUNTERSHAFT GEAR

SPACER

REVERSE IDLER GEAR

REVERSE IDLER SHAFT

BLOCKING RING

THRUST WASHER

FIG 6 : 3   Internal components of gearbox (non-synchromesh bottom gear)

FIG 6 : 4 Location of oil filler and drain plugs

Lift out the lever after unscrewing its ball cap from the top of the box. The engine and gearbox must now be supported by suitable blocks or similar, from underneath. Next unscrew the nut from the centre of the engine rear support member. The four bolts can now be removed from the rear support member, and the box lifted clear along with the support. The latter is detached by taking out the two bolts holding it to the extension housing.

6 : 2 Inspection

If it is desired to inspect the gearbox interior and selector mechanism, this can be done by removing the gearlever and the box top. The lever housing is secured by four bolts to the rear extension housing, and can be removed when these are taken out. The box cover plate is also attached by four bolts. Care is necessary when lifting the cover, as it retains the springs over the selector shaft locking balls, which can be seen on **FIG 6 : 2** at the rear end of the cover flange; these springs may fly out if the cover is removed carelessly. When replacing the cover, take care that the springs are properly located in their holes, and the gasket is sound.

When refitting the box to the engine, great care must be used when entering the input shaft into the clutch centre, as indicated in Chapter 1. The rear support member can then be refitted in position and bolted to the frame and box extension. The drive shaft coupling is bolted up, first sliding the front joint sleeve on to the output shaft splines; taking care that no damage is caused to the oil seal or bearing, also that the markings on the rear joint flange coincide. The clutch operating cylinder is then replaced as detailed in Chapter 5, and the starter motor refitted and connected up. Do not forget to replace the earthing strap, and ensure that it makes good contact.

6 : 3 Fault diagnosis

(a) Jumping out of gear

1 Broken spring behind locating ball for selector rod
2 Excessively worn locating groove in selector rod
3 Worn coupling dogs
4 Selector fork loose on rod

(b) Noisy gearbox

1 Insufficient oil
2 Excessive end play in gears
3 Worn or damaged bearings
4 Worn or damaged gear teeth

(c) Difficulty in engaging gear

1 Incorrect clutch pedal adjustment
2 Worn synchromesh cones

(d) Oil leaks

1 Damaged joint washers
2 Worn or damaged oil seals
3 Front, rear or side covers loose or faces damaged

NOTES

CHAPTER 7

REAR AXLE, PROPELLER SHAFT AND SUSPENSION

The rear axle is of the banjo-casing type, housing a two-star differential unit carried in bearing trunnions integral with the front banjo cover, which also incorporate the nosepiece for the final drive shaft, bearings and pinion; **FIG 7:1** shows the constructional details. The axle shafts are splined into the differential output bevels, but as the splines are an interference fit the shafts cannot readily be pulled out; they have to be driven free by means of a slide-hammer anchored to the outer shaft flange by the wheel studs. The general arrangement is clear from **FIG 7:2.** In the event of trouble internally, the complete axle assembly should be detached from the springs and sent for rectification, as a number of special tools and gauges are required for the adjustments on the pinion and crown wheel bearings (the degree of pre-loading being important as well as depth of mesh, etc.).

7:1 Lubrication

The hub bearings are prepacked with lubricant and sealed, so that attention is not normally required. The same also applies to most propeller shaft universal joints. There is a combined filler and oil level plug in the rear of the banjo housing. Drain plugs were fitted to some early axles, but this fitting is no longer used as it is not necessary to drain the oil at any time in normal service. The level of the oil should be checked after the first 500 miles, and subsequently at 5000 mile intervals. The level must be tested with the car on an even keel and maintained up to the bottom of the filler plug hole which is positioned as on **FIG 7:3.** Always tighten the plug securely after removal.

The oil used must be of hypoid type, and not ordinary gear oil; the correct specification is given in the handbook chart.

Whenever new gears are fitted in any part of the differential these should be run in with the same care as for a new car, for 500 miles, and the oil topped-up if necessary at that mileage.

7:2 Axle removal

To remove the axle assembly, the rear of the car is first jacked-up by placing supports under the frame side-members in front of the rear springs. Next take off the wheels, and place blocks under the axle casing to take its weight. Mark the universal joint flange as described in Chapter 6, and take out the flange bolts. The handbrake is next released to the 'off' position, and the cable disconnected at the left side brake backplate. Also uncouple the brake rod from the righthand backplate lever, and the fabric strap from the axle casing. (These items are also referred to in Chapter 10 dealing with the brakes.)

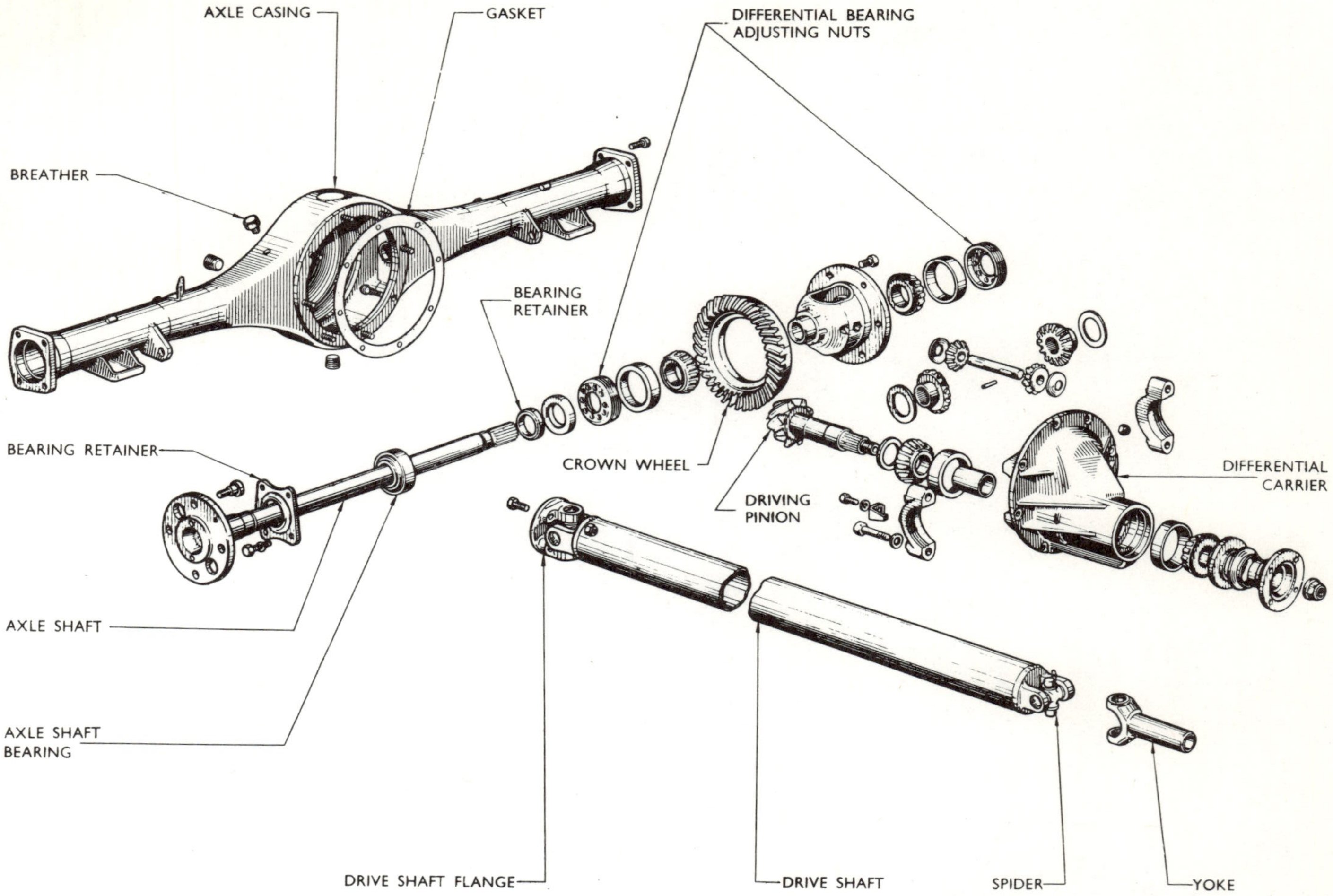

DIFFERENTIAL CARRIER

YOKE

SPIDER

DRIVE SHAFT

DIFFERENTIAL BEARING
ADJUSTING NUTS

DRIVING
PINION

CROWN WHEEL

BEARING
RETAINER

DRIVE SHAFT FLANGE

GASKET

AXLE CASING

BEARING RETAINER

AXLE SHAFT

AXLE SHAFT
BEARING

BREATHER

FIG 7 : 1   Components of rear axle, showing differential gear and propeller shaft

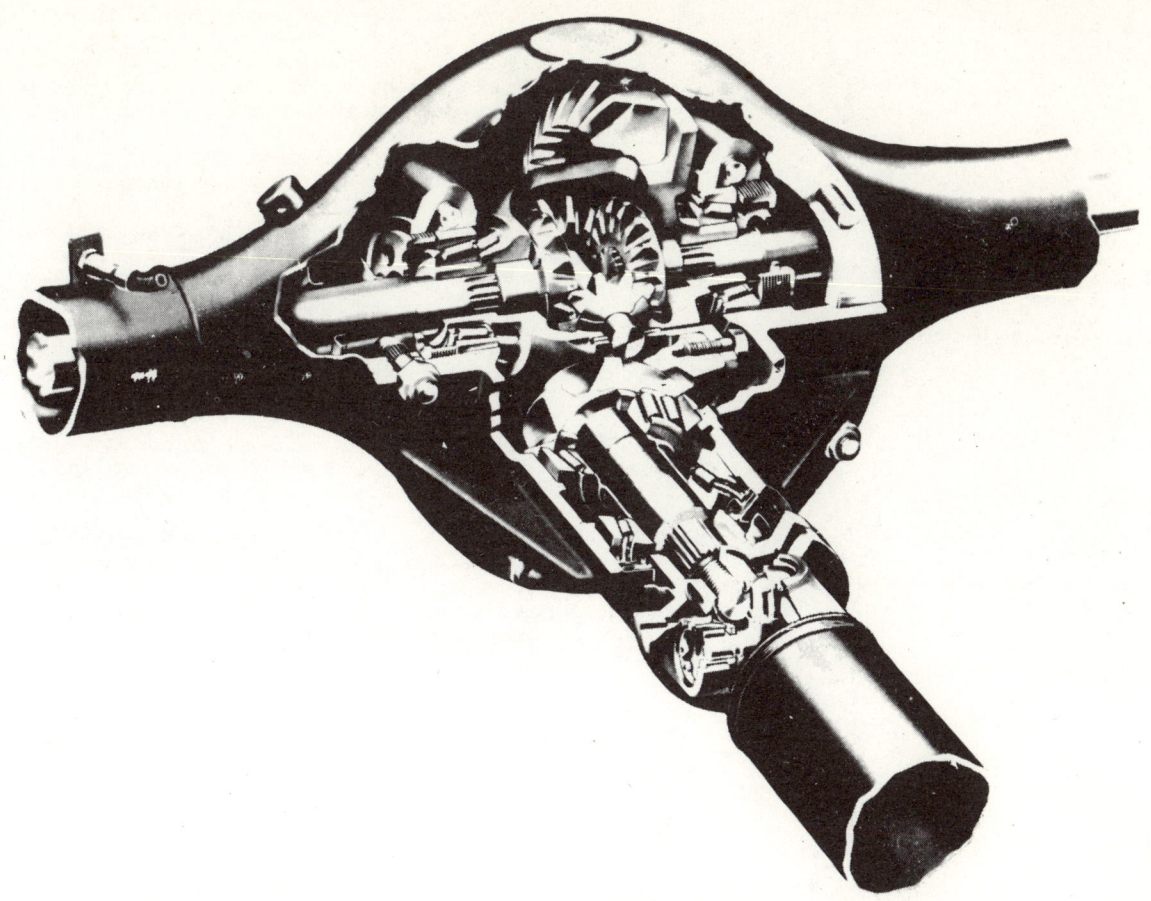

FIG 7:2   Part-sectional view of differential gear and final drive

Disconnect the shock absorber links from the axle spring seats, unscrew the union of the flexible brake pipe situated above the differential carrier, and fit a plug in the pipe-end to prevent loss of brake fluid.

The self-locking nuts on the U-bolts attaching the axle to the springs are then removed, and the plates taken off below the axle casing. This will free the casing, and the complete axle assembly is then withdrawn from the righthand side of the car. It should be noted that the inner and outer U-bolts are not identical, and care must be taken not to mix them, as otherwise it will be impossible to obtain a good fit on reassembly. The difference in type is shown on **FIG 7:4.**

When replacing the axle on the springs, make sure that the centre bolt head in the spring engages the recess in the axle mounting pad. Tighten the U-bolt nuts to a torque of 20-25 lb ft. Refit the brake pipe and handbrake system. The brakes must then be bled and adjusted in accordance with Chapter 10.

7:3 Propeller shaft joints

The propeller shaft universal joints are of the sealed needle roller bearing type, each bearing race containing 34 rollers. The wearing components are readily replaceable, and if after examination this is found necessary, a complete bearing set must be used, and never individual parts. The components for each joint comprise needle bearing assemblies, snap rings, and centre spider complete with seals and retainers. On earlier joints, a grease nipple is fitted to the spider, but this is deleted on later types, as it is unnecessary to add lubricant during the life of the joint in normal circumstances.

To overhaul the joints, the shaft is removed as described in Chapter 6, the rear end of the shaft being lowered to the floor to enable it to be withdrawn rearwards; this allows the front splines to disengage from the gearbox output end. The snap rings or circlips on the universal joints are of a type best dealt with by using circlip pliers, to avoid damage, and are removed by pinching their ends together and lifting out of the grooves. It may be found that the rings are caked with enamel or dirt, and this must be removed to avoid sticking. Also, as the bearing assembly may be hard up against the ring laterally, a tap on the end of the joint fork at the particular side being dealt with, will help to remove end-pressure on the ring. With the ring removed, gentle tapping on the

FIG 7:3 Location of axle filler plug which is positioned for correct oil level

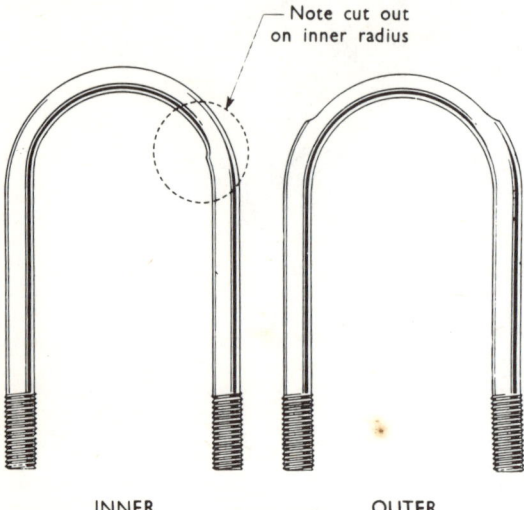

— Note cut out on inner radius

INNER   OUTER

FIG 7:4 Difference in design of inner and outer axle U-bolts, which must be correctly located

radius of the fork as shown on **FIG 7:5** will then cause the needle bearing assembly to emerge far enough to enable it to be pulled out by hand. This is best done from the bottom with the bearing vertical, as it is then easier to catch the needle rollers. The same operation is then repeated on the opposite bearing. This will leave the centre spider attached by its two bearings, and with two exposed journal faces on which the dismantled bearings work. The spider should be supported in soft faces to avoid damage to these ground faces, and the tapping process then used on the other fork to remove

its two races. If necessary, use a drift as shown on **FIG 7:6**. The spider with its four journals is now free, and the oil seals and retainers can be taken off. Wash all parts of the bearing assemblies, forks, and spider in petrol and inspect them carefully. If there is any sign of pitting, corrosion or abrasive wear, the parts must be replaced. The joint is shown dismantled on **FIG 7:7**.

To assemble a joint, first pack the bearings with an approved lubricant. This should be adequate not only to lubricate, but also to keep the rollers positioned during assembly. A multi-purpose lithium-base grease is recommended, and the housing and fork should be liberally smeared. The spider is then fitted into the yoke fork. First position the seals and retainers at the bottom of the four journals, with a little shellac varnish or other good jointing compound applied to the fork shoulders at this point to make a good seal. Tap the bearing assemblies into position with a copper drift of a shade less diameter than the yoke hole. Repeat this operation on the two bearings for the other fork. When all four races are firmly home refit the snap rings, making sure that they are located right down in their grooves. The joint may now appear tight in its articulating movement, but a few taps with a mallet on the yoke centre will remedy this, as it is simply due to the races being a little too far inwards. Finally, apply a little shellac to the area of the circlips to discourage the entry of moisture. It will be noted that renewal of the parts concerned does not compensate for wear in the bearing holes of the yoke forks taking the outer races. If for any reason these have worn oval or oversize to give a sloppy fit of the bearing races, the complete assembly must be replaced.

7:4 Shock absorbers

The shock absorbers are of the double-acting hydraulic type, and do not require attention. If faulty operation is suspected, the shock absorber must be removed, and the body suitably clamped in a vice. The movement can then be checked, and it should be possible to feel a consistent and even resistance on both up and down strokes. If resistance is erratic, and there is suspicion of free movement, with negligible resistance or even none at all, the complete shock absorber must be replaced. In such a case, it is obviously advisable to replace as a pair, to avoid any variation in action as between the two sides of the car.

In testing as described it is difficult to obtain a real guide to operating conditions without a lot of experience, because of the slow speed of movement in comparison with that which obtains in practice.

7:5 Spring overhaul

The rear springs are of conventional semi-elliptic type, and require no attention beyond keeping them clean and spraying the leaves periodically with penetrating oil, at the same time checking the tightness of the U-bolt nuts. If breakage is experienced, requiring removal of the spring, the car should be supported as already described, and the axle jacked-up sufficiently to take the weight off the spring attachments to the car frame. This enables the shackle bolt and plate assemblies to be removed from the rear of the spring after unscrewing the nuts, releasing the four loose rubber bushes. The front eye of the spring is disengaged by taking out the eyebolt. Removal of the

FIG 7:5 Method of extracting roller bearing from yoke of universal joint

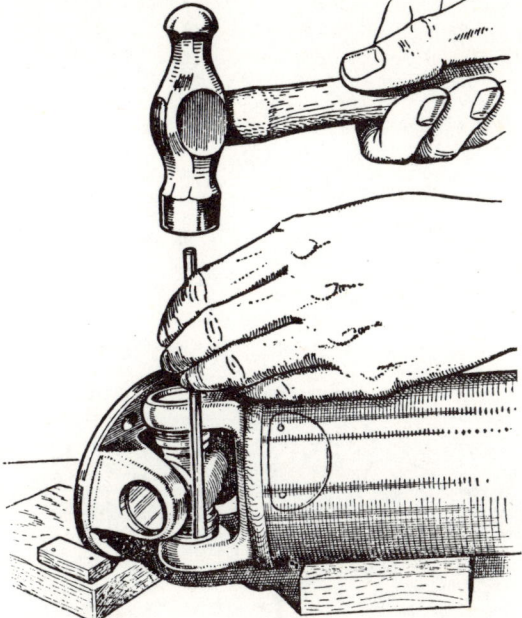

FIG 7:6 Use of drift for removing outer race from universal joint

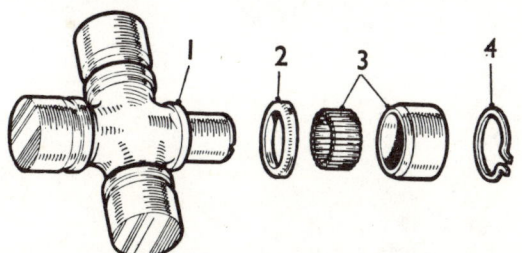

FIG 7:7 Spider and bearings of joint dismantled

Key to Fig 7:7   1 Spider   2 Rubber seal
3 Rollers and outer race   4 Circlip

U-bolts and plate will then allow the spring to be taken away from the car.

If the front bush in the spring eye requires replacement, this must be done by a Ford agent equipped with the necessary press, which removes the old bush concurrently with fitting a new one. The bushed eye is then located in the body bracket, the bolt fitted and lightly tightened. Fit the U-bolts, leaving the nuts slack. Fit new rubber bushes in the rear spring eye and body location which receives the shackle bolt. Position the spring end in relation to the body, insert the shackle bolts and assemble the plates, taking care that the rubber bushes are properly positioned. Fit the nuts, but do not tighten. The jack under the axle, and the car supports, can now be removed so that the car is resting on its wheels. Tighten the U-bolt nuts securely, followed by the front eye and the rear shackles in that order.

7:6 Fault diagnosis

(a) Noisy axle

1 Insufficient or incorrect lubricant
2 Worn bearings
3 Worn gears

(b) Excessive backlash

1 Worn gears, bearings or bearing housings
2 Worn universal joints
3 Loose or broken wheel studs

(c) Oil leakage

1 Defective seals in hub
2 Defective pinion shaft seal
3 Defective seals on universal joint spiders

(d) Vibration

1 Propeller shaft out of balance
2 Worn universal joint bearings

(e) Rattles

1 Rubber bushes in damper links worn through
2 Dampers loose
3 Spring 'U' bolts loose
4 Loose spring clips
5 Worn bushes in spring eyes and shackles
6 Broken spring leaves

(f) 'Settling'

1 Weak or broken spring leaves
2 Badly worn shackle pins and bushes
3 Loose spring anchorages

NOTES

CHAPTER 8

THE FRONT SUSPENSION

The front suspension is by two vertical coil spring and shock absorber units, each mounted at the top in a rubber-mounted thrust bearing attached to a reinforced bracket under the body structure at each side, as shown on **FIG 8 : 1**. To each unit, a track control arm is pivoted at the lower end, the outer ends of the arms being connected by a stabilizer or anti-roll bar which is pivoted on body brackets (see **FIG 8 : 2**). The inner ends of the track control arms have rubber bush bearings to the front crossmember of the car body, while the outer ends have ball joints allowing the steering joints to swivel, as well as for the up-and-down movement of the arms as the suspension operates. Two track rods of adjustable type connect the steering arms to a transverse rod, which moves on swinging links formed by an idler arm and the steering box drop arm itself. The idler arm and the drop arm are thus virtually parallel at all times. The various components of the whole assembly are illustrated on **FIG 8 : 3**.

The lock of the steering can be adjusted by means of

stops on the body sidemembers, which contact the drop arm on one side and the idler arm on the other under conditions of full lock. The wheel bearings are adjustable, also the toe-in or out of the front wheels. The camber, castor and kingpin angles are determined in manufacture, and are fixed.

Spring clips are available for restraining the powerful suspension coil springs when carrying out repairs, etc., and it is essential that these are employed to avoid difficulty and even accident. It is always necessary to check wheel alignment after any such dismantling, which could affect the accuracy of the settings.

The joints in the steering and suspension linkage are variously of the rubber bush and grease-lubricated type. In the case of the latter, some cars have grease nipples for periodic attention, but as development is continuous, prepacked and sealed joints may be found on later cars. When unserviceable, lubricated-type joints should be replaced as assembled components, and it is preferable for the work to be undertaken by a Ford agent.

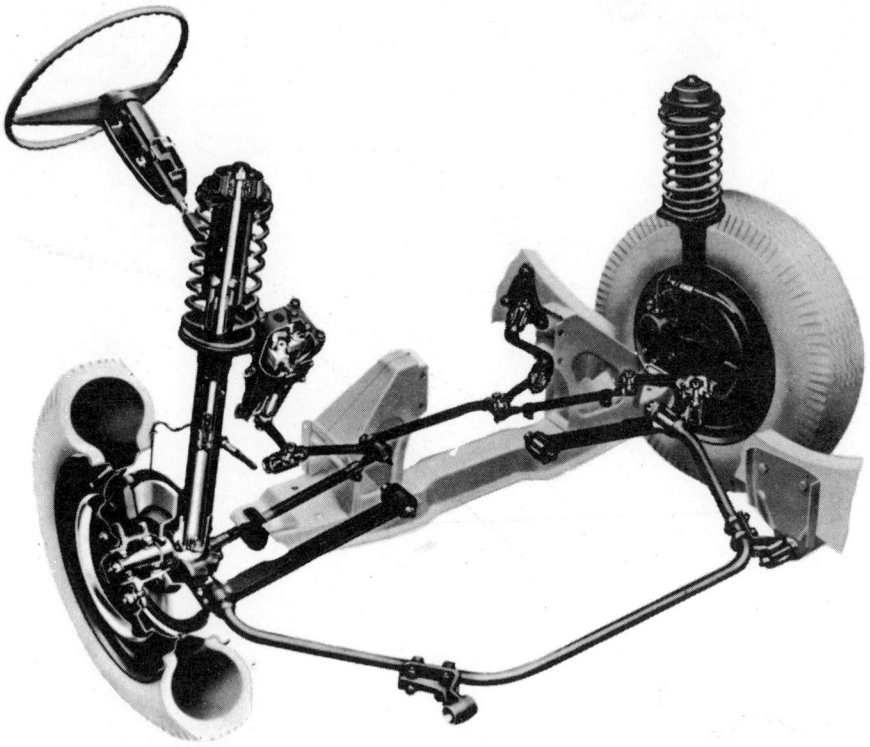

FIG 8:1 Suspension components and stabilizer bar (note—drum brakes are fitted as standard)

8:1 Wheel bearing adjustment

The front wheel bearings are of taper roller type, and adjustable. Every 5000 miles the hubs should be checked to ensure that the end float is not excessive. The method of adjustment is as follows.

The wheel is jacked-up, and the hub cap removed, followed by the bearing dust cap which is a press-fit and may be tapped free. Next remove the splitpin which locks the castellated nut, (these parts being shown on **FIG 8 : 4**), and fit a torque wrench to the nut with its reading set to 27-28 lb ft. Turn the hub and brake drum anticlockwise, and gently turn the wrench clockwise to reduce the bearing play, until the torque setting is reached; the method is shown on **FIG 8 : 5**. Then turn back the nut one castellation at a time, until there is just perceptible end float with the hub perfectly free to spin. Note that the spindle has two holes therein for the splitpin, at 90 deg., and this allows a very accurate positioning of the nut to be made. It is best to test for end float at the periphery of the road wheel.

It is possible to obtain good adjustment without the use of a torque wrench so long as the free movement is very carefully judged. It is obviously essential that influences such as dragging brake shoes must be eliminated before the adjustment is made, and if necessary the brake adjustment must be slacked-off, or the drums removed and cleaned as described in Chapter 10.

A new splitpin should always be used on the nut, with its legs bent over securely. Clean and refit the dust cap,

noting that it must not be packed with grease, as its purpose is for bearing protection only.

In service it is likely that tyre wear may be slightly uneven, and a periodic check with a balancing machine is advisable so as to avoid undesirable steering effects.

8:2 Hub overhaul

At each 15,000 miles, the front hubs should be removed, and the grease cleaned out and replaced with a recommended lubricant having a lithium base.

The front of the car is firmly supported, and the wheel and hub cap removed. The brake adjusters should also be slackened off. Next remove the splitpin, spindle nut and washer, and inner cone of the outer bearing, in that order. The roller cage of the outer bearing is then withdrawn. The hub and brake drum unit are then taken off the spindle, followed by the roller cage of the inner bearing.

The inner race of the inner bearing stays on the spindle, and need not be removed if it is in good condition; the same remark applies to the grease retainer behind the race. If however the condition is doubtful these parts should be removed. It should also be noted that in the case of wear in any bearing component, the whole bearing assembly must be replaced. The components are shown on **FIG 8 : 6.**

Assuming however, that all parts are serviceable, the hub and drum assembly should be thoroughly cleaned inside and out, and the roller cages and rollers washed in petrol and allowed to dry. On the clean spindle, pack the space between the cup locations with new grease,

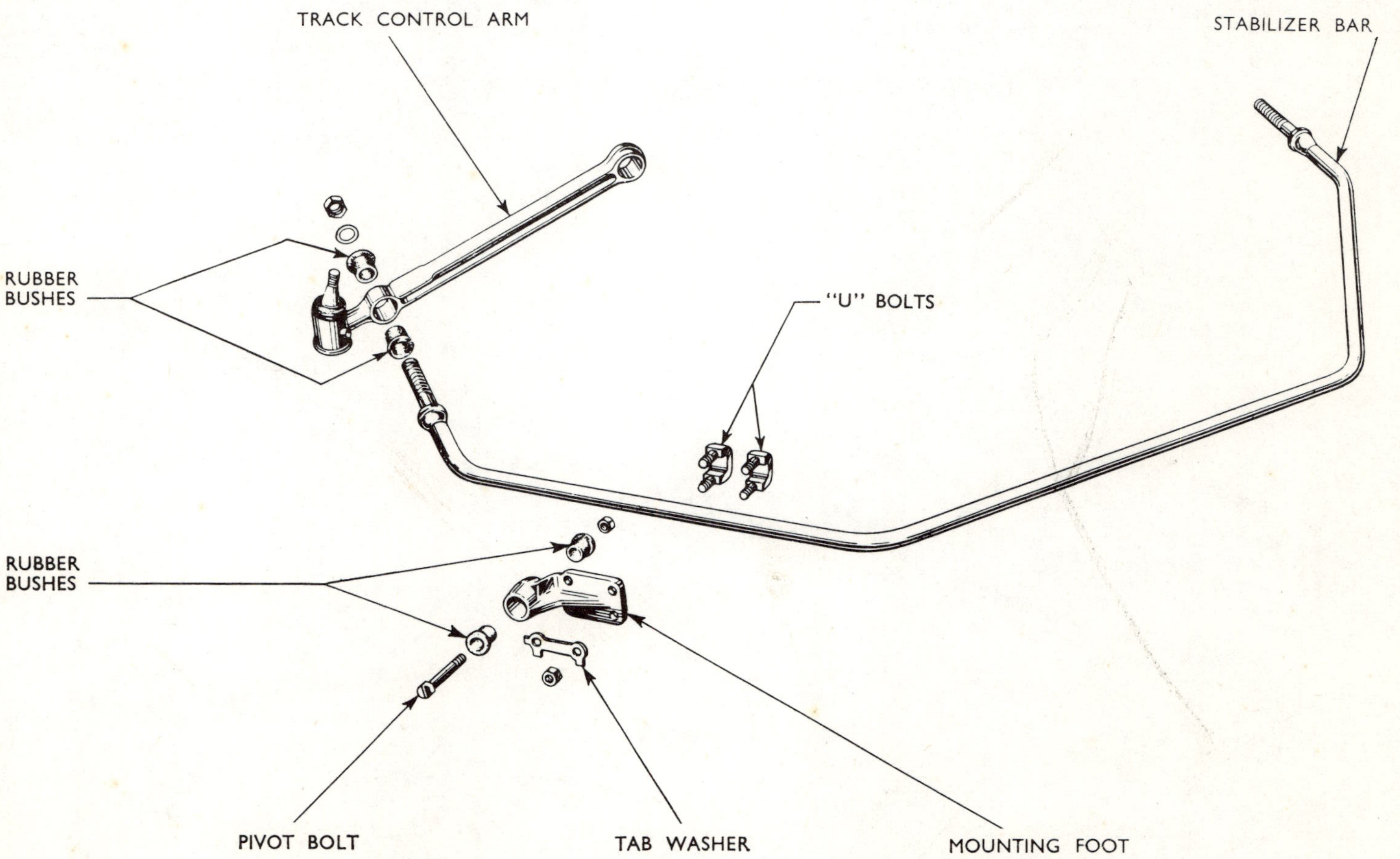

STABILIZER BAR

"U" BOLTS

MOUNTING FOOT

TAB WASHER

TRACK CONTROL ARM

PIVOT BOLT

RUBBER BUSHES

RUBBER BUSHES

FIG 8:2 Components of stabilizer bar and mountings

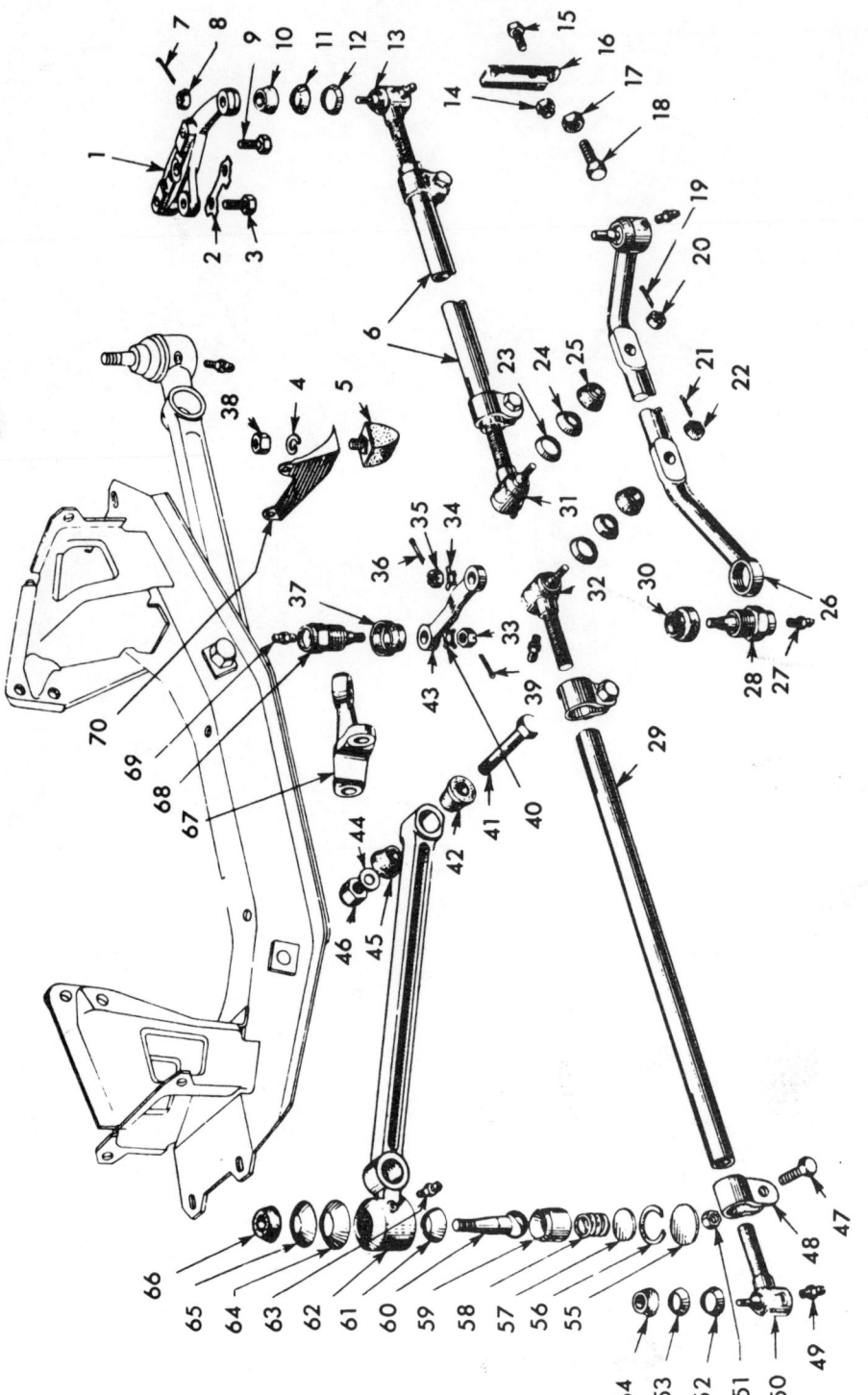

FIG 8:3   Exploded view of the steering layout and track control

Key to Fig 8:3   1 Steering arm   **2** Tab lockwasher   **3** Bolt   **4** Spring washer   **5** Bump stop (where fitted)   **6** Track rod   **7** Splitpin   **8** Nut   **9** Bolt   **10** Dust seal
11 Upper cap   **12** Lower cap   **13** Track rod ball joint assembly   **14** Self-locking nut   **15** Bolt   **16** Bracket   **17** Nut   **18** Bolt   **19** Splitpin   **20** Castellated nut
21 Splitpin   **22** Castellated nut   **23** Ball joint dust seal   **24** Cap   **25** Inner cap   **26** Steering drop arm to idler arm rod   **27** Grease nipple   **28** Stud   **29** Track rod
30 Seal   **31** Track rod end lefthand thread   **32** Track rod end righthand thread   **33** Castellated nut   **34** Tabwasher   **35** Castellated nut   **36** Splitpin   **37** Seal
38 Nut   **39** Splitpin   **40** Tabwasher   **41** Bolt   **42** Bush   **43** Steering idler arm   **44** Washer   **45** Bush   **46** Nut   **47** Bolt   **48** Track rod end clamp
49 Grease nipple   **50** Track rod end ball joint assembly   **51** Nut   **52** Cap   **53** Upper cup   **54** Dust seal   **55** Plug
56 Spring retaining ring   **57** Spring retaining plate   **58** Spring   **59** Ball joint seal   **60** Ball joint stud   **61** Ball stud bearing   **62** Track control arm assembly
63 Grease nipple   **64** Lower cap   **65** Upper cap   **66** Seal   **67** Steering idler arm bracket   **68** Stud   **69** Grease nipple   **70** Reinforcement bracket

but leave a good air space to allow for expansion when warm, otherwise the lubricant will be forced out. Pack the roller cages and rollers with similar grease and smear the outer races. Fit the cage and rollers over the inner race of the inner bearing, slide the hub over the spindle, and note that the inner bearing unites properly. At the outer end of the spindle, fit the cage and rollers into the outer race, ensuring that there is plenty of grease on the cage.

Refit the inner race, followed by the castellated nut and washer, and finally adjust the bearings as already detailed.

If on dismantling it has been decided to replace the brake drum this can be removed from the hub by releasing the locking tabs and taking out the four bolts holding the disc to the hub.

Before fitting a new drum the hub face must be thoroughly cleaned.

8 : 3 Suspension units

The suspension units, one of which is shown dismantled on **FIG 8 : 7,** have coil springs located between a lower seat fixed to the body of the unit, and another seat on the piston rod of the shock absorber. Inside the spring is a shroud to protect the surface of the piston rod. The top mounting comprises a steel sleeve having a rubber bush bonded internally to it. A pair of ball thrust bearings, catering for swivel steering action, are located in the mounting with their outer races bonded to the rubber bush and their inner races on the piston rod. The suspension unit body has an internal cylinder held at the top by the lower guide seat, and at the bottom by a compression valve assembly. The piston rod operates inside the cylinder being held in the ball thrust bearings at its upper end; the rod has piston and rebound valves at the bottom. It will be evident that in operation, the rod remains stationary relative to the car (being held in the top bearings) while the suspension unit body, with the cylinder, moves up and down on the rod. Operation of the various valves is such that when a bump is encountered and the body of the unit moves upwards, fluid is forced past the compression valve, lifting it. This fluid flows into the space between the cylinder and the unit casing. Simultaneously the piston valve is lifted off its seat, and fluid flows through ports in the rod to the space above the piston inside the cylinder. On downward movement of the suspension after the bump, the unit body moves (on rebound) downwards, creating a vacuum in the cylinder between the piston and the foot valve. The piston valve therefore closes, and fluid flows back through the ports in the piston rod, and into the cylinder via the rebound valve, which opens at a predetermined setting.

However this quantity is insufficient to relieve the vacuum which therefore lifts the foot valve from its seat and allows more fluid to fill the cylinder, drawn from the space between the body and cylinder.

There is a rubber sealing gland on the piston rod at the upper guide bearing, and thus the fluid is sealed inside the unit.

If the unit is fitted with a combined fluid level and filler plug on the outside of the body, the fluid quantity should be checked at the specified intervals, with the car standing unladen on level ground. Fluid must never be

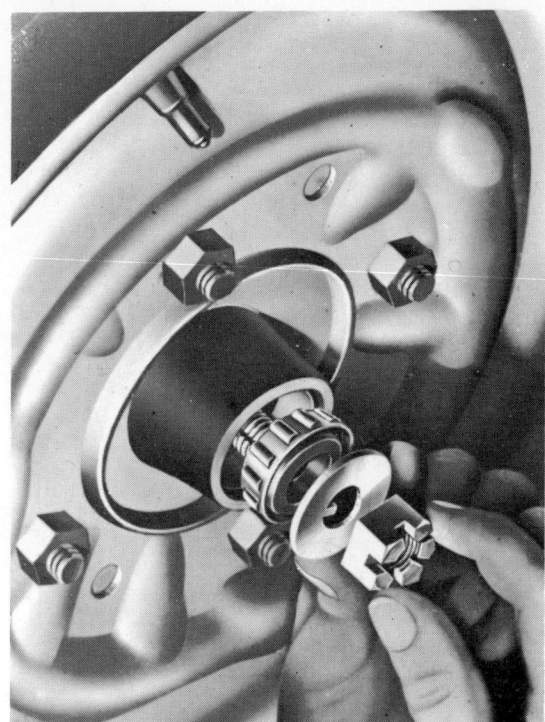

FIG 8 : 4 Outer bearing of front wheel with nut and roller cage removed

FIG 8 : 5 Method of wheel bearing adjustment (Disc brake shown is non-standard)

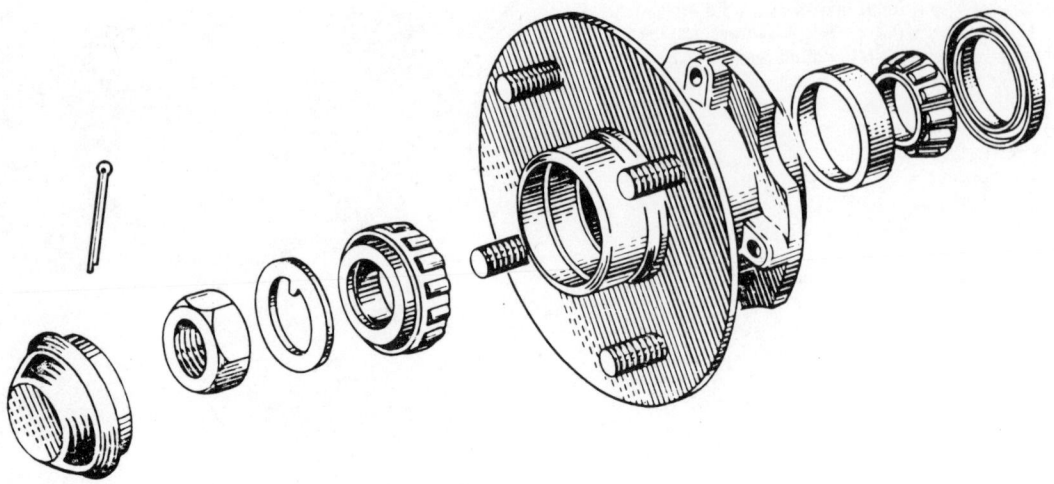

FIG 8:6   Front hub components, showing order of assembly

added by use of a pressure appliance, or when a wheel is raised off the ground.

If no plug is fitted the units are sealed for life, no attention being necessary. Suspension units should not be dismantled, exchange units being fitted when necessary.

8:4 Removing spring unit

To remove a suspension unit, the first requirement is to fit spring restraining clips (Ford Tool No. P5.010) over as many spring coils as possible, and secure with the safety strap. Jack-up the car, and put supports securely underneath. The road wheel, brake drum and hub assembly, and bearing components are then detached as already detailed. Take off the brake backplate by unscrewing the self-locking nuts from the studs. The plate must be supported so that the hydraulic fluid pipe is not distorted; if preferred, uncouple the pipe and plug its end to prevent fluid loss. This will then allow the back-plate assembly to be put on one side (see also Chapter 10). Take out the three bolts securing the steering arm to the foot. This assembly can then be pulled down and away from the suspension unit.

After lifting up the bonnet remove the plastic cover from over the upper bearing. Undo the three bolts which hold the upper support to the frame of the body. Hold the unit, ease the bottom track control arm and steering arm away from the bottom, and remove the unit from the car.

The steering arm and ball joint assembly should not be dismantled further, and if defective should be serviced by an agent.

To refit the suspension unit, first position a new gasket on the inner mounting assembly and bolt the top of the unit to the reinforcing plate of the body, tightening the nuts to a torque of 15-18 lb ft. The dust cap is then replaced. Fit the steering arm to the bottom of the suspension unit, taking care that the lugs on the arm are properly located. Fit the three bolts, tighten them evenly and securely, and lock them by bending over the tab washers.

When replacing the brake backplate, tighten the nuts to 15-18 lb ft torque. After reassembling the hub bearing and fitting the road wheel, the car is lowered to the ground and the clips removed from the suspension springs. It is necessary to bleed and adjust the brakes after this operation, as described in Chapter 10.

8:5 Track control arms

The inner ends of the bottom track control arms are attached to the crossmember by rubber bushed joints which are readily renewable. The ball joint at the outer end (see **FIG 8:8**) can only be serviced by a Ford agent and no attempt should be made to dismantle it. To remove a track control arm, clips must be fitted to the suspension spring, the car jacked-up and firmly supported and the three bolts securing the steering arm to the suspension unit removed as already detailed. After taking out the splitpin, unscrew the castellated nut of the ball joint which holds the steering arm to the control arm, and detach the joint. A special tool is necessary for this, Ford Part No. P.3073-9. Detach the dust seal and cap from the ball joint, take off the self-locking nut from the inner pivot of the control arm, and withdraw the pivot bolt. Remove the splitpin and castellated nut from the end of the stabilizer bar, and take out the bush and washer from the end of the bar. The track control arm is then completely free, and can be taken to a Ford agent for attention to the ball joint.

If the latter is in good condition, and only the inner rubber bushes of the track control arm need replacing, it is not necessary to take off the arm completely. Remove the inner pivot bolt and nut as already described, and pull down the arm, so that its inner end clears the crossmember; the bushes can then be removed. When fitting new bushes these must first be lubricated liberally with soapy water. Enter the arm with the bushes inserted, into position in the crossmember, and fit the pivot bolt and nut, tightening the latter finger tight. Lower the car to the ground, so that it is resting on its wheels, and tighten the pivot bolt nut to a torque of 22-27 lb ft.

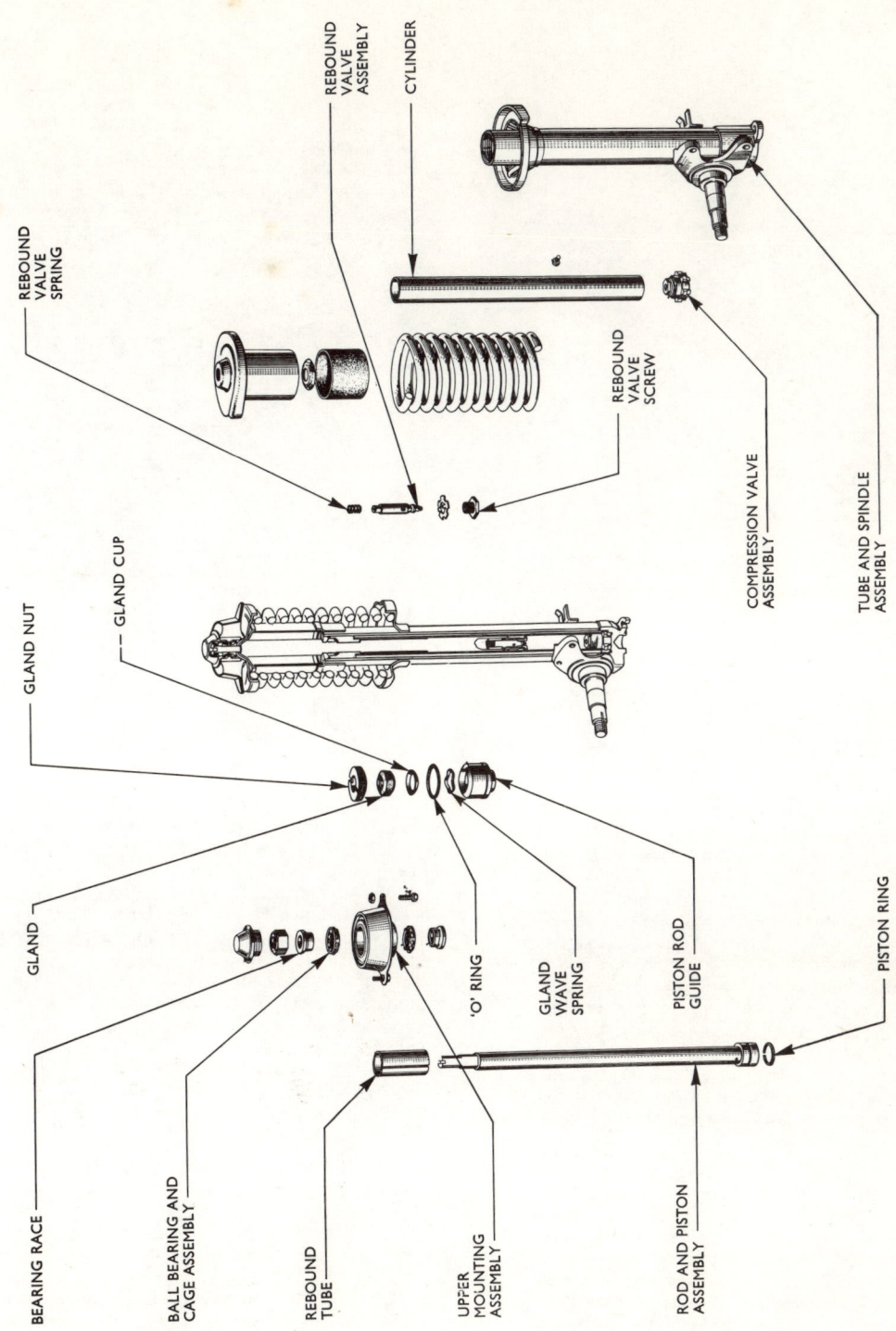

REBOUND VALVE ASSEMBLY

CYLINDER

REBOUND VALVE SPRING

REBOUND VALVE SCREW

COMPRESSION VALVE ASSEMBLY

TUBE AND SPINDLE ASSEMBLY

GLAND NUT

GLAND CUP

GLAND

PISTON RING

BEARING RACE

BALL BEARING AND CAGE ASSEMBLY

REBOUND TUBE

UPPER MOUNTING ASSEMBLY

ROD AND PISTON ASSEMBLY

'O' RING

GLAND WAVE SPRING

PISTON ROD GUIDE

FIG 8 : 7   Front suspension unit with components dismantled

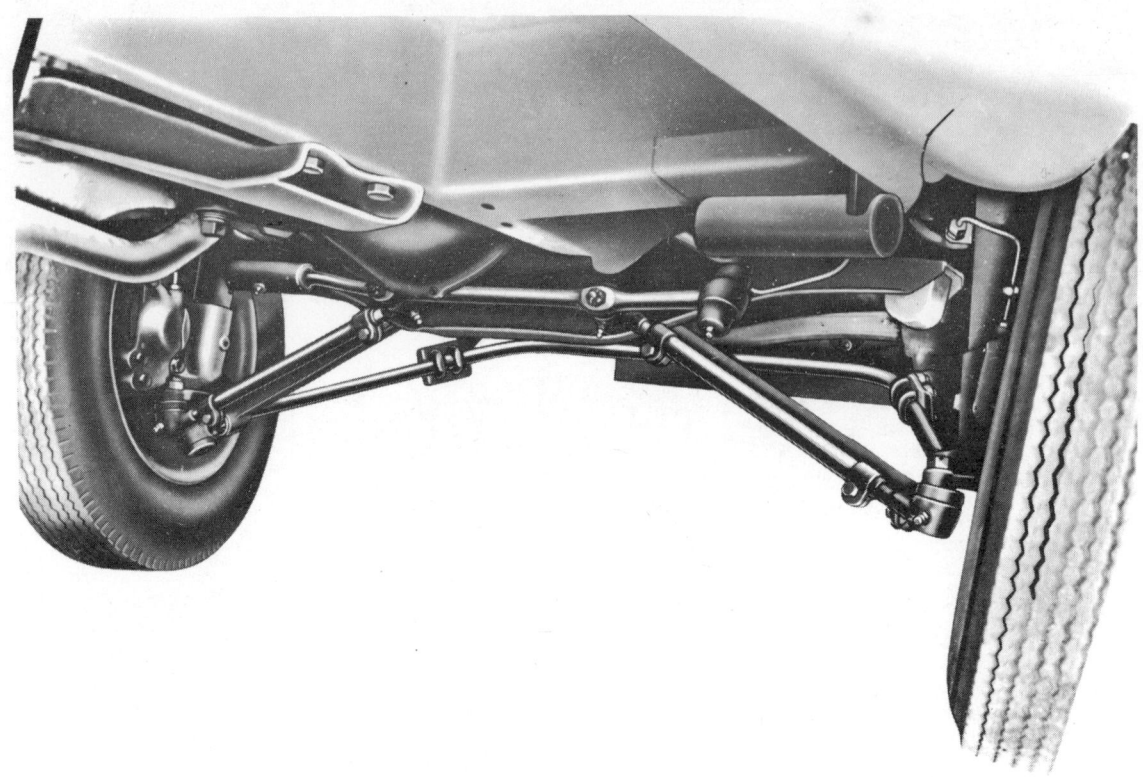

FIG 8 : 8 Arrangement of linkage joints. Note positioning of track rod clamps (Disc brakes shown are non-standard)

When replacing the complete track control arm, the inner pivot is dealt with as above, but first the outer end must be secured. The arm is first positioned on the end of the stabilizer bar, and the bush washer and nut fitted to the end of the bar. The inner end of the arm is then secured as just described. Next fit the dust cap and seal on to the outer ball joint, and enter the joint shank into the steering arm, screw on the nut, tighten to a torque of 40-45 lb ft, and secure with a new splitpin. Locate the steering arm lugs properly on the foot of the suspension unit, tighten the three bolts, and lock with the tab-washers as detailed earlier. The stabilizer bar end-nut can then be tightened to a torque of 25-30 lb ft and locked with a new splitpin. The car is then lowered, the inner nuts of the inner pivot bolts tightened as before, and the spring clips removed.

8 : 6 Stabilizer bar

To remove the stabilizer bar for renewal of bushes or other components, first support the car on stands as already detailed, and fit the spring clips. Referring to **FIG 8 : 2,** remove the stabilizer bar U-bolts, and after taking out the splitpins unscrew the nuts from the ends of the bar. Detach the conical rubber bushes from the track control arms, and take off the bar. The mounting foot (see **FIG 8 : 2**) is removed from the car sidemember by taking off the pivot bolt, flat washer and nut, and sliding the foot from its location.

To fit new bushes, first position the bushes in the mounting foot, and lubricate their flanges with soapy water. Enter the foot between the sidemember flanges, and fit the pivot bolt, flat washer and nut; leave the nut slack for the moment. Position a rubber bush on each end of the stabilizer bar with the flange facing the flange on the bar. Fit the bar to the track control arms, with the sweep of the bar facing upwards. (The bar will then slope upwards from the track control arms towards the attachment mounting feet) Fit a rubber bush to each end of the bar at the rear of the track control arm with its flange outwards, followed by the flat washer and castellated nut. Tighten the nuts to a torque of 25-30 lb ft, and lock them with new splitpins.

Next fit the U-bolts into the notches cut in the stabilizer bar, and replace their locking plates and nuts. Tighten the nuts to 15-18 lb ft torque, and bend over the locking plates securely. Lower the car to the ground, remove the spring clips, and tighten the nuts on the stabilizer bar mounting foot pivots, to a torque of 22-27 lb ft.

8 : 7 Steering joints

The steering arm at the base of each suspension unit is coupled to its respective track rod by a ball joint which when worn must be renewed as a unit. To detach this joint, the splitpin and castellated nut are removed from the joint stud, and the joint separated by using a suitable tool, such as Ford Part No. 3073–9. Take care not to damage the thread of the stud when removing. A similar type of joint is used on the inner ends of the track rods. When replacing the track rods after attention to joints or other items, first check that each track rod end is screwed into the tubular rod by an equal amount, and that there is a clamp in position at each end. Fit the large-diameter inner cap, and the outer cap, over each inner ball joint stud, place the rubber dust cap over the stud, and insert the stud through the crossrod hole, noting that the tapers are engaging properly. To ensure this, all the parts must be perfectly clean. Fit the nut, tighten to a torque of 18-22 lb ft, and secure with a new splitpin. The outer joints of the track rods are dealt with similarly. It is important to keep each track rod to its correct side of the car, and if necessary they should be marked for identification before removing. Before locking the two clamps at the ends of each track rod, make sure that the front wheels are in the dead-ahead position, and that all the ball joints are at mid-travel, so that when the rod is swivelled or turned radially, there is no danger of a joint binding or locking-up. Position each clamp in the pendant position, so that the clamp bolt is at the bottom as shown on **FIG 8 : 8,** and with the slot in line with the track rod slot. The toe-in or out can be adjusted if necessary as described later in this Chapter.

8 : 8 Transverse steering rod

The cross or transverse rod between the drop arm and the idler arm is provided with ball joints, which are dealt with in a similar manner to those already described. To separate the tapered shank of the joint from the location in the rod, a suitable type of forked tool is necessary.

When reassembling, the rubber dust cap is first fitted over the joint shank, the latter then being inserted through the tapered hole in the crossrod (note previous remarks regarding cleanliness), the nut fitted and tightened, and secured with a new splitpin.

8 : 9 Idler arm assembly

The idler arm to which the outer end of the crossrod is attached, consists of a bracket carrying an integral bearing bush with a stud for the pivotal action of the idler arm. The assembly must be removed if necessary for renewal of worn parts. First separate the crossrod ball joint the idler arm as just described. Remove the two bolts and nuts holding the bracket to the car body sidemember, and lift off the assembly complete. Unscrew the castellated nut on the stud-end after removing the splitpin, and detach the idler arm from the stud. The stud should be a good fit in the bush, without shake, and if undue wear is evident, the parts must be renewed as a pair. The bearing is of screw formation, and the stud is first screwed into the bush until it is tight, and then backed-off to a complete turn. Take care that this setting is not altered in subsequent operations. Fit the bracket to the sidemember and tighten the securing nuts to a torque of 25-30 lb ft. Place the rubber dust seal over the stud, position the steering in the dead-ahead position, and fit the idler arm to the stud. A new tab washer is now placed on the stud followed by the castellated nut which is loosely tightened. Move the tab washer until the two longest and widest spaced tabs lie on either side of the idler arm. Bend them down so that they securely grip the arm, and tighten the nut tightly.

Next check that there is a distance of $\frac{35}{64}$ inch approximately, between the lower face of the idler arm and the upper face of the crossrod. The same dimension applies also to the distance between the upper face of the idler arm at its inner end, and the lower face of the support bracket. If correct, these measurements ensure correct working of the screwed bush bearing and stud assembly.

Tighten the idler arm securing nut tightly, and fit a new splitpin. Then turn up the two remaining tabs of the tab washer against the nut flats.

8 : 10 Alignment checks

Front wheel alignment can only be checked correctly when all items affecting it are known to be in order. These can be summarized as: tyres at correct pressure, wheels and tyres running true, bearings correctly adjusted, and all joints in steering and suspension in good condition. The car must also rest on a really level surface, being then wheeled to and fro to allow the wheels to settle into the dead-ahead position, and 'bounced' a few times so that the suspension takes up its natural position. It is of course highly desirable to use the correct alignment gauges for testing (made by V. L. Churchill & Co. Ltd., Feltham, Middlesex).

For checking the toe-in, the measurement is taken at the front and rear of the wheels, and at the same height in each case. Toe-in should be between $\frac{1}{8}$ and $\frac{3}{16}$ inch. If it is found incorrect, slacken the clamp bolts at each end of each track rod, which will be seen on **FIG 8 : 8,** first noting that there is an equal amount of thread available at all four ends. If not, the offending rod or rods must be removed and the ends screwed in or out to correct. Assuming this point is in order, both rods are turned an equal amount to make the adjustment. When the rod is turned so that its top arc moves rearwards, this decreases the toe-in; if moved the opposite way, the toe-in is increased. This is of course the result of the lefthand and righthand threads on each rod-end. When the toe-in is correct the rod clamps can be tightened, making sure the clamps are nicely positioned so that the open-ended portion with the bolt through, hangs downwards to give good accessibility. The open ends of the clamps should then line-up with the split in the track rod ends. Tighten the clamps sufficiently to hold them in position, and then move the steering through the whole of its travel to ensure that nothing is fouling. In particular, note that at full lock to left or right, it must be possible to rotate each track rod slightly, through the amount allowed by the ball joint movement; this confirms that the ball joints are not binding in themselves. Then tighten the clamp bolts securely, and check the adjustment again.

If inaccuracy is suspected for any reason in the angles of the kingpin inclination, castor or camber, checking can only be done by the special Ford gauges, and the car should be taken to the local agent.

8 : 11 Fault diagnosis

(a) Wheel wobble

1 Worn hub bearings
2 Broken or weak front springs

3 Uneven tyre wear
4 Worn suspension linkage
5 Loose wheel fixings

(b) 'Bottoming' of suspension

1 Check 2 in (a)
2 Dampers not working

(c) Heavy steering

1 Neglected lubrication
2 Inaccurate suspension geometry

(d) Excessive tyre wear

1 Check 4 in (a), 2 in (b) and 2 in (c)

(e) Rattles

1 Check 2 in (a)
2 Linkage lubrication neglected, rubber bushes worn
3 Damper mountings loose
4 Suspension arm mountings loose or worn
5 Anti-roll bar mountings loose, bushes worn

(f) Excessive 'rolling'

1 Check 2 in (a), 2 in (b) and 5 in (e)

CHAPTER 9

THE STEERING GEAR

The steering gear is of the worm and nut type, with the nut running on a recirculatory ball bearing. The general arrangement of the steering gearbox is clarified from the component view (see **FIG 9 : 1**). The linkage from the drop arm to the front wheels has already been detailed in Chapter 8, and is shown on **FIG 8 : 3**. There are two adjustments provided in the steering gearbox, these being for rocker shaft end float and for wear in the ballbearings of the steering wheel shaft. It is possible to carry out the former with the assembly in position on the vehicle, but in general it is preferable for all adjustments to be done away from the car, as in any case the presence of excessive lost motion usually indicates the need for complete overhaul.

The condition of the rocker shaft adjustment can be checked quite easily by first disconnecting the steering linkage from the drop arm end, to which it is secured by a splitpinned castellated nut. Next turn the wheel fully from lock to lock, counting the number of turns. Then turn the wheel through half this number from one lock, which should give the dead-ahead position of the gear. In this position the drop arm should point forwards and also be parallel to the steering wheel shaft. A spring balance is now attached to the steering wheel periphery, at its junction with a spoke, and a pull applied to the balance at right angles to the spoke. 1.25 to 1.5 lb pull should suffice to move the wheel in an arc through the dead-ahead position.

9 : 1 Rocker shaft adjustment

If less pull is required it is usually a sign that adjustment is necessary, and this must be verified. First unscrew the four bolts securing the cover of the box, and remove the cover and shim pack. Check that the steering mechanism is at the straight-ahead halfway position, and that all appears in order inside the box. Refit the cover plate, with the gaskets and shims just as when removed, and measure the amount of shaft end float by moving the shaft axially. The float can be estimated, but it is more satisfactory to use a dial gauge suitably mounted with its button against the lower (drop arm) end of the shaft. The permissible end float is .003 to .006 inch. If this is not obtained, take off the cover and remove sufficient shims from the pack to correct the end float. When this is satisfactory, again detach the cover, discard the paper gaskets on each side of the shim pack, and replace with new ones. The adjustment should then be rechecked.

The shims available for adjustment are of .0035 and .010 inch thickness in steel, and .010 inch made of paper. The minimum number of shims should always be used with which correct end float can be achieved.

Finally reconnect the steering crossrod to the drop arm as described in Chapter 8, and top-up the steering box to the level of the filler plug hole bottom. The position of the plug is shown on **FIG 9 : 2** and the level should be checked at each 5000 miles.

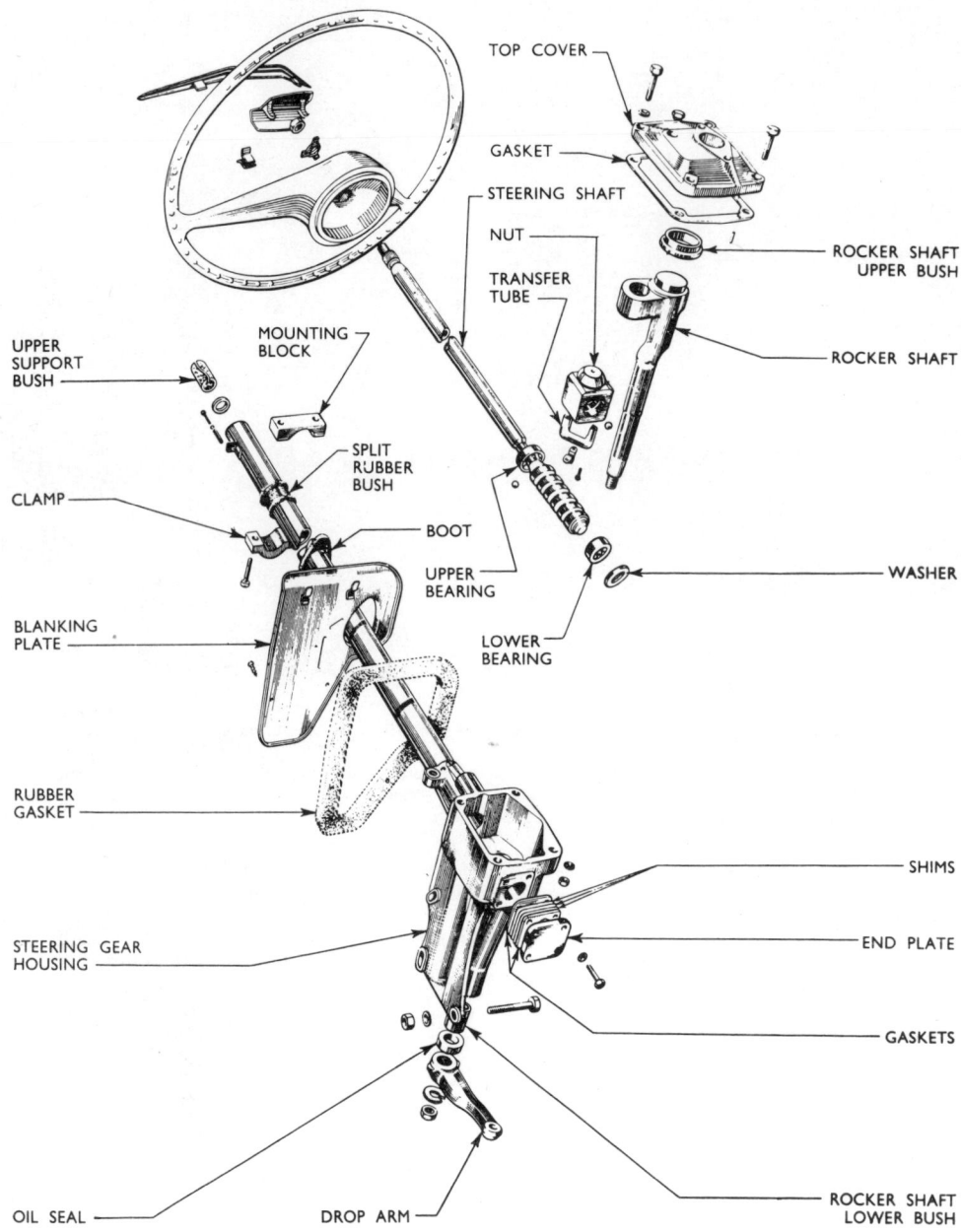

TOP COVER

GASKET

STEERING SHAFT

NUT

TRANSFER
TUBE

ROCKER SHAFT
UPPER BUSH

ROCKER SHAFT

UPPER
SUPPORT
BUSH

MOUNTING
BLOCK

SPLIT
RUBBER
BUSH

CLAMP

BOOT

UPPER
BEARING

WASHER

BLANKING
PLATE

LOWER
BEARING

RUBBER
GASKET

SHIMS

STEERING GEAR
HOUSING

END PLATE

GASKETS

ROCKER SHAFT
LOWER BUSH

OIL SEAL

DROP ARM

FIG 9:1   Components of steering column and gearbox

FIG 9 : 2   Position of oil filler plug on steering box

9 : 2   Column removal

To remove the steering column assembly from the car in the event of overhaul being necessary, the first requirement is to disconnect the battery. The steering wheel should then be placed dead-ahead, and its centre motif removed by prising it up gently. Bend the locking tab from the nut, and take off the nut and wheel. Next take out the four screws which clamp the two half housings to the steering column and detach the housings. Unscrew the two screws which hold the direction indicator and horn switch assembly to the column and release the switch. Deal similarly with the dipswitch. The switches can then be supported or tied out of the way, leaving the electrical wiring intact; there is no need to disconnect the latter.

Take out the two screws securing the column bracket to the parcels tray, and detach the bracket; also remove the two screws holding the upper mounting of the column to the underside of the facia panel, and the two screws attaching the floor opening coverplate and draught excluder to the floor.

The car front must now be jacked-up and firmly supported as was done for dealing with the steering linkage, and some dismantling of the linkage carried out as detailed in Chapter 8. First disconnect the drop arm to crossrod joint at the drop arm, and uncouple the track rods from the crossrod. Take off the idler arm bracket complete from the body and remove it from the car complete with the crossrod.

FIG 9 : 3 Bottom bearing of column shaft removed. Note shims for adjustment

After removing the three nuts and bolts which hold the steering gear to the body member, the assembly can be withdrawn downwards and out of the car. The lubricant is then drained off.

9 : 3 Dismantling

Take out the two screws which hold the spring retainer plate at the rocker shaft end to the coverplate, and detach the retainer and spring. Then remove the cover as already detailed, taking care to keep the shim pack intact. Note that the cover bolts include two of the fitted type for precise location of the cover. Next take out the four bolts securing the endplate on the box end, at the bottom bearing of the steering shaft (see **FIG 9 : 3**). Take off the plate, gaskets and shims; keep the shims as removed, and note that a gasket is fitted on each side of the pack. Lever the direction indicator cam from the top end of the steering shaft, and partially remove the shaft from the box, by turning it so as to screw downwards through the steering nut in the box; this will displace the spacing washer and lower shaft bearing assembly. The ten balls in the upper bearing will be released by this operation, and must not be lost. Also watch that the ten balls from the lower bearing are retrieved as the bearing cup comes out.

The shaft can then be screwed down, right through the nut; there are thirty balls in the nut, which must be collected as this is done. Then pull out the rocker shaft and nut from the box, and the cup of the steering shaft upper bearing. The rocker shaft bushes can now be examined, and if considered unserviceable the bushes and oil seal must be attended to by a Ford agent. There is one bush in the box cover plate as well as the lower one at the drop arm end. The felt bush at the top end of the steering column tube is next withdrawn, along with its washer if fitted.

9 : 4 Reassembly

All parts of the assembly should be thoroughly cleaned and examined for wear. Commence reassembly by fitting a new felt bush to the top of the column tube, first soaking it in hot heavy grease or tallow. The washer is fitted into the tube first, then the bush, until they contact the register inside the tube. Next examine the bearing cups and all the balls, including those in the steering nut. The same size ball is used throughout, ten in each bearing and thirty in the nut. If any worn ones are found, replace the whole set, along with the races.

Fit the upper bearing cup of the steering shaft into its housing, making sure it is squarely home. Smear the transfer tube and balltrack of the nut with grease, so that it will retain the balls, and carefully fit the balls into the nut and tube. Put the nut into the housing (taking care not to displace any of the balls) with its spherical top upwards. Fit the rocker shaft into the bottom bush, taking care not to damage the new oil seal, and locate its rocker recess in the spherical top of the nut; the nut can be fitted either way round. Now pass the steering shaft carefully up through the steering box from the bottom, and rotate it when the worm enters the nut so that the shaft will screw into position. When the upper bearing track formed at the top of the worm is about half-an-inch from the top bearing cup, hold the box with the column downwards and fit ten balls into the bearing, using grease

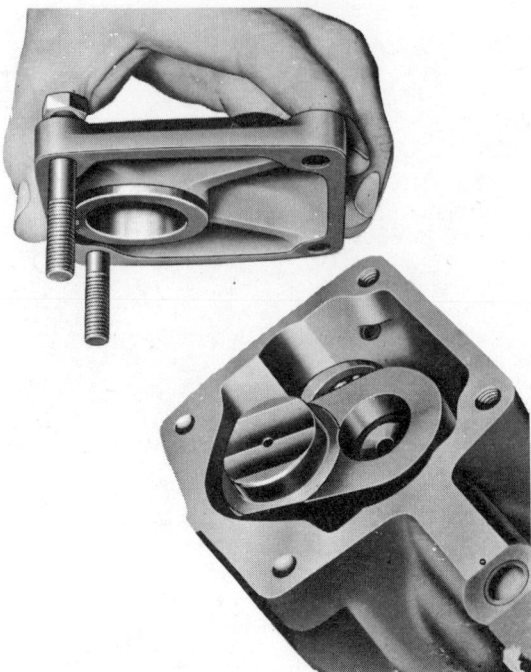

FIG 9 : 4 Top cover with integral upper bearing for rocker shaft

to keep them positioned. Screw the shaft further into the nut so as to close the bearing, making sure that the balls stay in position. Next fit ten balls to the lower bearing cup, using grease to hold them as before. Fit the cup into the box register, followed by the spacing washer against the cup. Again make sure that the balls are properly in the bearing.

To adjust the steering shaft bearings finally, a preload is required of .002 to .004 inch. To obtain this, shims of .004 and .010 inch and paper washers of .025 and .010 inch are available. Proceed by positioning a new .010 inch paper gasket against the box face (see **FIG 9 : 3**), followed by the shim pack originally removed, and then a second new gasket. Fit the endplate, and retain by finger tightening the screws. Tighten the bolts evenly while rotating the steering shaft, so that any binding, roughness or other defects will be immediately apparent; this would indicate insufficient shim thickness. It is important that a paper gasket is always positioned on either side of the pack.

If end float can be felt on the shaft, take off the plate and decrease the pack thickness by removing shims or washers until there is about .001 inch end float. Finally remove one .004 inch shim, which will give the necessary pre-load.

The top cover can now be fitted to the box, along with its gasket. It is important to insert the fitted bolts first, tightening them lightly before inserting the other two. The fitted bolts are then tightened to a torque of 17-22 lb ft, followed by the other two. The rocker shaft must then be adjusted if required, as already detailed, the cover of course being again removed for that purpose, (**FIG 9 : 4**).

9:5 Column replacement

Refitting the column to the car is mainly a reversal of the dismantling procedure. The assembly is first passed through the floor opening, and the steering box located against the frame and held by its three nuts and bolts. Note that two of the bolts also hold the steering lockstop bracket, and these must be passed first through the bracket, then through the body member and finally through the steering box flange. Do not tighten any of the nuts at this stage, as the column must be secured first at its upper mounting. Fit the draught excluder and plate to the floor opening from inside the car, and secure the plate with its screws while holding the brake and clutch pedals fully depressed. The split rubber bush is now fitted around the column and positioned along with the packing piece, against the underside of the facia, with the gasket between the facia and packing. The clamp is then placed over the bush and the two long screws inserted, passed through the holes in the packing, gasket and facia, and tightened. Be careful to line-up all these holes otherwise difficulty will be experienced in fitting the screws, and the column may be misaligned. The three nuts securing the steering box to the body member can then be tightened to a torque of 25-30 lb ft. The idler arm bracket crossrod and steering linkages are reassembled as described in Chapter 8. Next fit the switches to the column, securing by the two screws for each switch. With the road wheels in the dead-ahead position, place the direction indicator cam on the steering shaft, and check the switch for its cancelling operation; the steering wheel can be temporarily fitted for this purpose. When the cam is properly set, remove the steering wheel and fit the two half housings. Take care that the wiring is not twisted or trapped and that the connections are tight, before finally securing the housings with their two screws. The steering wheel is then replaced, with its spoke horizontal and the larger open section at the top to give full visibility to the panel. Tighten the steering shaft end-nut to a torque of 20-25 lb ft, and bend up the tab washer to lock it

securely. Press the ornamental motif into the wheel centre. Finally reconnect the battery, lower the car to the ground, and top-up the steering box to the correct oil level with approved lubricant.

9:6 Fault diagnosis

(a) Wheel wobble

1 Unbalanced wheels and tyres
2 Slack steering connections
3 Incorrect steering geometry
4 Excessive play in steering gear
5 Broken or weak front springs
6 Worn hub bearings

(b) Wander

1 Check 2, 3 and 4 in (a)
2 Front suspension and rear axle mounting points out of line
3 Uneven tyre pressures
4 Uneven tyre wear
5 Weak dampers or springs

(c) Heavy steering

1 Check 3 in (a)
2 Very low tyre pressures
3 Neglected lubrication
4 Wheels out of track
5 Steering gear maladjusted
6 Steering column bent or misaligned
7 Steering column bearings too tight

(d) Lost motion

1 End play in steering column
2 Loose steering wheel.
3 Worn steering box and idler
4 Worn ball joints
5 Worn suspension system and kingpin bearings

NOTES

CHAPTER 10

THE BRAKING SYSTEM

The braking system on all types of car is of the hydraulic type, using drums all round. A general layout is shown on **FIG 10 : 1.** Operation is by a pendant pedal, which is incorporated in the assembly already described (in Chapter 5) in connection with the clutch. It operates a hydraulic master cylinder of identical design to that used for clutch operation. Earlier cars have eccentric bolts on the pedal bracket between the master cylinder pushrods and the pedals, by which the pedal height can be adjusted; later cars have concentric shouldered bolts. However, this does not affect overhauling procedure.

Each front brake is of the two leading shoe type having a separate hydraulic cylinder to operate each shoe as shown on **FIG 10 : 2.** The rear brakes have single cylinders on each backplate to operate the pair of shoes, the cylinder being allowed to float so as to equalize the shoe pressure. This assembly also embodies a mechanical expander and centralizer for operation by the handbrake mechanism and an adjusting device, as shown on **FIG 10 : 3.**

10 : 1 Pipe system

The pipeline from the master cylinder is connected to a union from which separate pipes lead to the front brakes, and a single pipe to the rear brakes. A stoplight switch operated by hydraulic pressure is mounted on the union (early cars may have a mechanical switch). From the separate pipes to each front brake, flexible connections lead from the car body sides to each brake assembly.

The pipe to the rear brakes is taken along the propeller shaft tunnel to a bracket under the floor just ahead of the axle casing. A flexible connection from this point is carried to another bracket on the axle casing. At this bracket is a three-way union, from which rigid pipes are taken, one to each of the rear wheel brake cylinders.

Bleed valves are fitted to each brake assembly and are accessible from the outside of the backplates. (Some cars may have only one bleed valve at the rear, on the nearside backplate.) When the fluid level is topped-up in the hydraulic reservoir, it is essential to maintain the level about half-an-inch from the top rim, and when bleeding the brakes involving pumping through of fluid, it is important not to allow the level to fall too much, as otherwise air is liable to enter the system.

10 : 2 Handbrake layout

The handbrake lever operates the rear brake shoes by a cable system which is shown in detail on **FIG 10 : 4.** From the central handbrake lever, a cased flexible cable runs rearwards, to an equalizer bracket which is flexibly mounted on the rear axle casing. To this bracket, the casing of the cable is attached, while the operating cable is coupled to the nearside backplate brake lever. From the offside backplate lever, a pullrod is connected to the flexible bracket. The cable casing is supported inside the propeller shaft tunnel by means of a bracket, and there is an adjustment for the cable at the attachment point to the handbrake lever. Van versions are different, these having two cables, one to each backplate lever.

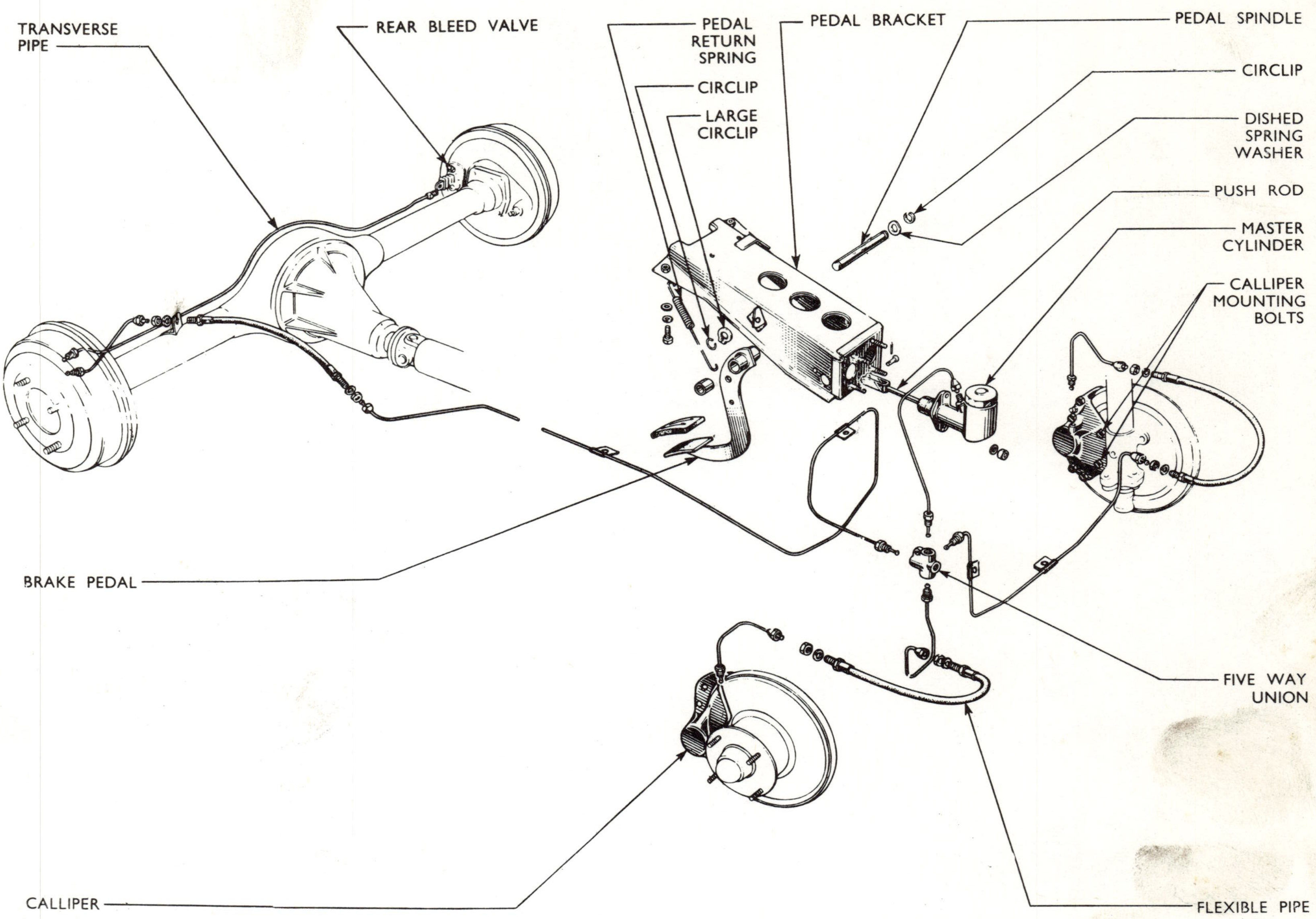

PEDAL SPINDLE

CIRCLIP

DISHED SPRING WASHER

PUSH ROD

MASTER CYLINDER

CALLIPER MOUNTING BOLTS

FIVE WAY UNION

FLEXIBLE PIPE

PEDAL BRACKET

PEDAL RETURN SPRING

CIRCLIP

LARGE CIRCLIP

REAR BLEED VALVE

TRANSVERSE PIPE

BRAKE PEDAL

CALLIPER

FIG 10:1 Hydraulic brake pipeline layout (note—drum front brakes are fitted as standard)

FIG 10:3 Rear brake with drum removed, showing adjusting device between shoes

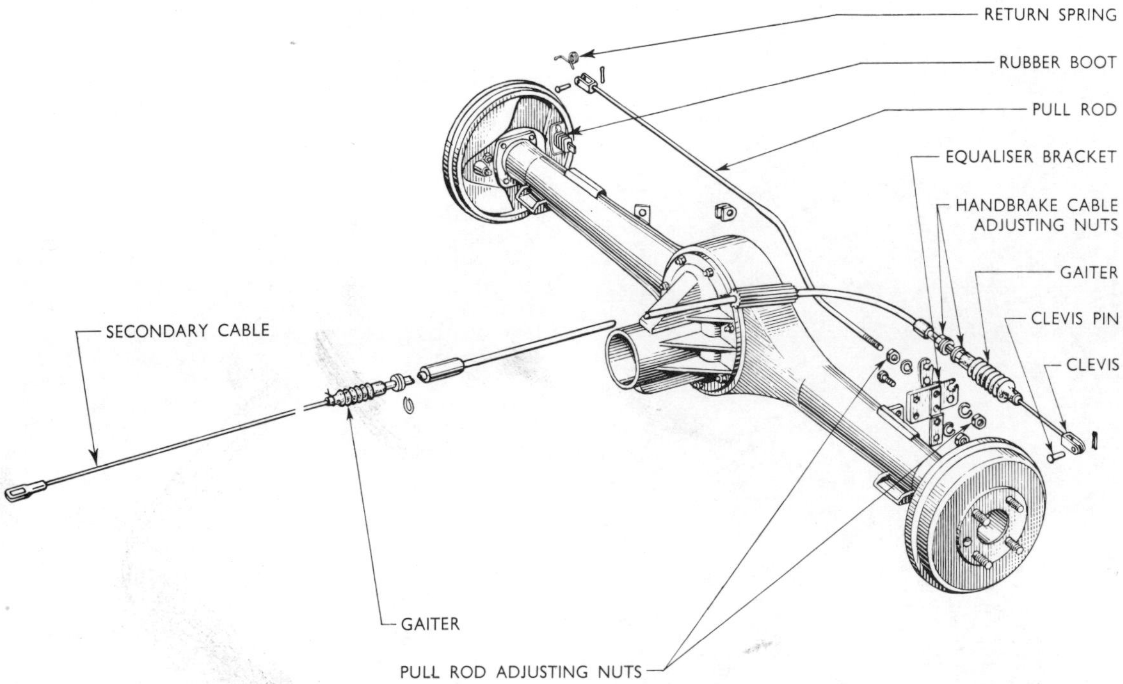

FIG 10:2 Two-leading-shoe front brake with drum removed

RETURN SPRING

RUBBER BOOT

PULL ROD

EQUALISER BRACKET

HANDBRAKE CABLE ADJUSTING NUTS

GAITER

CLEVIS PIN

CLEVIS

SECONDARY CABLE

GAITER

PULL ROD ADJUSTING NUTS

FIG 10:4 Handbrake cable mechanism

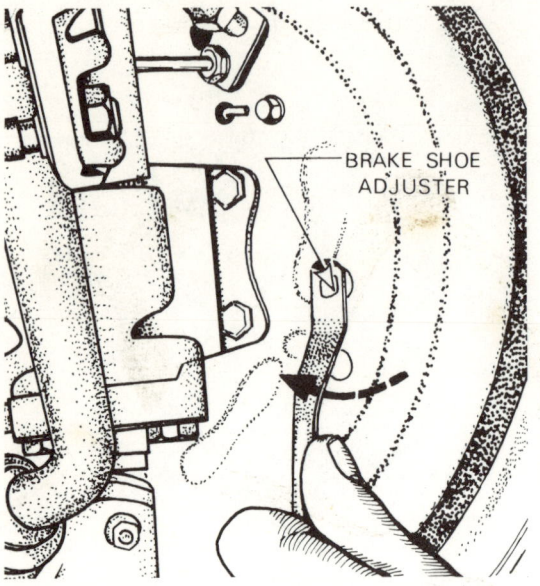

BRAKE SHOE ADJUSTER

FIG 10:5 Method of adjusting front brake (as described in text)

FIG 10:6 Position of rear brake adjuster on backplate

10:3 Brake adjustment

As each front brake shoe has its own hydraulic cylinder, it is also provided with an individual adjustment. On each brake backplate, two square-headed studs can be seen, these operating snail-cams which contact the shoes; the latter are thus moved nearer to the brake drum when the studs are turned with a spanner, and the increased volume in the hydraulic cylinders as a result of this, is automatically compensated for, by fluid from the reservoir of the master cylinder. To adjust the front brakes, jack the car up until each wheel is clear of the ground. Spin the wheel and note if there are any noises suggesting that foreign matter or some defect is causing binding or difficulty in rotation. If all is in order, turn one of the adjusters anti-clockwise to bring the shoe well clear of the drum. Then turn the other adjuster clockwise, as shown on **FIG 10:5,** with the wheel spinning, until it brings the shoe firmly against the drum, thus braking the wheel. The adjuster is then slackened back until the wheel is just free to rotate. The adjuster previously backed-off is then dealt with in a similar manner. The operation must be painstakingly carried out, as the less shoe clearance is required the less free motion will be felt at the pedal. At the same time, the shoes must not be so close as to bind against the drum, even lightly. An assistant who can apply the brakes while the wheel is being spun, can be useful in ensuring that the ideal position of adjustment is arrived at.

These general requirements apply also to the rear brakes. The latter however have only one cylinder on each backplate, which is allowed to float within limits in order to equalize the pressure on the pair of shoes; a single adjuster is fitted at the opposite side of the backplate to the cylinder. In addition, on some cars a snail-cam adjuster of the type already described is provided on the leading shoe only.

To adjust the rear brakes, jack-up the wheel, and turn the main adjuster, which is positioned in front of and above the axle housing, as shown on **FIG 10:6.** It will be noted that the adjuster is of the clicker type, and locks into definite positions. It should be turned until the shoes are hard up against the brake drum, and the spinning wheel is firmly braked. If a snail-cam adjuster is also fitted at the leading shoe, this must now be turned until the cam is felt to be just touching the shoe. The main adjuster should now be backed-off to the extent of two clicks anticlockwise, and also (if fitted) the snail-cam adjuster to the extent of about one-twelfth of a turn, which is equal to a 2 inch movement at the end of a 4 inch long spanner. If a shoe appears to bind, turn the snail-cam until it is free. With new or relined shoes, it may be necessary to back-off the main adjuster to the extent of three clicks, but this should only be temporary until the linings have settled down, and the correct setting must be restored as early as possible, bearing in mind previous remarks regarding lost motion at the pedal.

It is possible if the brakes are allowed to rub or bind even to a small degree, for a lot of heat to be generated. Under some conditions this could lead to aeration of the fluid in the operating cylinder, in which case the system must be bled after cooling-down. Apart from incorrect adjustment of the shoes, brake drag can also be the outcome of the handbrake not releasing properly even though its lever is fully off.

10 : 4 Handbrake adjustment

Before carrying out adjustments on the handbrake, its mechanism should be carefully examined. See that the operating links on the brake backplates are quite free, and that the expander slides on the cylinder mounting without binding. All clevis pins must be renewed if badly worn or otherwise faulty. When operating the lever the action at the backplates should be watched, to see that the linkage retracts correctly to the 'off' position. Finally, ensure that there are no sharp bends introduced in the run of the cable and casing.

With the rear wheels clear of the ground and the car firmly supported, check the distance along the transverse pushrod. This should measure between 31.875 and 32.03 inches, measured between the centre of the right-hand clevis and the inside face of the equalizer where the casing of the cable abuts it. If necessary, adjust the rod to obtain this dimension.

With the handbrake lever in the 'off' position, turn the main adjusters on each backplate until the brakes are locked as already described. Next slacken the locknut of the adjuster sleeve fitted to the outer casing of the handbrake cable at the bracket inside the shaft tunnel under the car (see **FIG 10 : 7**). Tighten the threaded sleeve by its adjusting nut until there is no play left in the operating cable, and tighten the locknut. It is important not to overtighten the cable, as this may affect the main brake adjustment and lead to incorrect operation. The shoe adjusters must then be backed-off, to give the required clearance as described for adjustment procedure. If all is correct, the handbrake lever should pull-on through four or five notches of the ratchet to lock the wheels. Note also that with the brake pulled on, the flexible mounting of the equalizer should be parallel to the centre line of the car. On van versions, adjust each cable to pull equally at the two backplate levers.

10 : 5 Brake bleeding

If for any reason the brake fluid has become aerated, or if any part of the hydraulic system has been dismantled allowing air to enter, it is necessary to bleed the system. Ensure that all unions and connections are tight and free from leaks. In the case of the master cylinder and wheel cylinders, fluid leaks may show up on the outside of the rubber boots and cylinders, and this must be rectified at once.

It should also be emphasized that if any fluid other than brake fluid of an approved type has been put in the system, it must be completely flushed out with methylated spirits, and all the rubber seals and piston cups replaced with new ones. The system is then refilled with fluid, and bled.

The bleed valves and surrounding areas are cleaned, and work started on the front brake which has the shortest pipeline to the multiple union. Take off the rubber cap and fit a rubber or plastic bleed tube to the valve (a set of four tubes is available, Ford Tool No. P.2006). Lead the free end of the tube into a jar containing brake fluid, ensuring that the end is below the fluid surface. Next open the bleed valve half a turn, and pump the brake pedal to the floor, taking care that the pedal movement is not impeded in any way by the floor covering. Release the pedal smartly, and take time to allow the master cylinder to fill from the reservoir. Then repeat the process

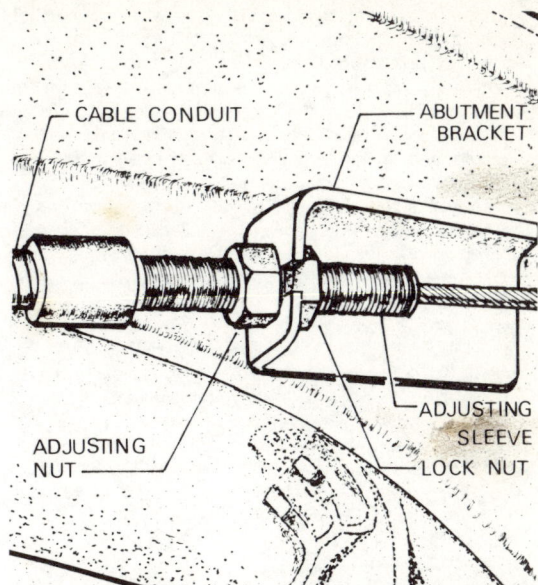

FIG 10 : 7   Components of handbrake cable adjuster

several times, checking always that there is plenty of fluid in the reservoir. Fluid plus any air present will be discharged into the jar from the bleed tube at each stroke. If this does not happen check that the bleed valve is properly open and that the pipeline is not blocked. When fluid which is completely free from air bubbles emerges from the tube throughout the pedal stroke, this is satisfactory, and the bleed valve must then be shut off while the pedal is fully depressed. Tightening torque for the valve is 5-7 lb ft.

The bleeding operation is then performed on the other front brake, followed by the lefthand rear brake, the righthand rear brake (if a valve is fitted here), and finally repeated on the original front one. If after completion of the whole process, the brake pedal feels spongy, the brake shoes must be locked against the drums by means of their adjusters (as when adjusting the shoes). This pushes the pistons in the wheel cylinders fully inwards, and provides the minimum fluid capacity in the wheel cylinder, which reduces the possibility of an air content. The system is then re-bled as before.

Finally, the fluid reservoir should be refilled to the correct level, and the rear shoes adjusted if necessary.

Fluid bled out of the system must not be reused, as it may contain dirt or air bubbles.

10 : 6 Brake shoe removal

The brake drums must at all times be maintained free of foreign matter, and it is necessary to inspect the interior periodically for this purpose, and also to check the lining condition. With riveted-on linings there should be at least $\frac{1}{32}$ inch thickness of lining above the heads of the rivets. Regardless of wear, shoes which have become contaminated by oil or grease must be replaced as a pair. New linings can be riveted to the existing shoes after removal of the old ones, but some skill and familiarity with the job are essential. It is thus considered best that worn shoes be exchanged for new ones, complete with linings and retracting springs. To obtain access to a rear brake, first remove the wheel nuts and jack-up the wheel firmly. Fully release the handbrake, and take off the wheel and brake drum; the latter is located by a countersunk head screw. Then remove the holding-spindle and retaining clip from each shoe by depressing the clip, releasing the spindle and withdrawing the latter from the backplate. Take out the splitpin from the handbrake link to the web of the leading shoe. Each shoe can then be pulled out of its engagement with the tappet at the adjuster end and the expander at the operating cylinder end. Both shoes are removed in this way. It is next advisable to fit some kind of clip or rubber band around the hydraulic cylinder and pistons, to ensure that the pistons do not come out of the cylinder accidentally. The retracting springs between the shoes are of course stretched in order to remove the latter, after which they can be unhooked. Note when refitting the springs, that the one having two sets of coils is located adjacent to the expander housing, while the other, which is shorter, fits at the adjuster end of the shoes.

10:7 Shoe replacement

Before fitting replacement shoes, the backplate and all its components must be thoroughly cleaned, and the wheel cylinder examined for any sign of fluid leakage. Apply an approved type of grease very sparingly to the support pads of the shoes and the recesses into which they fit. Position one of the shoes with its ends located in the adjuster tappet and the hydraulic cylinder piston, and retain with its spindle and clip. Take care that the springs are fitted in the correct holes, that is in the second hole counting inwards from the end of the shoe. Stretch the springs to allow the second shoe to be fitted similarly to the first. Check that the shoe ends are firmly in position and that the retracting springs do not foul any part of the cylinder, adjuster or axle components. Apply a little approved grease very sparingly to the shoe retaining spindles and clips. Check the handbrake link to ensure that it is properly located in the web of the leading shoe, and fit a new splitpin. The brake drum can then be replaced after inspecting for cleanliness and absence of scoring.

As the front brakes are of the two leading shoe type, the construction differs in detail from that already described, though the same principle is followed. Each shoe has one end located at the piston-end of its operating cylinder, the other end abutting a hardened steel pad which is fitted into a recess cast on the back end of the opposite hydraulic cylinder. A single return spring is used to retract each shoe, this being anchored to the shoe at one end, and to a hole in the backplate at the other. Steady spindles and clips are used to retain the shoes, as in the case of the rear brakes.

To remove the shoes it is first necessary to dismantle the hub and brake drum assembly as detailed in Chapter 8, leaving the hub spindle clear. The clips are next removed from the shoe spindles, and each shoe can then be pulled out of its end-locations and the retracting springs removed.

The procedure for fitting new shoes is similar to that already described in regard to cleaning and greasing of the parts. Hook the return spring ends into the holes in the backplate and shoe, stretch the spring and locate the shoe ends in the registers; the wider end of the shoe web is fitted into the slot cast at the blank end of the wheel cylinder in each case. When all is correct, fit the clips to the shoe spindles. Examine the brake drum for cleanliness and scoring, and deal with the hub components as described in Chapter 8. The hub and brake drum may then be reassembled.

10:8 General

When applying grease to the brake components as detailed, this must be done very sparingly, and any surplus wiped off before replacing the drums. If fluid leaks are apparent at the wheel cylinders, the advice of a Ford Agent should be sought, as removal of the cylinders and replacement by exchange assemblies is the best course. Note that even with trouble-free operation, it is essential to replace the whole of the hydraulic seals and non-metallic components of the system at intervals of about 35,000 miles, or two years if below that mileage. The fluid is of course changed at the same time. This is a sensible safety measure which should be strictly adhered to. When fitting new flexible brake pipes which are included in the parts to be changed, take care that these are not twisted. It is perfectly simple to tighten the unions adequately without doing this, if a second spanner is employed to hold the stationary hexagon on the pipe-end.

Minor brake squeal, though of course annoying, is usually very temporary, and is caused by overnight atmospheric conditions which leave a film of moisture and incipient rust on the drum surface. This disappears after the first few brake applications, and should not then recur. Excessive dust or grit in the drums may of course cause noise, but is in any case detrimental to the linings and drums, and should not be allowed to accumulate. If therefore squeal becomes persistent, an examination must be made. It is naturally assumed that the correct grade of lining is used at all times, as otherwise quite unpredictable effects result, apart from the foregoing.

10:9 Handbrake cable overhaul

In the event of fraying or breakage of the handbrake operating cable, this can be removed complete with the outer casing. First disconnect the cable at the handbrake lever by removing the splitpin and clevis pin. Take off the locknut holding the outer casing to the tunnel bracket. Pull the adjusting sleeve on the outer casing to the rear, when the inner operating cable can then be slid out of the bracket. Undo the nut and bolt securing the equalizer to the flexible mounting on the axle casing, and uncouple the inner cable and actuating rod respectively from their slotted holes at each backplate. The cable complete can then be withdrawn from the car.

If the handbrake operating lever requires removal, this is done by taking out the eight self-tapping screws which hold the gaiter retainer and gaiter, lifting these components up the lever, and unscrewing the two bolts which secure the lever assembly to the car floor.

To reassemble the handbrake system, bolt the lever to the floor, position the gaiter and retainer, and secure with the eight screws. Fit the equalizer to the flexible mounting on the axle casing, complete with the cable assembly. Locate the cable and rod ends in their respective attachments at the backplates, and pass the inner cable through the slot in the shaft tunnel bracket. Fit the adjusting sleeve into the bracket and screw up the locknut. Using a new splitpin, attach the front end of the cable to the handbrake lever by means of its clevis and pin. The handbrake linkage must then be adjusted as already described. A light application of grease to the more accessible moving parts, e.g. ratchet and clevises, of the handbrake system will encourage smooth operation.

10:10 Fault diagnosis

(a) 'Spongy' pedal

1 Leak in the system
2 Worn master cylinder
3 Leaking wheel cylinders
4 Air in the system
5 Gaps between shoes and underside of linings

(b) Excessive pedal movement

1 Check 1 and 4 in (a)
2 Excessive lining wear
3 Very low fluid level in supply reservoir
4 Worn bushes etc. on pedal assembly

(c) Brakes grab or pull to one side

1 Brake backplate loose
2 Scored, cracked or distorted drum
3 High spots on drum
4 Unbalanced shoe adjustment
5 Wet or oily linings
6 Worn or loose rear spring fixings
7 Front suspension or rear axle anchorages loose
8 Worn steering connections
9 Mixed linings of different grades
10 Uneven tyre pressures
11 Broken shoe return springs
12 Seized or maladjusted handbrake cable

NOTES

CHAPTER 11

ELECTRICAL EQUIPMENT

The electrical system is of the 12-volt type with the positive pole of the battery earthed. The components and circuits are of normal automobile electrical design, and as is generally accepted, faults in components are usually dealt with by substitution of exchange units. The equipment required for testing is of a type marketed for service-station use and thus it would seem that there is little scope for owner-attention. However, for readers possessing adequate electrical knowledge, some tests applicable to the charging circuit are described in detail, as it is possible to carry these out with the aid of standard precision-type electrical meters. It is however emphasized that the latter must be of high-grade pattern, applied with proper knowledge, and that rough-and-ready methods can only lead to further trouble.

For assemblies such as the starter and generator, it is quite feasible, in the event of bearing or other replacement being required, partly to dismantle the units by using standard tools; this can result in a cost saving.

Wiring diagrams are included in the Appendix. In regard to the smaller electrical units, it may be found that in some cases, access is not easy, and a good deal of prior dismantling of the surrounds may be called for. In such cases, it is preferable to seek the advice of a Ford electrical specialist as being the most economical course.

Accessories such as lamps and horn follow established patterns, with ready accessibility for exchange of faulty components, bulbs, etc. While both styling and lamp reflector designs for example, are liable to change, in no case should there be added difficulty in respect of the essential requirements referred to. As these are substantially the same for all modern cars, it is not considered necessary to reiterate familar details. The practice should be followed of using only lamp bulbs of an established and reliable make, and of the power stipulated. Also, if lamp alignment is suspect, this should be tested by an agent equipped with the necessary precision apparatus; hit-and-miss methods must never be relied on. The reliable functioning of the system depends to a very large extent on the battery, but this is a component whose life is inherently limited by the nature of its work. Long and trouble-free service is however obtainable, provided maintenance is carried out at stipulated intervals. Neglect will obviously encourage early failure.

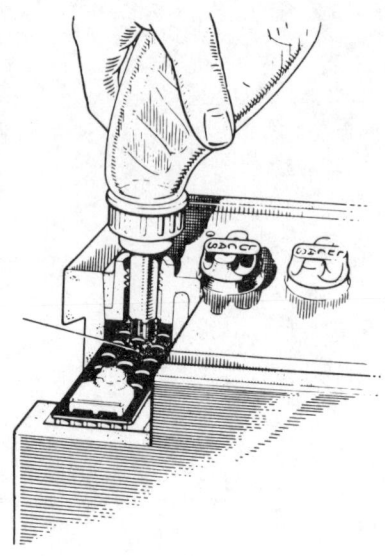

FIG 11 : 1   A Lucas filler for battery topping-up

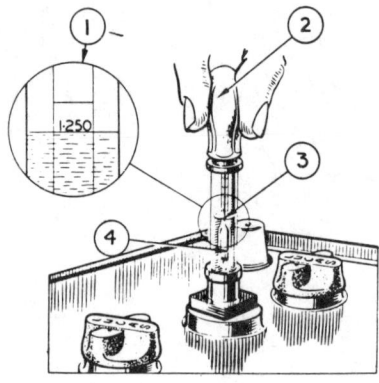

FIG 11 : 2   Hydrometer in use for testing specific gravity of battery electrolyte

Key to Fig 11 : 2   1 Hydrometer scale   2 Bulb
3 Liquid level   4 Float

11 : 1 Battery

The battery is of the lead/acid type with a capacity of 38 amp/hr. A heavy duty battery of 51 amp/hr capacity is available for cold climates, and details of the two types will be found in the Appendix.

In normal maintenance the battery exterior should be kept clean at all times, as a film of moisture and dirt encourages electrical leakage and the building up of resistance in the terminal connections. Corrosion in particular must be avoided; thus the terminals must have their connections kept tight, and a film of petroleum jelly smeared over the metal. Topping-up is facilitated by the quick-fill feature common to this type of battery, but at all times spillage of liquid whether water or electrolyte, is to be avoided. Any such spillage must be mopped up immediately. The correct electrolyte level is .25 inch above the plates. If the level requires topping-up it is preferable to do this just before a journey, as the electrolyte becomes mixed quickly in running conditions. A useful container for topping-up is shown on **FIG 11 : 1**, but whatever kind is used must be of glass or earthenware and not metal.

The necessity for frequent topping-up indicates either excessive charging or a leaking case. The latter is likely to be the cause if one cell requires more fluid than another to maintain the level. Repair of a minor leak in the case is possible, but should be entrusted to a service station. If excessive charging is suspected, the regulator unit can be adjusted, subject to earlier comments on the knowledge and use of electrical instruments.

11 : 2 State of charge

The state of charge of the battery can be checked at any time with a hydrometer, which measures the specific gravity of the electrolyte. When using, make sure that sufficient electrolyte is drawn into the instrument, and repeat the test on each cell as shown on **FIG 11 : 2**. At a temperature of 16°C the battery condition is indicated by the following readings:

Hydrometer reading	Battery condition
1.280	100% charged
1.240	75% charged
1.200	50% charged
1.160	25% charged
1.120	0% charged

At electrolyte temperatures other than 16°C, the hydrometer reading should be adjusted by adding .004 for each 5.5°C above 16°C, and subtracting the same amount for each 5.5°C below 16°C. Should one of the cells show a reading of approximately .030 lower than its neighbours, it may be failing, but this should be confirmed by giving the battery a slow charge on the bench. If the readings are generally irregular, with one or more cells .050 lower than the remainder, the battery should be scrapped. If the readings are reasonably uniform, but low, the battery is quite probably in fairly good condition but in need of a good charge on the bench. The hydrometer is a very satisfactory instrument for ascertaining both the condition of the electrolyte and the state of charge. However, service stations are equipped to carry out a quick check. For example, a high rate discharge test is carried out by connecting the appropriate tester across the main battery terminals and maintaining the test for 10 seconds. With a discharge of 150 amp, there should be virtually no fall-off in the voltage reading of approximately 9.6 volts. If the voltage drop is appreciable it indicates that the battery is nearing the end of its life, and if the voltage shown is below 5, the battery should be scrapped. The foregoing tests should obviously be done when the battery is in a supposedly good state of charge. When the battery is likely to be out of action for a long period, it must be given a topping-up charge at least one per month.

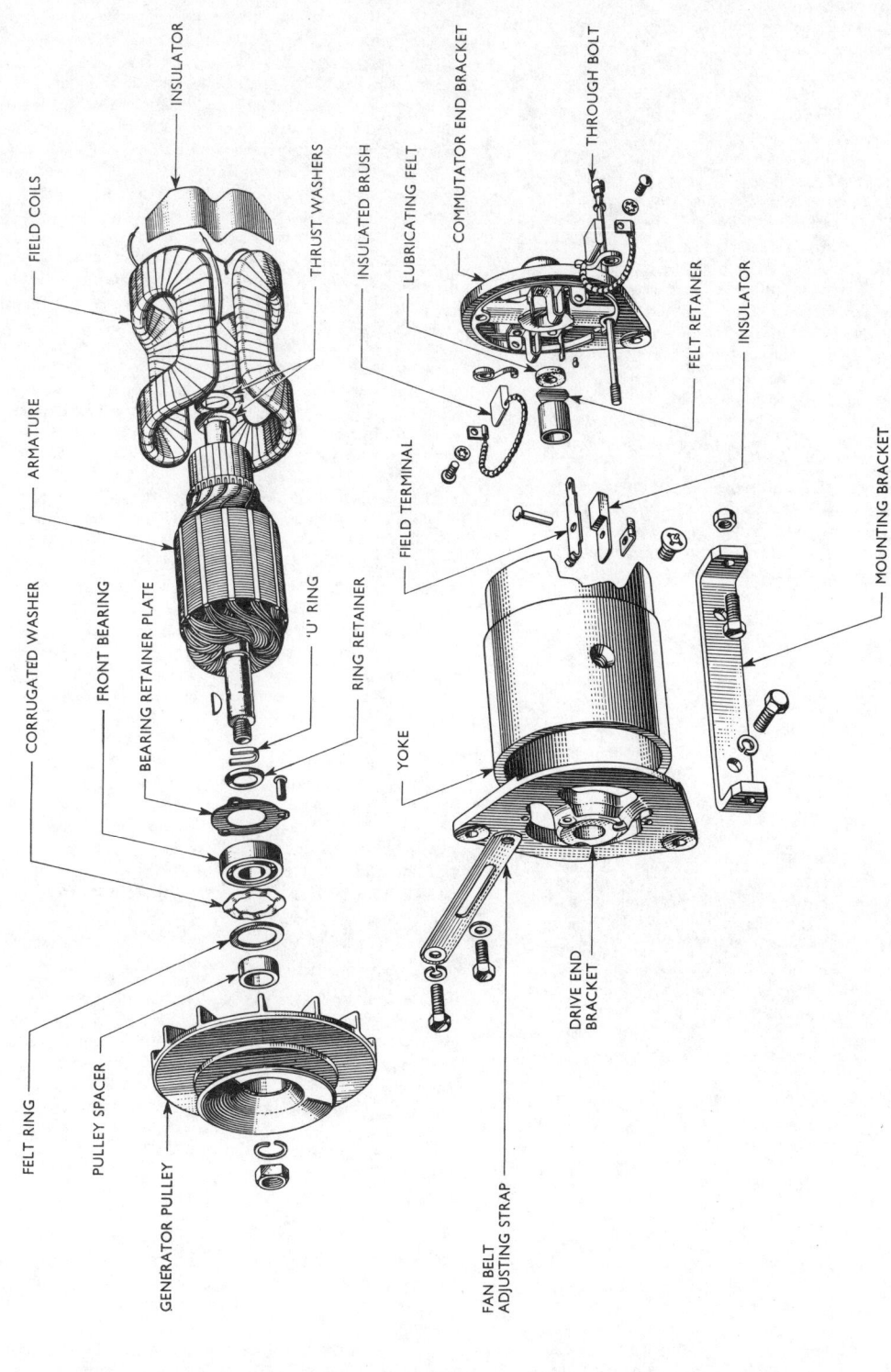

INSULATOR

FIELD COILS

THRUST WASHERS

INSULATED BRUSH

LUBRICATING FELT

COMMUTATOR END BRACKET

THROUGH BOLT

ARMATURE

FELT RETAINER

INSULATOR

CORRUGATED WASHER

FRONT BEARING

BEARING RETAINER PLATE

'U' RING

RING RETAINER

FIELD TERMINAL

MOUNTING BRACKET

FELT RING

PULLEY SPACER

GENERATOR PULLEY

YOKE

FAN BELT
ADJUSTING STRAP

DRIVE END
BRACKET

FIG 11 : 3   Components of generator

11 : 3 Generator

The generator is of the two-brush type, belt driven at 1.5 times engine speed and having an output of 20 amp. It operates in conjunction with an automatic voltage regulator and cut-out unit. The output voltage of the generator can be checked by disconnecting the main and field leads from the two terminals on the generator marked 'D' and 'F', joining them with a loop of wire, and connecting a voltmeter reading 0/30 between the loop and earth. At a crankshaft speed of 1000 rev/min the reading should be at least 24. The speed must not be increased to try to obtain this voltage, as it should be obtained at the fast idling speed indicated. If a very low reading, or none at all, is the result the brushgear and windings of the machine must be examined. To assist in tracing faults a further test can be applied if an ammeter is available. Slacken the generator mountings and remove the belt. Then connect the ammeter (reading 0-30-0) between the terminals joined as before, and the negative terminal of the battery. This will cause the machine to run as a motor, with the ammeter reading 4 to 6 amp. If this reading is higher, it indicates excessive friction, e.g. tight bearings, or possible short circuits. A low reading generally shows high resistance, which could be caused by a commutator in poor condition, or faulty brush contact giving generally bad commutation.

The field resistance can be checked by taking the lead off the 'F' terminal, and connecting this to an independent battery, with the ammeter in series. A lead from the other battery terminal is then touched on the generator casing. The voltmeter must also be connected between the 'F' terminal and the casing. Using Ohm's Law, the voltage reading is divided by the current reading to obtain the resistance in ohm. This should be 6 ohm for the 22 amp generator and 5.9 ohm for the 25 amp generator, at a normal room temperature of 20°C. The car battery (disconnected of course from its normal circuit) may be used for this test.

The generator may be partially dismantled for inspection or rectification, by first removing it from the engine (Chapter 1) after which the nut and lockwasher are removed from the shaft end and the pulley and spacer taken off. As the pulley is of a plastic material, reasonable care must be taken to avoid damage. Work is facilitated by reference to **FIG 11 : 3** for identification of the parts.

The two long bolts are next unscrewed from the driving end of the machine. The bearing end bracket at the opposite or commutator end can then be taken off, and the driving end bracket complete with shaft and armature pulled from the other end. Take out the pulley key from this end.

Should it be considered that the drive-end bearing, windings or commutator require attention this work should be given to a Ford electrical service station. The same remark applies to renewal of the bush in the commutator-end bracket.

11 : 4 Brushes

The brushes can be renewed by lifting up the springs, taking out the brushes from their holders, and removing the screws securing the ends of the brush leads to the holders. To reassemble after repairs, etc., the brushes are first positioned in their holders and held in the raised position by allowing the brush springs to ride with their ends on the sides of the brushes instead of on the top. Then fit the end bracket over the armature, with its bush on the shaft, release the brushes and position their springs properly. Pull each brush in turn away from its contact with the commutator, by pulling on its lead. The brush movement must be free without shake, but if at all imprecise or sluggish, take the brush out of the holder and carefully ease it on the sides as shown to be appropriate. Do not overdo this process, as this will introduce undue shake; and always fit brushes in the same original positions. Renewal is necessary when the brushes are worn below $\frac{5}{16}$ inch long.

The commutator end bracket is now again removed and the brush leads secured by their screws to the holders. The driving end bracket complete with armature can be fitted, with the dowel in the bracket engaging the hole in the groove of the machine casing. Raise the brushes in their holders and locate them in this position as previously. Fit the fibre thrust washer over the end of the shaft, and put the end bracket over the shaft end. Then position the bracket with its dowel engaging the machine body as for the other end. The two long bolts are then inserted from the driving end, and securely tightened.

By using a small screwdriver or similar thin tool, the brush springs can now be levered up into their correct position with the ends on the tops of the brushes, and the brushes correctly contacting the armature. The pulley spacer, shaft key, pulley, washer and locknut are then replaced in that order, which completes the work.

The commutator-end bearing bush must be lubricated, by forcing a few drops of thin engine oil into the lubrication hole at the end of the bearing boss. The machine is then replaced on the engine in accordance with details given in Chapter 1.

The ignition warning light on the dashboard indicates that the generator is charging. It should light when the ignition is switched on, and will remain illuminated when the engine is stationary, or idling very slowly. As the speed increases the generator voltage builds up. This opposes the battery voltage applied to the lamp, causing light to fade until the voltage build-up is sufficient to operate the cut-out. This action short-circuits the lamp, which then goes out.

11 : 5 Starter motor

The starter motor is constructed mechanically on generally similar lines to the generator, but of course its design electrically is quite different; components are arranged as on **FIG 11 : 4**. The generator has four sets of field coils and four brushes, the main electrical input being taken to the field coils the other ends of which are connected to two of the brushes. From these brushes the current passes to the commutator and armature, and thence back to the remaining two brushes, which are earthed.

The armature shaft has a square machined thereon at the commutator end, which enables a spanner to be used to turn the shaft in the event of the starter pinion jamming. The square is normally covered by a metal cap.

It is necessary to remove the starter from the engine, as detailed in Chapter 1, before carrying out any maintenance work. Having done this, the cover band can be taken off, and both end brackets removed by with-

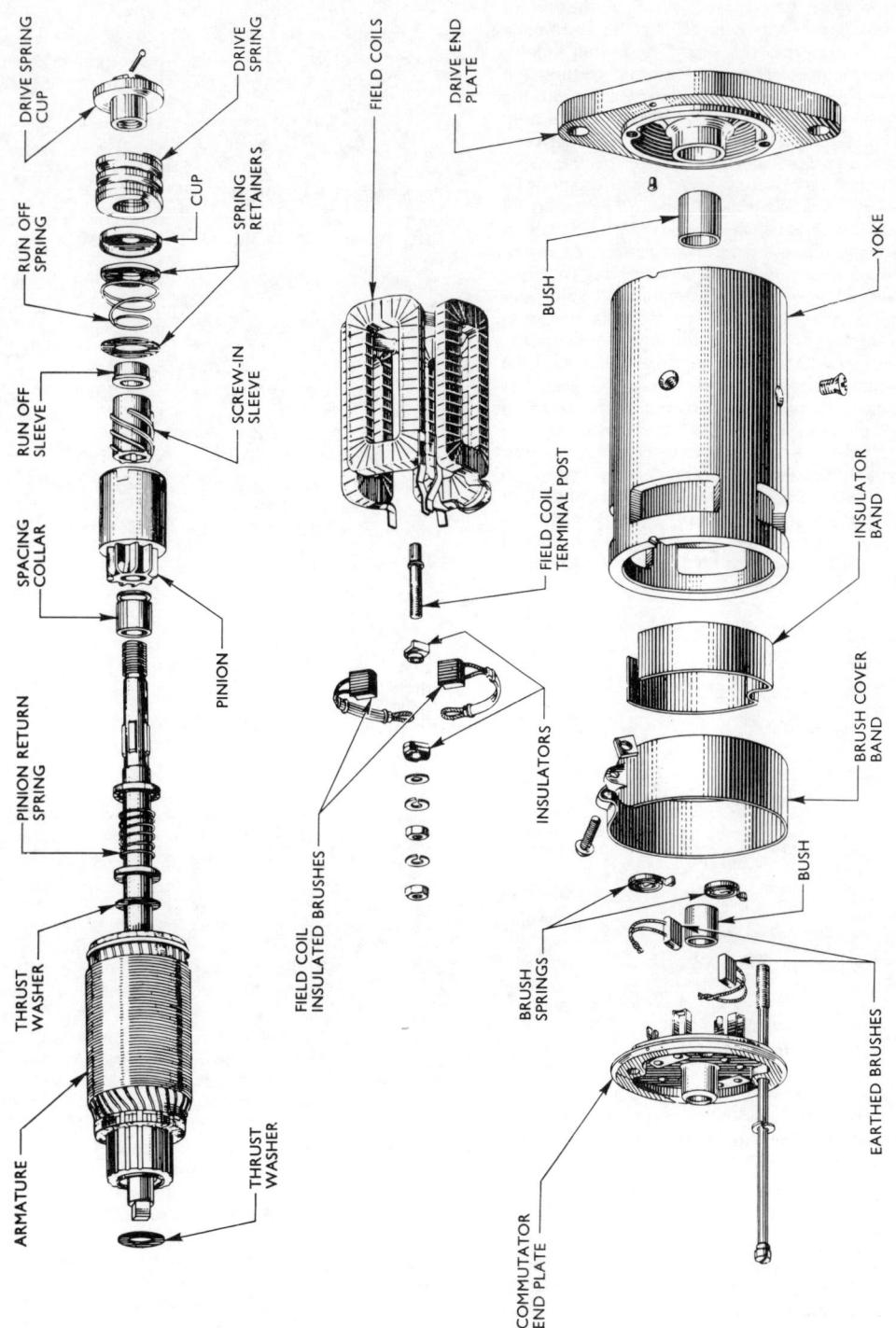

DRIVE SPRING CUP

DRIVE SPRING

FIELD COILS

DRIVE END PLATE

CUP

RUN OFF SPRING

SPRING RETAINERS

RUN OFF SLEEVE

SCREW-IN SLEEVE

BUSH

YOKE

SPACING COLLAR

FIELD COIL TERMINAL POST

PINION

PINION RETURN SPRING

INSULATOR BAND

BRUSH COVER BAND

THRUST WASHER

FIELD COIL INSULATED BRUSHES

INSULATORS

BUSH

ARMATURE

THRUST WASHER

BRUSH SPRINGS

COMMUTATOR END PLATE

EARTHED BRUSHES

FIG 11:4 Components of starter motor and pinion drive

drawing the two long bolts, as in the case of the generator. This will of course withdraw the armature complete with driving pinion assembly.

The brush springs are next lifted, and the brushes examined for free movement up and down in their holders. They may require cleaning with a cloth dampened in petrol, and if considered advisable may also be eased on their sides to ensure free movement as in the case of the generator brushes. Brush replacement is necessary when the length is reduced to $\frac{5}{16}$ inch. The brush leads are sweated to their connections, and after unsoldering them, the new leads must be carefully secured by the same means. Note that the leads of the brushes attached to the field coils have a braided covering and that they are longer than the earthed brushes. If the strength of the springs is inadequate these may be renewed, taking care to close the ends of the spring posts after fitting new springs. The insulation of the brush holders can also be tested with a battery and telltale lamp.

The two field coil brushes must also be positioned so that they point to the main input terminal located on the inner periphery of the machine casing, and which is connected to the other end of the field windings. This post should have fibre washers thereon, and also a fibre sleeve which insulates it from the hole through which it passes in the commutator-end bracket. There is also an internal band of insulating material between the casing interior and the ends of the four field coils at this end; make sure this is positioned correctly.

11 : 6 Starter assembly

Assuming that no specialist work is required on the field coils, the commutator end bracket can be refitted to the casing, but first the brushes attached to the field coils must be passed through the openings in the casing. Locate the end bracket on the casing, with its dowel engaged properly in the notch on the casing. Then pass the two earthed brushes through the other two openings in the casing. Fit a fibre washer, flat washer, spring washer, nut, spring washer, and nut, in that order on the terminal post, and securely tighten the first of the nuts fitted. If no special work is required on the armature, bearing, or pinion and drive, this unit may be replaced. The dowel pin in the end bracket is engaged in the notch at this end of the frame; the two long bolts may then be replaced and securely tightened.

The brush springs are now lifted by means of a hooked wire, and the brushes put back into their holders, noting that the field coil brushes must be in the insulated holders. Check that all is correct and replace the cover band. The machine may then be refitted to the engine.

When the armature is withdrawn, the commutator can be cleaned with a cloth dampened with petrol. It is not advisable to use any abrasive; judicious use of fine glasspaper may have some effect, but is probably hardly worthwhile. There are obvious dangers in employing anything more drastic, such as emery cloth, and in general faulty commutation is best remedied properly, by having the commutator expertly skimmed in a lathe.

Armature trouble such as a bent shaft, or faulty pinion or drive, is properly remedied by fitting a replacement component. The bearings also comprise porous metal bushes, and should have specialist attention if replacement is necessary.

11 : 7 Regulator unit

The regulator system controlling the generator output consists of a two-bobbin unit having a voltage regulator and cut-out mounted side by side on an insulated base as shown on FIG 11 : 5. If malfunctioning is suspected, the action may be investigated, subject to the comments made at the beginning of this chapter; elementary causes such as loose battery terminals, faulty earth connections or a slipping drive belt, should not be overlooked. The generator output should also be tested as already described. If all this is in order, further tests must be made on the regulator unit itself; for this purpose an accurate 30 scale voltmeter and a moving-coil ammeter scale 40-0-40 are required.

Remove the regulator cover and disconnect the two leads from the terminals marked 'A' and 'A1'. Join the two leads together temporarily so as to retain the ignition circuit, taking care that the bare ends of the leads do not come in contact with any part of the vehicle.

Now connect the voltmeter leads to the terminals marked 'D' and 'E'. Start the engine and gradually increase its speed until the voltmeter needle flicks and then remains steady, which should occur at about 1500 generator rev/min (or 1000 engine rev/min). The voltage reading is dependent on the temperature of the regulator unit coil; as this will be equal to atmospheric when the engine is cold, the latter temperature should be noted. The limits are as follows:

Ambient temperature	Open circuit voltage
10°C (50°F)	15.7 to 16.1
20°C (68°F)	15.6 to 16.0
30°C (86°F)	15.5 to 15.9
40°C (104°F)	15.4 to 15.8

If the reading is not within the appropriate range the regulator needs adjusting. Gradually increase the generator speed until the voltmeter reading shows a small increase of not more than .5 volt above the stated figure. If the reading rises appreciably with engine speed and the needle possibly swings well over, either the regulator points are not opening, or there is a fault in the earth connection between the regulator and the vehicle body. Should the points not be opening it is likely that they are short-circuited or welded together, or that the magnet coil is faulty; the unit must then be replaced with an exchange assembly. However, if the voltmeter steadies but does so outside the range stated, the regulator can be adjusted. Stop the engine and turn the screw on the voltage regulator shown on FIG 11 : 7, to obtain the correct setting. The screw is turned clockwise to increase and anticlockwise to decrease the voltage. Between very small movements of the screw, start the engine and check the voltmeter reading. When all is correct, remove the voltmeter and restore the connections. It should be noted that when running on open-circuit, the generator builds up a high voltage. Thus when adjusting the regulator the engine speed must be increased slowly; if the throttle is blipped sharply a false reading will be shown, leading to incorrect adjustment. When all is correct, restore the connections, remove the voltmeter and replace the cover.

If it is desired to check the charging rate, the ammeter is connected in series with terminal 'A' and its lead, after taking the latter off the terminal. The ammeter reading will depend on the state of battery charge; if fully charged, a very low reading will be shown.

11 : 8 Cut-out action

To check the operation of the cut-out (see **FIG 11 : 6**), it is necessary first to ascertain the cut-in voltage of the generator. The headlamps should be switched on, and the voltmeter connected between terminal 'D' and earth. The engine is then started and slowly speeded up. Watch the voltmeter closely and note the voltage reading obtained at the point when the reading suddenly drops as the cut-out points close. This should be between 12.6 and 13.4 volts. If the reading is outside these limits, adjustment is effected by slackening the locknut on the adjusting screw and turning the screw clockwise for increase of cut-in voltage and oppositely for decrease. The engine must be stopped when adjusting the points, and restarted to check subsequent readings, and the screw moved a little at a time between tests.

The drop-off voltage at which the cut-out breaks circuit can be checked by disconnecting the leads from the 'A' and 'A1' terminals and joining the leads as was done when testing the voltage regulator action. Join the terminals 'A' and 'A1' with a jump-wire, and connect the voltmeter between the terminal pair and earth. Run the engine up gently to about 3000 rev/min, and allow it to decelerate slowly. Note the reading at the point when the needle drops to zero, indicating that the cut-out contact points have opened. This should be between the limits of 8.5 and 11 volts. If the reading is outside these limits the fixed contact height must be adjusted by carefully bending the blade, towards the bobbin to reduce, or away from the bobbin to increase, the voltage; this is done with a pair of thin-nose pliers. The voltage must then be rechecked, and further adjustments made if necessary.

11 : 9 Setting of points

It is important that both the regulator and cut-out points should meet squarely and also have the correct gapping. To achieve this it is necessary to make use of thin-nose pliers. In the case of the cut-out points the two armature securing screws must first be slackened, and the adjustment screw turned so as to be well clear of the tension spring. Then press the armature squarely down against the core-face, hold it there and retighten the screws. Note that the core-face may either be copper-sprayed or fitted with a square of copper foil. No gauge is necessary for this operation. Next with the armature still pressed against the core-face, adjust the gap between the armature stop-arm and the armature tongue by carefully bending the stop-arm with the pliers. The correct gap is .025 to .040 inch, when the armature is squarely down as shown on **FIG 11 : 6**.

At the same time, the fixed contact blade under these conditions, should deflect or follow-through for a distance of .10 to .20 inch, as indicated in the illustration. When this setting has been achieved, the electrical setting must be checked and corrected if necessary, as already described.

To set the regulator points the locking nut of the fixed contact is slackened and the contact screw backed-off until it is well clear of the moving contact (see **FIG 11 : 7**). The voltage adjusting screw is also slackened simultaneously until it is clear of the tension spring of the armature. The two screws holding the armature assembly

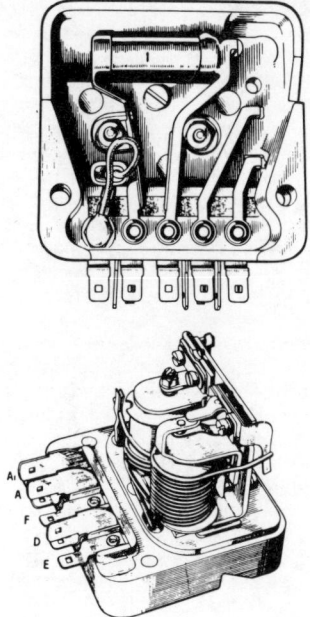

FIG 11 : 5   Voltage regulator and cut-out unit, showing also underside of base

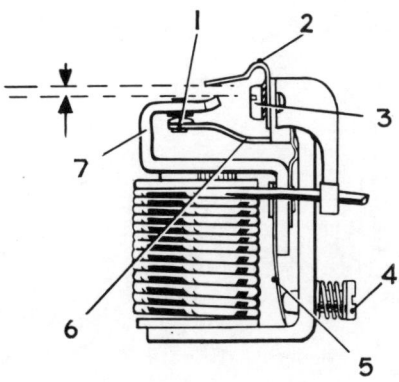

FIG 11 : 6   Air-gap setting and details of cut-out

Key to Fig 11 : 6   1 Fixed contact   2 Stop arm
3 Armature adjusting screws   4 Cut-out adjustment
5 Armature tension spring   6 Fixed contact blade
7 Armature tongue and moving contact
Arrowed gap shows follow-through movement

are next slackened. Insert a feeler gauge blade which is sufficiently wide to cover completely the core face, into the gap between the core shim and the armature; be careful not to damage the shim edge. If the shim is round, use a .015 inch feeler; if the shim is square, .021 inch. Press the armature down squarely against the feeler blade, and tighten the assembly securing screws. Leave the feeler blade in position and tighten down the adjustable contact until it just touches the armature contact, and tighten the locking nut. The regulator must then be checked for electrically correct settings as already detailed. When setting the points as described, the main lead should be disconnected from the battery. In fact it is really advisable to take off the wiring from the regulator unit and remove the latter to the workbench, where the precise settings required can be obtained much more conveniently.

When testing any of the items it should be appreciated that the coil will heat up quite quickly, affecting the winding resistance and thus the meter reading. To prevent false readings, the test for any one reading should be performed within half a minute, or of course less if possible.

Regulator contacts can be trued if necessary with a fine carborundum stone or silicon carbide paper. The contacts are then cleaned with methylated spirits. The contacts on the cut-out are dealt with differently, and it is essential that no carborundum or emery cloth is used here, as the contacts are of soft metal. The correct method is with a strip of fine glasspaper.

Before attempting to clean regulator contacts, the wiring must be disconnected and the complete regulator removed from the car. The adjustable contacts of the two regulators may then be taken off, which will facilitate cleaning of all the contacts.

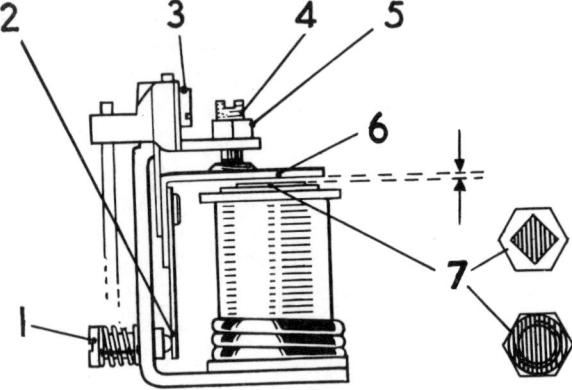

FIG 11 : 7 Adjustment points and details of voltage regulator

Key to Fig 11 : 7   1 Voltage adjustment   2 Armature tension spring   3 Armature securing screws
4 Fixed contact adjustment   5 Locknut   6 Armature
7 Alternative core faces
Arrowed gap shows armature movement

11 : 10 Fault diagnosis

(a) Battery discharged

1 Terminals loose or dirty
2 Lighting circuit short circuited
3 Generator not charging
4 Regulator or cut-out unit not working properly
5 Battery internally defective

(b) Insufficient charging current

1 Loose or corroded battery terminals
2 Generator driving belt slipping

(c) Battery will not hold a charge

1 Low electrolyte level
2 Battery plates sulphated
3 Electrolyte leakage from cracked casing or top
4 Plate separators ineffective

(d) Battery overcharged

1 Voltage regulator needs adjusting

(e) Generator output low or nil

1 Belt broken or slipping
2 Regulator unit out of adjustment
3 Commutator worn, burned or short circuited
4 Insulation proud between commutator segments
5 Brushes sticking, springs weak or broken
6 Field coil wires short circuited, broken or burned

(f) Starter motor lacks power or will not operate

1 Battery discharged, loose cable connections
2 Starter pinion jammed in mesh with flywheel gear
3 Starter switch faulty
4 Brushes worn or sticking, leads detached or short circuiting
5 Commutator dirty or worn
6 Starter shaft bent
7 Engine abnormally stiff

(g) Starter motor runs but does not turn engine

1 Pinion sticking on screwed sleeve
2 Broken teeth on pinion or flywheel gears

(h) Noisy starter pinion when engine is running

1 Restraining spring weak or broken

(i) Starter motor inoperative

1 Check 1 and 4 in (f)
2 Armature or field coils faulty

(j) Starter motor rough or noisy

1 Mounting bolts loose
2 Damaged pinion or flywheel gear teeth
3 Main pinion spring broken

(k) Lamps inoperative or erratic

1 Battery low, bulbs burned out
2 Faulty earthing of lamps or battery
3 Lighting switch faulty, loose or broken wiring connections

(l) Wiper motor sluggish, taking high current

1 Faulty armature
2 Bearings out of alignment
3 Commutator dirty or short circuited
4 Wheelbox spindle binding, cable rack tight in housing

(m) Wiper motor operates but does not drive arm

1 Wheelbox gear and spindle worn
2 Cable rack faulty
3 Gearbox components worn

(n) Panel gauge does not register

1 No battery supply to gauge
2 Gauge casing not earthed
3 Cable between gauge and sender unit earthed

NOTES

CHAPTER 12

THE BODYWORK

Because of the highly specialized form of modern body construction, it is usually necessary to take any typical modern car to an agent having a completely equipped body shop, should any exacting work be required such as replacement of glass, hanging of doors, panel-beating, etc.; these Ford models are no exception. However, it is quite feasible for the skilful owner to carry out certain work concerned with maintaining the body in a weather-tight condition, so that there need be no falling-off in comfort or roadworthiness as mileage mounts up. Water ingress, draughts and so on are apt to be too readily accepted on older cars, or those that have had a lot of service; but due to the wide use of readily applied sealing compounds as standard practice, such defects can be overcome so long as method is applied to the work.

12 : 1 Body sealing

On a new car, the bodywork is well sealed against the entry of both water and dust. In use however the continuous flexing which is a consequence of road motion, is liable to prejudice the original effectiveness of the seals at certain points.

Any joint or aperture in the body which connects to the outside is a potential source of entry for water and dust. To prevent this, it is essential that the rubber weatherstrips around the doors and boot lid are in good condition and cemented firmly in the correct position; also that the wind cords on the trim are properly located. When investigating water entry, for example, it is useless to try a hit-and-miss investigation. The precise point of leakage must be ascertained, when it can then be decided whether the standard practice is to use a simple sealer at that point, or if there is a fault which requires more complicated attention.

A good check for water leakage is to apply a low-pressure water jet from a hose on the upper parts of the body, after first removing the carpets, seats, and trim panels from the interior. The welded joints under the mudguards can also be tested with a high-pressure jet. Actual holes in the panelling can sometimes be seen if a bright light is held outside the suspected panel and close to it, while an assistant checks whether the light can be seen from the inside.

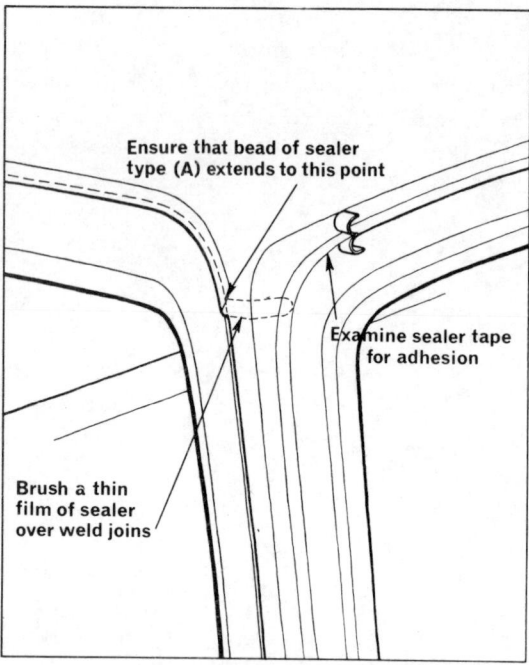

FIG 12:1 Sealing points at top of screen pillars

In the figure:
- Ensure that bead of sealer type (A) extends to this point
- Examine sealer tape for adhesion
- Brush a thin film of sealer over weld joins

12:2 Sealing material

There are plenty of universal sealing compounds marketed, but for the best results it is essential to use the correct type of compound for any particular locations. It is practicable to refer to sealers under the following descriptions.

A. A compound for general application to joints of panels, where a neat fillet of water-resistant sealer is called for. This should be fairly fluid so that it may be applied by use of a pressure-gun or similar nozzle. It will dry to a rubbery consistency, and have good adhesion to the surface to which it is applied.

B. A sealer for application by brush, water resistant and with good adhesive properties, and drying fairly hard. This is for application in places where bombardment by small stones and grit is likely, as on the inside of the wheel arches and mudguards. Due to its hard-setting, this sealer can withstand such conditions without penetration.

C. A liquid sealer having a consistency suitable for application by force-feed oilcan or gun, and employed for sealing fixed window and windscreen weather-strips to both the glass and body metal.

D. A bulk sealer which is used in locations where the joint is not exposed to the weather.

E. A plastic sealing tape with a width of .75 inch, which is used around the windscreen and rear window apertures.

F. An adhesive for reattaching carpet underfelts, sponge weather-strips and similar furnishings to body and door metal.

12:3 Applying sealers

No form of sealing compound will be effective unless the surfaces to which it is applied are absolutely clean and free from moisture, dirt or rust, and really thorough cleaning is necessary. Due to the general requirement of getting a car back on the road as soon as possible, many types of sealer are fast-drying, and may thus feel dry to the touch about an hour after application. It is however most advisable to allow at least 24 hours drying period even with this type; on slower-drying sealers the makers' instructions must be rigidly adhered to. In general, the longer the drying period that can be allowed, the better.

Smoothing-off after application of a fillet of sealer can be done with the finger if well moistened. If sealer is accidentally put on paintwork it can be removed with petrol or white spirit. Sealer which has of necessity to be visible on the body should be touched-up with paint of the correct body colour. When refitting weather-strips on doors and windows, the old adhesive is removed by using Bostik cleaner or cellulose thinner. If the latter is used however, on no account must it come into contact with cellulose paintwork.

12:4 Water leakage

It will be useful to detail some of the more usual sources of water-drips into the body interior, and the method of remedying these. Dripping on to the front carpet is often caused by defective roof drain channels, and the latter should be examined at the joints of the channel and roof panel. Seal the joints along the underside and inner edges of each channel, applying a smooth fillet of the sealer described under type A from a pressure-gun or nozzle.

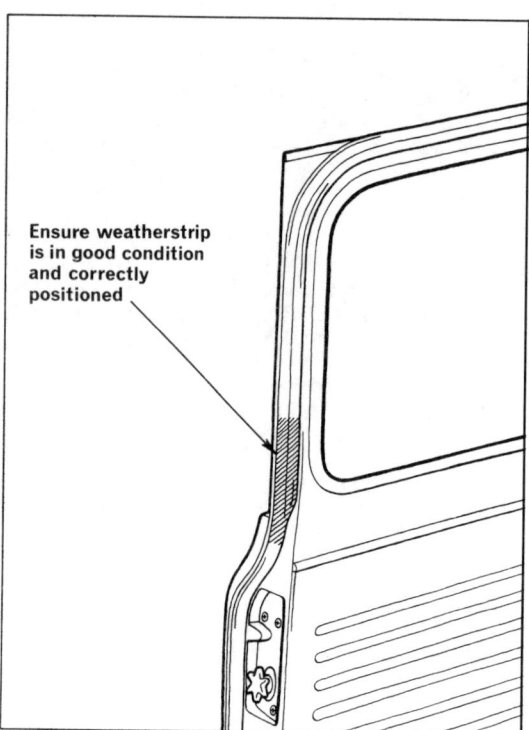

FIG 12:2 Location of door weatherstrips

In the figure:
- Ensure weatherstrip is in good condition and correctly positioned

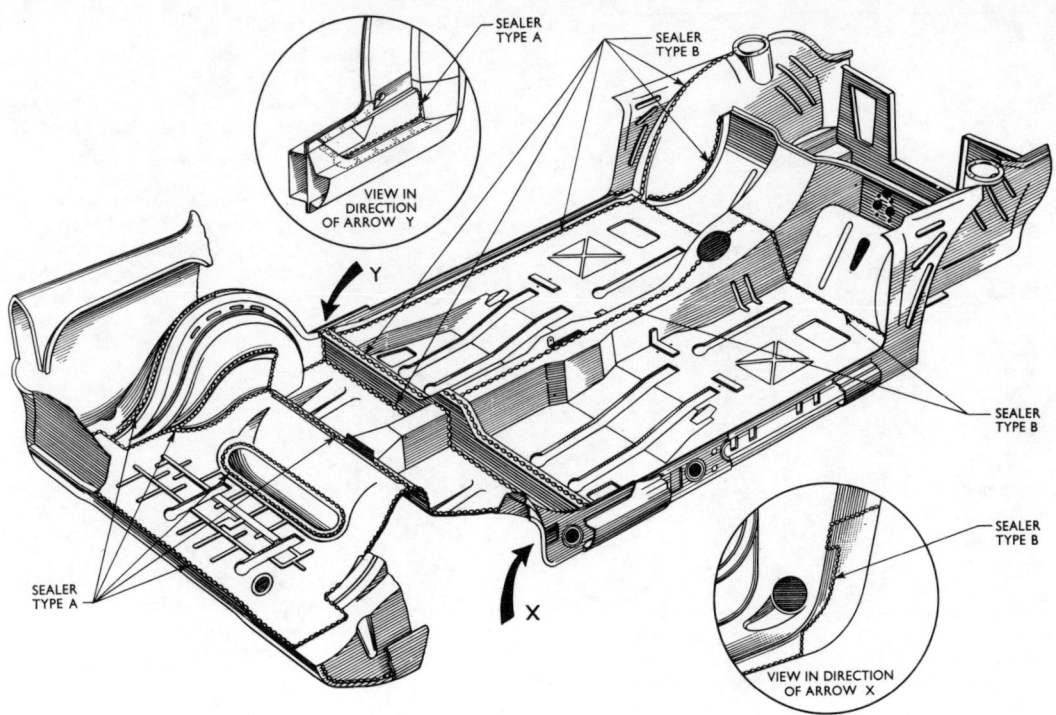

FIG 12 : 3 Main floor frame and bulkhead joints showing sealing points

The full length of each channel joint should be treated on both sides of the car. With this kind of leakage it is possible for water to enter the windscreen pillars at the front end of the channels, and thus to drip down into the corners of the belt-rail panel. If this occurs the chromium plated mouldings on the screen pillars must be removed by drilling out the three rivets holding each moulding. Sealer can then be applied so that the fillet extends right to the front ends and the top of the screen pillars (see **FIG 12 : 1**). At the same time, see that the waterproof tape which covers the flange joint between the roof panel and the screen-opening panel is well covered with a thin film, particular attention being paid to the top corners. For this purpose, type C sealer is preferable.

There are two further welded joints on the windscreen pillar which for additional proofing, can be covered with sealer type A.

While the chrome strips are removed it is a good opportunity to examine the windscreen weather-strip. If its adhesion is in doubt, apply type C sealer to both the inner and outer lip, using a force-feed oilcan or similar device, and give particular attention to the top corners. Any surplus sealer must be immediately cleaned from the rubber strip and glass.

The joints should also be examined between the dash-panel and the cowl-side panel to the windscreen-opening panel in each case. If leakage is suspected, use type C sealer applied as before, achieving a smooth fillet.

If the windscreen wiper grommets below the screen are allowing water to enter, it is necessary to remove the wiper arms, blades, nuts, grommets and wiper motor. Fit new rubber grommets and apply type C sealer to the front face of the aperture before reassembling the motor, nuts and wiper arms and blades to the car. Adjust the blades to ensure that when parked they are on the glass and not on the screen weather-strip. At the same time, do not fit the blades in a position where they prejudice vision.

12 : 5 Door pillar weather-strips

The doors are fitted with rubber weather-strips which can be tested with a hose-jet as already described. If water runs down the pillar faces, the door seal shown on **FIG 12 : 2** should be checked by trapping a piece of paper between the rubber strip on the pillar and the weather-strip on the door, with the latter closed. The paper should be firmly nipped, but if not, first make sure that the door alignment is correct. If this is in order, the weather-strip must be packed out from the door by inserting slivers of rubber strip behind it. When satisfactory, cement the strip firmly into position with adhesive type F.

At the front body pillar which carries the door hinges, a rubber strip is attached by five clips in addition to a sealing adhesive. Check that the clips are correctly positioned and in good order, and firmly clenched to the flange of the pillar. Apply sealing adhesive type F between the strip and the metal of the pillar if necessary.

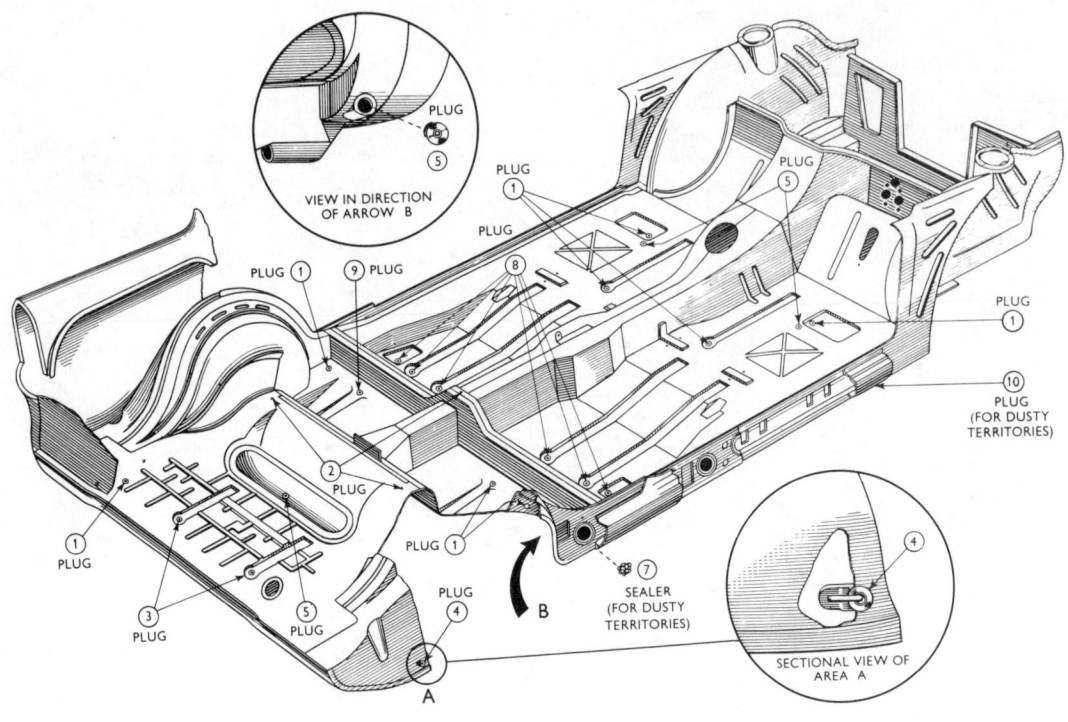

FIG 12 : 4 Location of blanking plugs in floor

The rubber weather-strips on the front ventilator windows must be in good condition, and when shut the windows should seat firmly against the rubber. If there is a gap shown between the rubber and the window, remove the latter. The self-locking stud on the threaded end of the lower pivot stud can then be adjusted until the gap is eliminated, but at the same time the window must be free to pivot without excessive effort.

The door trim panels are removed after taking off the interior handles and carefully easing the clips out of their holes in the door frame. This gives access to the door-lock and window-winder mechanism. In the event of trouble with these items, exchange assemblies should be fitted. A plastic sheeting is fixed to the metal door panel under the trim panel. If this requires renewal at any time, take care not to cover the drain holes at the bottom of the door frame either with surplus sheeting or adhesive.

12 : 6 Floor and bulkhead sealing

Should leakage take place at any of the various welded joints of the floor and bulkhead, this will probably be due to failure of the sealer, and renewal of this should effect a remedy; great care must be taken to clean the metal properly, as already emphasized. The various joints and method of sealing are partly shown on **FIG 12 : 3**, and are as follows:

Windscreen-opening panel to front mudguard panel joint. Cover with a liberal coat of type A sealer and brush it over the joint.

Windscreen-opening panel to dash panel joint. A liberal coat of type A sealer is applied along the joint.

Windscreen-opening panel to front mudguard apron joint. Type A sealer should be flowed along the joint.

Front mudguard to cowl side, and front mudguard to front mudguard apron joint. A continuous bead of type A sealer is applied along the joint.

Front suspension spring attachment reinforcing plate to side apron joint. Press sealer type D firmly into position from beneath the mudguard.

Junction of front mudguard apron with dash panel. Press sealer type D firmly into position.

Bonnet weather-strip retainer to windscreen-opening panel joint. Apply type A sealer in a continuous bead, and brush neatly in.

Hydraulic master cylinder bracket to dash panel joint. A continuous bead of type A sealer is applied around the bracket perimeter.

The cover plate of the steering column has a rubber gasket and is secured by screws. If required, the latter may have type D applied for further proofing.

The bonnet lock assembly is fitted with rubber washers, and these also can be additionally sealed by an application of type D sealer between the front faces of the washers and the bulkhead, after the former have been carefully positioned. Where pipes and cables, etc. pass through the bulkhead, rubber grommets are used, and these must be replaced when perished or damaged. If there are holes in the bulkhead that are unused for any such purpose, rubber blanking plugs should be positioned therein. If these are missing, fit new ones and secure in position by sealer type F.

Sealer type D may also be applied to the retaining

screws of the rubber boots fitted on the gearchange and handbrake levers at their floor attachments.

It is possible for moisture to enter where the front seat mounting bolts pass through the floor. If this occurs, remove the seats and bolts, apply a liberal quantity of type A to the bolt holes, and refit the bolts before it becomes tacky.

At the point where the rear wheel housings meet the well section of the body, leakage may occur; this is remedied by applying sealer type B from the underside of the wheel housings. The body floor is provided with paint drainage holes for use in manufacture, there being subsequently blanked off with rubber plugs. If any of the plugs are loose or missing, fit new ones, and secure them in position with sealer type B liberally applied. The location of the plugs is shown on **FIG 12 : 4.**

12 : 7 Rear boot sealing

The rear window weather-strip can be examined by carefully easing the chromium mouldings from around the window to expose the strip. If rectification is called for, this is done as described earlier in the case of the windscreen (see **FIG 12 : 5**), particular attention should be given to the condition of the plastic sealer tape which covers the flange of the window aperture and the rear quarter panel. The boot lid is fitted with weather-strips which must be firmly cemented along their whole lengths; they should also seat securely on the edges of the water drain channels with the lid closed. If repositioning or renewal is required, pay particular attention to the junctions between the strips near the bottom edge of the lid.

If water leaks through the spot-welded joints of the water drainage channels, run a small fillet of sealer type A along the inside of the channel. Do not let excess sealer harden in the channel as it will obstruct the water drainage. To assist drainage later cars have a $\frac{3}{16}$ inch hole drilled in the lid reinforcement strip, immediately under the lock handle.

Weather-sealing of the boot is impossible if the lid or body have become appreciably distorted. However, very slight distortion can be accommodated by lifting the weather-strip along the upper edge of the lid, and fitting a rubber packing strip between metal flange and the weather-strip. This will add further compression to the strip when the lid is closed. The packings and strip must of course be firmly cemented in position with type F sealer.

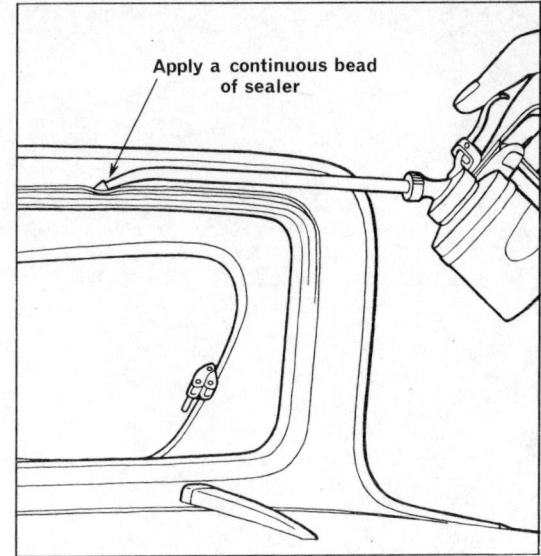

Apply a continuous bead of sealer

FIG 12 : 5   Application of sealer to rear window

12 : 8 Dust exclusion

If the body is properly weather-sealed, it also follows that a large amount of dust is automatically excluded. However, due to the differential air pressure caused by the car movement, dust entry may be induced even when the general sealing is satisfactory. The trim fittings and windcords are important in excluding dust, and any deterioration should be remedied by fitting new parts. The trim clips generally have polyurethene packings incorporated, likewise the door-frame drain holes, and these packings must be positioned correctly. In some earlier cars, dust can enter the boot through the lock assembly, and to prevent this, a cover plate is available as fitted to later cars. This is Ford Part No. E.2854.AA.1, and is supplied complete with two self-tapping screws by which it is secured to the inside of the lid over the lock body.

It is also possible for dust to enter via the fuel filler neck grommet, but is excluded by applying sealer type A around the periphery of the rubber.

NOTES

APPENDIX

TECHNICAL DATA

        Engine details   Piston data   Ignition system
        Cooling system   Carburetter details   Gearbox
        Battery and generator

WIRING DIAGRAMS

        Fig 13:1   Anglia
        Fig 13:2   Prefect
        Fig 13:3   Anglia (August 1965 to March 1967)
        Fig 13:4   Anglia (March 1967 on)

HINTS ON MAINTENANCE AND OVERHAUL

GLOSSARY OF TERMS

CAR PERFORMANCE

        Explanatory definitions   Catalogue information
        Engine output   Torque and brake mean pressure
        Compression ratio

   INDEX

NOTES

TECHNICAL DATA
ENGINE DETAILS
Dimensions in inches unless otherwise stated
Engine performance figures are nett

997 cc engine, low compression:
Bore and stroke (mm)	80.96 c 48.41
Compression ratio	7.5 : 1
Max. bhp at rev/min	37 at 5000
Max. torque (lb ft) at rev/min	50 at 2700

997 cc engine, high compression:
Bore and stroke (mm)	80.96 x 48.41
Compression ratio	8.9 : 1
Max. bhp at rev/min	39 at 5000
Max. torque (lb ft) at rev/min	52.5 at 2700

1198 cc engine, low compression:
Bore and stroke (mm)	80.96 x 58.17
Compression ratio	7.3 : 1
Max. bhp at rev/min	46 at 4800
Max. torque (lb ft) at rev/min	60 at 2700

1198 cc engine, high compression (pre-October 1964):
Bore and stroke (mm)	80.96 x 58.17
Compression ratio	8.7 : 1
Max. bhp at rev/min	48.5 at 4800
Max. torque (lb ft) at rev/min	63 at 2700

1198 cc engine, high compression (October 1964 on):
Bore and stroke (mm)	80.96 x 58.17
Compression ratio	9.0 : 1
Max. bhp at rev/min	50 at 4900
Max. torque (lb ft) at rev/min	69 at 2700

Main bearings, journal diameter	2.1255–2.1260
Crankcase bore for bearing liners (diameter) ...	2.271–2.2715
Bearing liners, wall thickness	.072–.07225
Bearing running clearance	.0005–.002
Crankshaft end float	.003–.001
Crankshaft thrust washer thickness	.091–.093
Crankpin diameter	1.9370–1.9375
Crankshaft run-out (max.)	.006
Flywheel face run-out (max.)	.004
Flywheel centre, spigot bearing type	Sintered bronze bush
Camshaft journal diameter	1.56

Camshaft bearing length:
Front	.75
Centre	.64
Rear	.75

Camshaft bearings, inside diameter	1.5165–1.5635
Camshaft bearings, clearance	.001–.002
Camshaft bearings, end float	.002–.007
Camshaft thrust plate thickness	.176–.178
Timing chain, type	Single roller
Timing chain, pitch	.375
Timing chain, roller diameter	.225
Timing chain, length, pitches	46
Cam lift, inlet	.2108
Cam lift, exhaust	.2176

Connecting rod centres:
997 cc	4.611–4.612
1198 cc	4.419–4.421

Big-end bearing clearance to crankpin	.0005–.0022
Big-end bearing wall thickness	.719–.7225
Big-end bearing housing bore...	2.0825–2.2083
Gudgeon pin diameter...	.812–.8123
Small-end bush diameter	.8122–.8125
Clearance, pin to small-end bush	.0001–.0003
Connecting rod end float in crankpin	.002–.008
Oil sump capacity—up to November 1964 (approx.)	4.5 pints
Oil sump capacity—after November 1964 (approx.)	5.5 pints
Oil filter capacity	.5 pint
Warning light, minimum operating pressure	5–7 lb/sq in
Oil pump delivery volume (gpm) at rev/min:	
bi-rotor type	2/2000
vane type	2.8/2000
Oil pump, bearing inside diameter	.500–.501
Oil pump, shaft diameter	.498–.4985
Oil pump, shaft clearance to body	.0015–.003
Oil pump, bi-rotor type, lobe clearance to inner and outer rotors (max.)	.006
Oil pump, clearance between outer rotor and housing (max.)...	.0055–.0075
Oil pump, shaft end float (max.)	.005
Oil pump, vane type, clearance of vanes in rotor	.005
Oil pump, clearance between endplate and rotor/vanes ...	.005
Oil pressure (normal)	35–40 lb/sq in
Pistons—type	Aluminium alloy
Number of piston rings	3
Offset of gudgeon pin in piston	.040
Ring groove width, compression rings	.77–.78
Ring groove width, oil control ring	.155–.156
Gudgeon pin bore	.8121–.8124
Gudgeon pin clearance in boss (selective)	Zero to .0002
Valve head diameter—inlet	1.262–1.272
exhaust	1.183–1.193
Valve stem diameter—inlet	.3095–.3105
exhaust	.3086–.3096
Valve guide bore diameter	.3113–.3125
Valve stem clearance in guide	.0018–.003
Valve lift—inlet	.2893
exhaust	.2904
Valve seat angle	45 deg.
Valve rocker clearance at operating temperature—inlet ...	.010
exhaust ...	.017
Valve rocker clearance, cold—inlet	.008
exhaust	.018
Valve spring, free length	1.48
Valve spring, fitted length/lbs load	1.263/44–49

	Inlet Opens Before TDC	Inlet Closes After BDC	Exhaust Opens Before BDC	Exhaust Closes After TDC
Valve timing with cold clearance of inlet .015, exhaust .027:				
997 cc	10	50	44	10
1198 cc	17	51	51	17

Tightening torque (lb ft):

Cylinder head bolts	65/70
Manifold bolts/nuts...	12/15
Flywheel bolts	45/50
Main bearing caps	55/60
Big-end bearing caps	20/25

PISTON DATA

Piston grade						Standard bore	.030 o/s bore
1	...	...	...	...	...	3.1858–3.1861	3.2158–3.2161
2	...	...	...	...	...	3.1861–3.1864	3.2161–3.2164
3	...	...	...	...	...	3.1864–3.1867	3.2164–3.2167
4	...	...	...	...	...	3.1867–3.1870	3.2167–3.2170
5	...	...	...	...	...	3.1870–3.1873	3.2170–3.2173
6	...	...	...	...	...	3.1873–3.1876	3.2173–3.2176

Note—Grades 5 and 6 only supplied in service. Piston fit 3-7 lb. pull on .0015 inch feeler blade, .5 inch wide.

IGNITION SYSTEM

Initial advance (crankshaft degrees):

997 cc engine, low compression	10
997 cc engine, high compression (pre-September 1963) ...	10
997 cc engine, high compression (post-September 1963) ...	8
1198 cc engine, low compression (pre-February 1965) ...	6
1198 cc engine, low compression (post-February 1965) ...	10
1198 cc engine, high compression	6
Contact breaker gap, Lucas distributor	.014–.016
Contact breaker gap, Ford distributor	.025
Spark plug type	14 mm Autolite AG.32

COOLING SYSTEM

Capacity—Imperial pints, without heater (997 cc)	10.25
(1198 cc)	9.0
Capacity—Imperial pints, with heater (997 cc)	11.25
(1198 cc) ...	10.5

Approx. volume of antifreeze in system (ME.1167.B or equal)	Min. ambient temp.	Antifreeze
	17°F (—8°C)	10 per cent
	7°F (—13°C)	15 per cent
	3°F (—19°C)	20
	—20°F (—29°C)	25

Radiator cap blow-off pressure	4–7 lb/sq in

CARBURETTER DETAILS

Engine type:	997 cc		1198 cc
	Up to Jan. 1960	After Jan. 1960	After May 1962
Main jet	115	115	97.5	110
Main air correction jet	175	175	160	200
Economizer jet	140	140	—	—
Idling jet	50	40	50	50
Idling air jet	120	150	—	—
Choke tube (mm)	22	22	21.5	23
Needle valve	—	—	1.3	1.6
Accelerator pump jet	—	—	45	40
Economizer air jet	195	195	—	—
Starter jet	125	125	—	—
Idling air bleed	—	—	.85	60

Fuel pump, type	Mechanical diaphragm
Delivery pressure	1.25–2.0 lb/sq in
Diaphragm spring test length, 997 cc	.468
Diaphragm spring test length, 1198 cc	.59
Diaphragm spring test pressure, 997 cc	3.25–3.5 lb
Diaphragm spring test pressure, 1198 cc	4.0–4.5 lb

GEARBOX

Oil capacity (Imperial pints)	...	...	...	...	...	1.75
Gearbox ratios—4th gear	...	...	...	...	...	1.00:1
3rd gear	...	...	...	...	...	1.412:1
2nd gear	...	...	...	...	...	2.396:1
1st gear	...	...	...	...	...	4.118:1
Reverse	...	...	...	...	...	5.404:1
Overall gear ratios with 33/8 axle—4th gear	...	...	...	...	4.125:1
3rd gear	...	...	...	...	5.826:1
2nd gear	...	...	...	...	9.884:1
1st gear	...	...	...	...	16.998:1
Reverse	...	...	...	...	22.292:1
Overall gear ratios with 31/7 axle—4th gear	...	...	...	...	4.44:1
3rd gear	...	...	...	...	6.275:1
2nd gear	...	...	...	...	10.648:1
1st gear	...	...	...	...	18.283:1
Reverse	...	...	...	...	24.018:1

BATTERY AND GENERATOR

Battery:
  type ... ...   Lead/acid, positive earth
  capacity, normal ... ...   38 amp/hr 9 plates per cell
  capacity, heavy duty ... ...   51 amp/hr 11 plates per cell
  electrolyte level ... ...   .25 inch above separators
Generator:
  type 2-brush
  drive ratio 1.5:1
Cut-out:
  cut-in voltage 12.6–13.4
  drop-off voltage 8.5–11.0
Voltage regulator:
  open-circuit voltage (normal) 14.2–14.8
  open-circuit voltage, correction for temperature ...

Ambient temp.	O.C. voltage
10°C	15.7–16.1
20°C	15.6–16.0
30°C	15.5–15.9
40°C	15.4–15.8

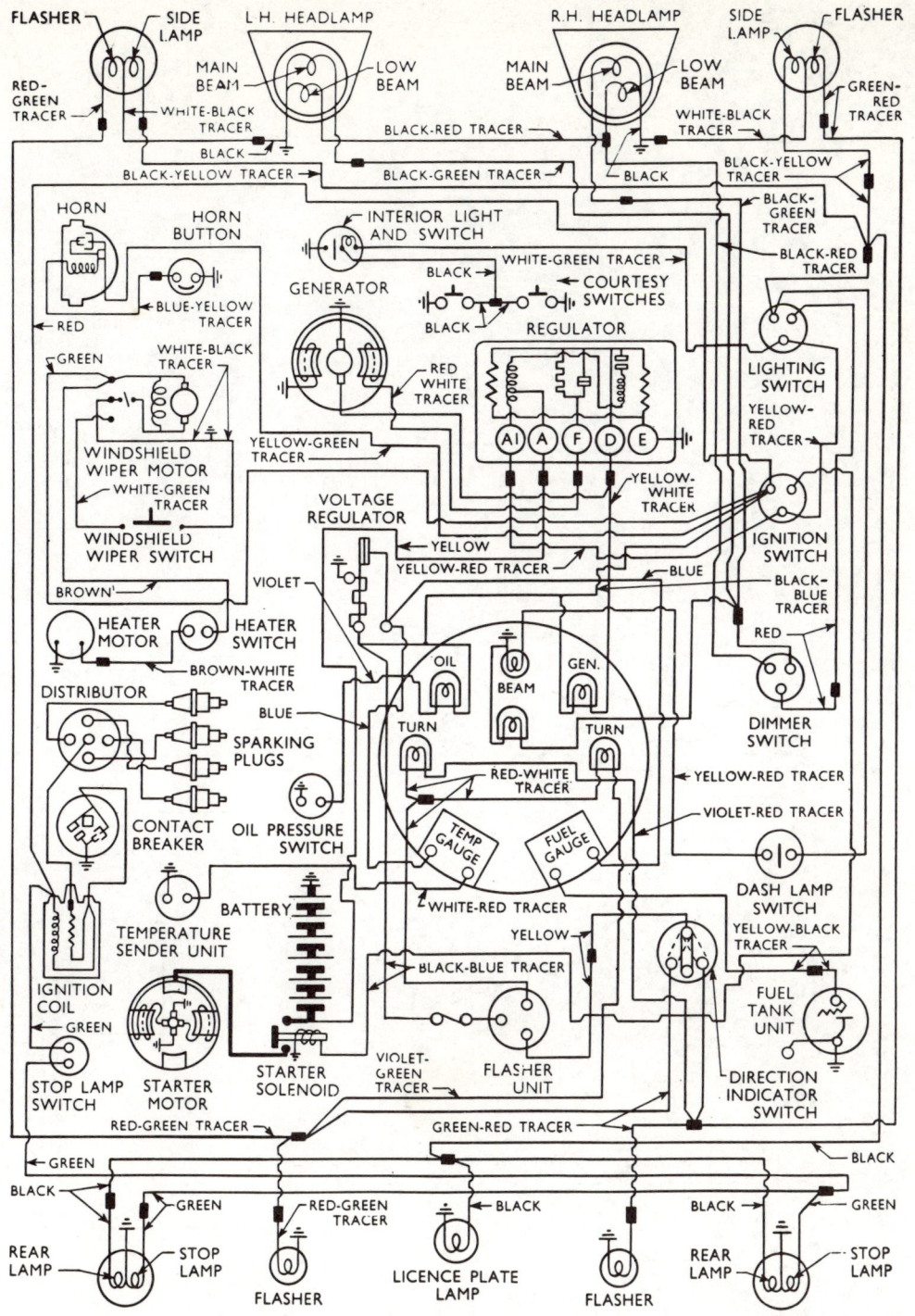

FIG 13:1 Anglia wiring diagram

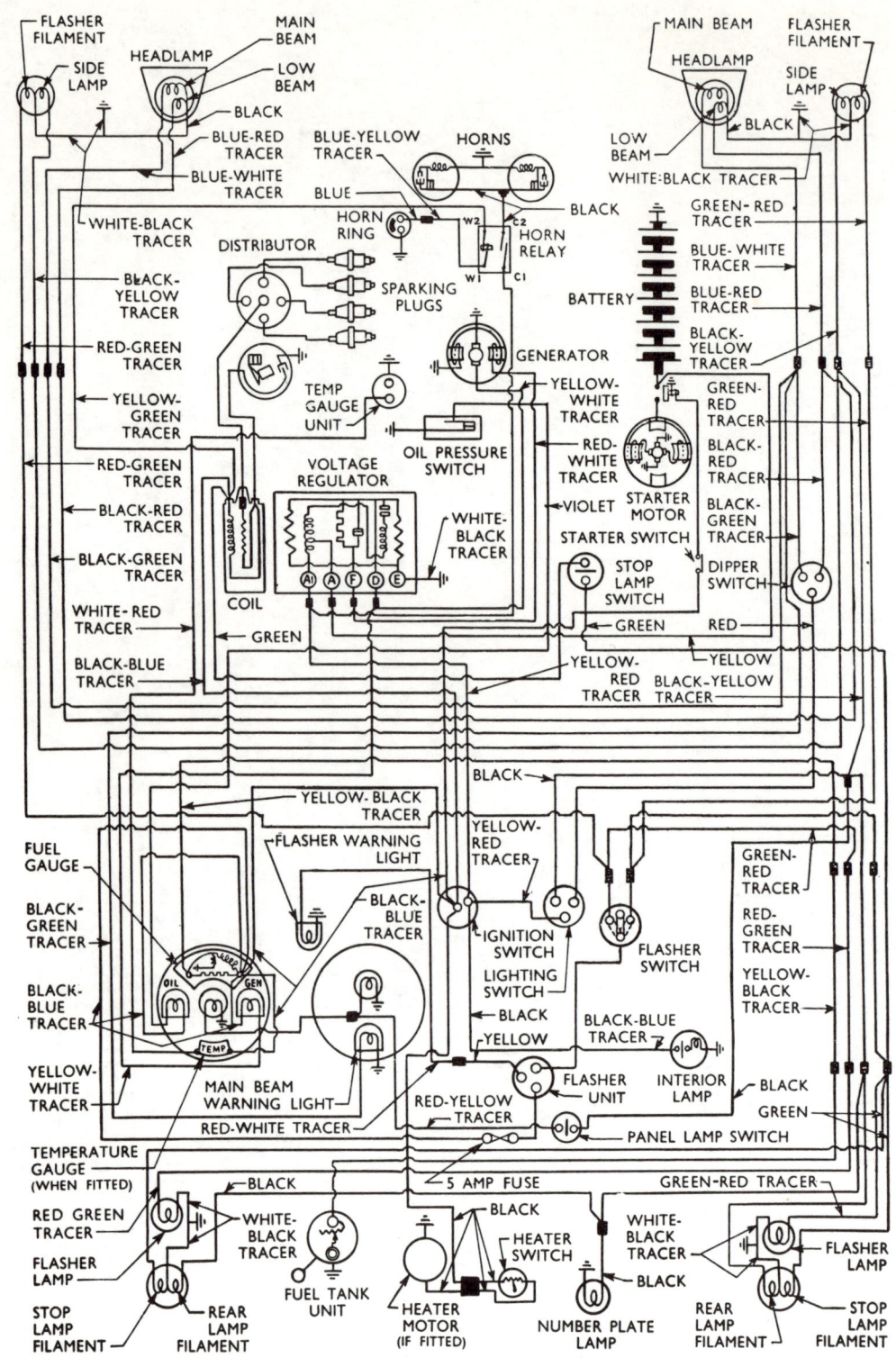

FIG 13:2 Prefect wiring diagram

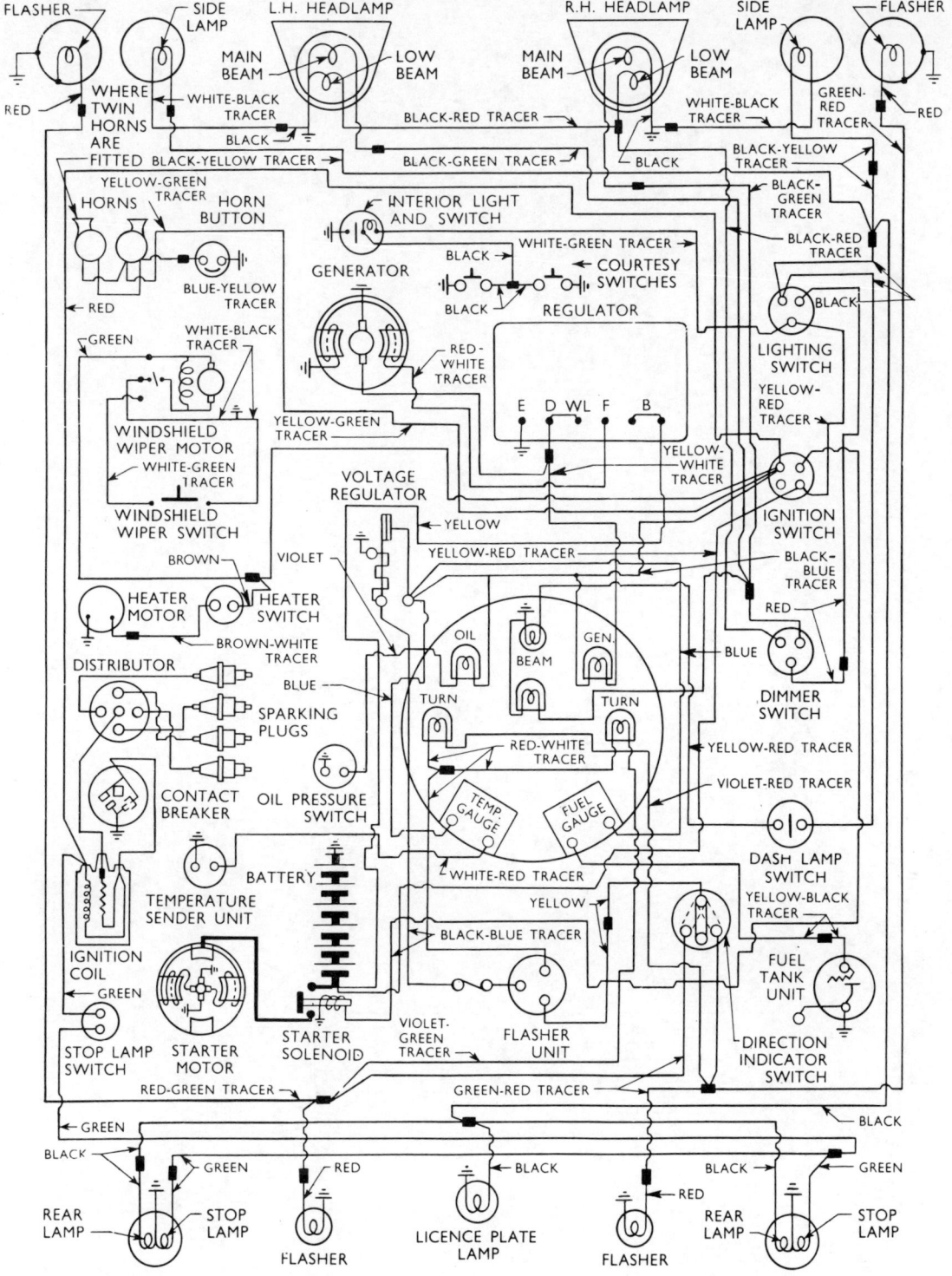

FIG 13:3   Anglia range (August 1965 to March 1967)

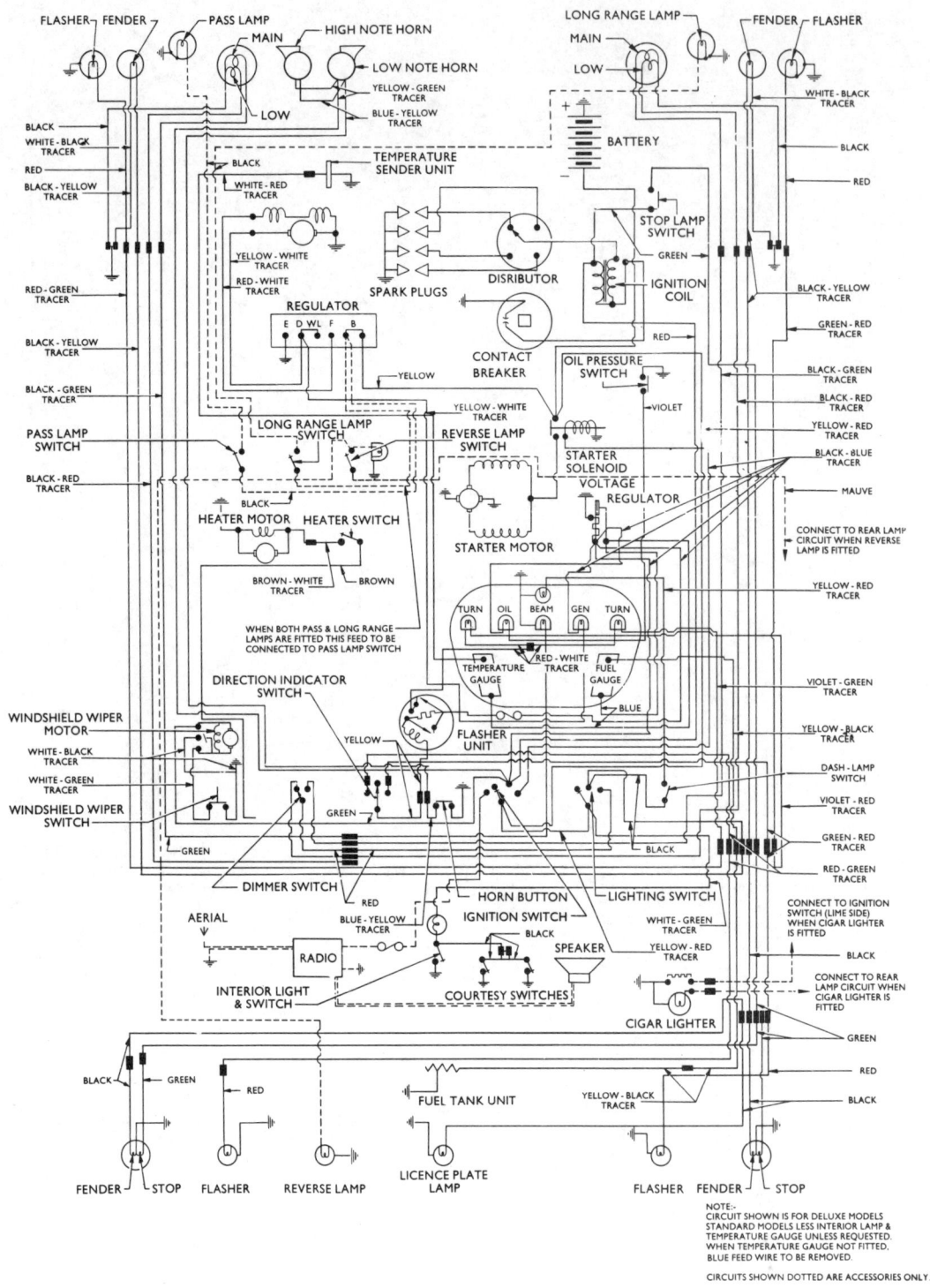

FIG 13:4 Anglia (March 1967 on)

Inches	Decimals	Milli-metres	Inches to Millimetres Inches	mm	Millimetres to Inches mm	Inches
1/64	.015625	.3969	001	.0254	.01	.00039
1/32	.03125	.7937	.002	.0508	.02	.00079
3/64	.046875	1.1906	.003	.0762	.03	.00118
1/16	.0625	1.5875	.004	.1016	.04	.00157
5/64	.078125	1.9844	.005	.1270	.05	.00197
3/32	.09375	2.3812	.006	.1524	.06	.00236
7/64	.109375	2.7781	.007	.1778	.07	.00276
1/8	.125	3.1750	.008	.2032	.08	.00315
9/64	.140625	3.5719	.009	.2286	.09	.00354
5/32	.15625	3.9687	.01	.254	.1	.00394
11/64	.171875	4.3656	.02	.508	.2	.00787
3/16	.1875	4.7625	.03	.762	.3	.01181
13/64	.203125	5.1594	.04	1.016	.4	.01575
7/32	.21875	5.5562	.05	1.270	.5	.01969
15/64	.234375	5.9531	.06	1.524	.6	.02362
1/4	.25	6.3500	.07	1.778	.7	.02756
17/64	.265625	6.7469	.08	2.032	.8	.03150
9/32	.28125	7.1437	.09	2.286	.9	.03543
19/64	.296875	7.5406	.1	2.54	1	.03937
5/16	.3125	7.9375	.2	5.08	2	.07874
21/64	.328125	8.3344	.3	7.62	3	.11811
11/32	.34375	8.7312	.4	10.16	4	.15748
23/64	.359375	9.1281	.5	12.70	5	.19685
3/8	.375	9.5250	.6	15.24	6	.23622
25/64	.390625	9.9219	.7	17.78	7	.27559
13/32	.40625	10.3187	.8	20.32	8	.31496
27/64	.421875	10.7156	.9	22.86	9	.35433
7/16	.4375	11.1125	1	25.4	10	.39370
29/64	.453125	11.5094	2	50.8	11	.43307
15/32	.46875	11.9062	3	76.2	12	.47244
31/64	.484375	12.3031	4	101.6	13	.51181
1/2	.5	12.7000	5	127.0	14	.55118
33/64	.515625	13.0969	6	152.4	15	.59055
17/32	.53125	13.4937	7	177.8	16	.62992
35/64	.546875	13.8906	8	203.2	17	.66929
9/16	.5625	14.2875	9	228.6	18	.70866
37/64	.578125	14.6844	10	254.0	19	.74803
19/32	.59375	15.0812	11	279.4	20	.78740
39/64	.609375	15.4781	12	304.8	21	.82677
5/8	.625	15.8750	13	330.2	22	.86614
41/64	.640625	16.2719	14	355.6	23	.90551
21/32	.65625	16.6687	15	381.0	24	.94488
43/64	.671875	17.0656	16	406.4	25	.98425
11/16	.6875	17.4625	17	431.8	26	1.02362
45/64	.703125	17.8594	18	457.2	27	1.06299
23/32	.71875	18.2562	19	482.6	28	1.10236
47/64	.734375	18.6531	20	508.0	29	1.14173
3/4	.75	19.0500	21	533.4	30	1.18110
49/64	.765625	19.4469	22	558.8	31	1.22047
25/32	.78125	19.8437	23	584.2	32	1.25984
51/64	.796875	20.2406	24	609.6	33	1.29921
13/16	.8125	20.6375	25	635.0	34	1.33858
53/64	.828125	21.0344	26	660.4	35	1.37795
27/32	.84375	21.4312	27	685.8	36	1.41732
55/64	.859375	21.8281	28	711.2	37	1.4567
7/8	.875	22.2250	29	736.6	38	1.4961
57/64	.890625	22.6219	30	762.0	39	1.5354
29/32	.90625	23.0187	31	787.4	40	1.5748
59/64	.921875	23.4156	32	812.8	41	1.6142
15/16	.9375	23.8125	33	838.2	42	1.6535
61/64	.953125	24.2094	34	863.6	43	1.6929
31/32	.96875	24.6062	35	889.0	44	1.7323
63/64	.984375	25.0031	36	914.4	45	1.7717

UNITS	Pints to Litres	Gallons to Litres	Litres to Pints	Litres to Gallons	Miles to Kilometres	Kilometres to Miles	Lbs. per sq. In. to Kg. per sq. Cm.	Kg. per sq. Cm. to Lbs. per sq. In.
1	.57	4.55	1.76	.22	1.61	.62	.07	14.22
2	1.14	9.09	3.52	.44	3.22	1.24	.14	28.50
3	1.70	13.64	5.28	.66	4.83	1.86	.21	42.67
4	2.27	18.18	7.04	.88	6.44	2.49	.28	56.89
5	2.84	22.73	8.80	1.10	8.05	3.11	.35	71.12
6	3.41	27.28	10.56	1.32	9.66	3.73	.42	85.34
7	3.98	31.82	12.32	1.54	11.27	4.35	.49	99.56
8	4.55	36.37	14.08	1.76	12.88	4.97	.56	113.79
9		40.91	15.84	1.98	14.48	5.59	.63	128.00
10		45.46	17.60	2.20	16.09	6.21	.70	142.23
20				4.40	32.19	12.43	1.41	284.47
30				6.60	48.28	18.64	2.11	426.70
40				8.80	64.37	24.85		
50					80.47	31.07		
60					96.56	37.28		
70					112.65	43.50		
80					128.75	49.71		
90					144.84	55.92		
100					160.93	62.14		

UNITS	Lb ft to kgm	Kgm to lb ft	UNITS	Lb ft to kgm	Kgm to lb ft
1	.138	7.233	7	.967	50.631
2	.276	14.466	8	1.106	57.864
3	.414	21.699	9	1.244	65.097
4	.553	28.932	10	1.382	72.330
5	.691	36.165	20	2.765	144.660
6	.829	43.398	30	4.147	216.990

NOTES

HINTS ON MAINTENANCE AND OVERHAUL

There are few things more rewarding than the restoration of a vehicle's original peak of efficiency and smooth performance.

The following notes are intended to help the owner to reach that state of perfection. Providing that he possesses the basic manual skills he should have no difficulty in performing most of the operations detailed in this manual. It must be stressed, however, that where recommended in the manual, highly-skilled operations ought to be entrusted to experts, who have the necessary equipment, to carry out the work satisfactorily.

Quality of workmanship:

The hazardous driving conditions on the roads to-day demand that vehicles should be as nearly perfect, mechanically, as possible. It is therefore most important that amateur work be carried out with care, bearing in mind the often inadequate working conditions, and also the inferior tools which may have to be used. It is easy to counsel perfection in all things, and we recognize that it may be setting an impossibly high standard. We do, however, suggest that every care should be taken to ensure that a vehicle is as safe to take on the road as it is humanly possible to make it.

Safe working conditions:

Even though a vehicle may be stationary, it is still potentially dangerous if certain sensible precautions are not taken when working on it while it is supported on jacks or blocks. It is indeed preferable not to use jacks alone, but to supplement them with carefully placed blocks, so that there will be plenty of support if the car rolls off the jacks during a strenuous manoeuvre. Axle stands are an excellent way of providing a rigid base which is not readily disturbed. Piles of bricks are a dangerous substitute. Be careful not to get under heavy loads on lifting tackle, the load could fall. It is preferable not to work alone when lifting an engine, or when working underneath a vehicle which is supported well off the ground. To be trapped, particularly under the vehicle, may have unpleasant results if help is not quickly forthcoming. Make some provision, however humble, to deal with fires. Always disconnect a battery if there is a likelihood of electrical shorts. These may start a fire if there is leaking fuel about. This applies particularly to leads which can carry a heavy current, like those in the starter circuit. While on the subject of electricity, we must also stress the danger of using equipment which is run off the mains and which has no earth or has faulty wiring or connections. So many workshops have damp floors, and electrical shocks are of such a nature that it is sometimes impossible to let go of a live lead or piece of equipment due to the muscular spasms which take place.

Work demanding special care:

This involves the servicing of braking, steering and suspension systems. On the road, failure of the braking system may be disastrous. Make quite sure that there can be no possibility of failure through the bursting of rusty brake pipes or rotten hoses, nor to a sudden loss of pressure due to defective seals or valves.

Problems:

The chief problems which may face an operator are:
1 External dirt.
2 Difficulty in undoing tight fixings.
3 Dismantling unfamiliar mechanisms.
4 Deciding in what respect parts are defective.
5 Confusion about the correct order for reassembly.
6 Adjusting running clearance.
7 Road testing.
8 Final tuning.

Practical suggestions to solve the problems:

1 Preliminary cleaning of large parts—engines, transmissions, steering, suspensions, etc.,—should be carried out before removal from the car. Where road dirt and mud alone are present, wash clean with a high-pressure water jet, brushing to remove stubborn adhesions, and allow to drain and dry. Where oil or grease is also present, wash down with a proprietary compound (Gunk, Teepol etc.,) applying with a stiff brush—an old paint brush is suitable—into all crevices. Cover the distributor and ignition coils with a polythene bag and then apply a strong water jet to clear the loosened deposits. Allow to drain and dry. The assemblies will then be sufficiently clean to remove and transfer to the bench for the next stage.

On the bench, further cleaning can be carried out, first wiping the parts as free as possible from grease with old newspaper. Avoid using rag or cotton waste which can leave clogging fibres behind. Any remaining grease can be removed with a brush dipped in paraffin. If necessary, traces of paraffin can be removed by carbon tetrachloride. Avoid using paraffin or petrol in large quantities for cleaning in enclosed areas, such as garages, on account of the high fire risk.

When all exteriors have been cleaned, and not before, dismantling can be commenced. This ensures that dirt will not enter into interiors and orifices revealed by dismantling. In the next phases, where components have to be cleaned, use carbon tetrachloride in preference to petrol and keep the containers covered except when in use. After the components have been cleaned, plug small holes with tapered hard wood plugs cut to size and blank off larger orifices with greaseproof paper and masking tape. Do not use soft wood plugs or matchsticks as they may break.

2 It is not advisable to hammer on the end of a screw thread, but if it must be done, first screw on a nut to protect the thread, and use a lead hammer. This applies particularly to the removal of tapered cotters. Nuts and bolts seem to 'grow' together, especially in exhaust systems. If penetrating oil does not work, try the judicious application of heat, but be careful of starting a fire. Asbestos sheet or cloth is useful to isolate heat.

Tight bushes or pieces of tail-pipe rusted into a silencer can be removed by splitting them with an open-ended hacksaw. Tight screws can sometimes be started by a tap from a hammer on the end of a suitable screwdriver. Many tight fittings will yield to the judicious use of a hammer, but it must be a soft-faced hammer if damage is to be avoided, use a heavy block on the opposite side to absorb shock. Any parts of the steering system which have been damaged should be renewed, as attempts to repair them may lead to cracking and subsequent failure, and steering ball joints should be disconnected using a recommended tool to prevent damage.

3 It often happens that an owner is baffled when trying to dismantle an unfamiliar piece of equipment. So many modern devices are pressed together or assembled by spinning-over flanges, that they must be sawn apart. The intention is that the whole assembly must be renewed. However, parts which appear to be in one piece to the naked eye, may reveal close-fitting joint lines when inspected with a magnifying glass, and, this may provide the necessary clue to dismantling. Left-handed screw threads are used where rotational forces would tend to unscrew a right-handed screw thread.

Be very careful when dismantling mechanisms which may come apart suddenly. Work in an enclosed space where the parts will be contained, and drape a piece of cloth over the device if springs are likely to fly in all directions. Mark everything which might be reassembled in the wrong position, scratched symbols may be used on unstressed parts, or a sequence of tiny dots from a centre punch can be useful. Stressed parts should never be scratched or centre-popped as this may lead to cracking under working conditions. Store parts which look alike in the correct order for reassembly. Never rely upon memory to assist in the assembly of complicated mechanisms, especially when they will be dismantled for a long time, but make notes, and drawings to supplement the diagrams in the manual, and put labels on detached wires. Rust stains may indicate unlubricated wear. This can sometimes be seen round the outside edge of a bearing cup in a universal joint. Look for bright rubbing marks on parts which normally should not make heavy contact. These might prove that something is bent or running out of truth. For example, there might be bright marks on one side of a piston, at the top near the ring grooves, and others at the bottom of the skirt on the other side. This could well be the clue to a bent connecting rod. Suspected cracks can be proved by heating the component in a light oil to approximately 100°C, removing, drying off, and dusting with french chalk, if a crack is present the oil retained in the crack will stain the french chalk.

4 In determining wear, and the degree, against the permissible limits set in the manual, accurate measurement can only be achieved by the use of a micrometer. In many cases, the wear is given to the fourth place of decimals; that is in ten-thousandths of an inch. This can be read by the vernier scale on the barrel of a good micrometer. Bore diameters are more difficult to determine. If, however, the matching shaft is accurately measured, the degree of play in the bore can be felt as a guide to its suitability. In other cases, the shank of a twist drill of known diameter is a handy check.

Many methods have been devised for determining the clearance between bearing surfaces. To-day the best and simplest is by the use of Plastigage, obtainable from most garages. A thin plastic thread is laid between the two surfaces and the bearing is tightened, flattening the thread. On removal, the width of the thread is compared with a scale supplied with the thread and the clearance is read off directly. Sometimes joint faces leak persistently, even after gasket renewal. The fault will then be traceable to distortion, dirt or burrs. Studs which are screwed into soft metal frequently raise burrs at the point of entry. A quick cure for this is to chamfer the edge of the hole in the part which fits over the stud.

5 **Always check a replacement part with the original one before it is fitted.**

If parts are not marked, and the order for reassembly is not known, a little detective work will help. Look for marks which are due to wear to see if they can be mated. Joint faces may not be identical due to manufacturing errors, and parts which overlap may be stained, giving a clue to the correct position. Most fixings leave identifying marks especially if they were painted over on assembly. It is then easier to decide whether a nut, for instance, has a plain, a spring, or a shakeproof washer under it. All running surfaces become 'bedded' together after long spells of work and tiny imperfections on one part will be found to have left corresponding marks on the other. This is particularly true of shafts and bearings and even a score on a cylinder wall will show on the piston.

6 Checking end float or rocker clearances by feeler gauge may not always give accurate results because of wear. For instance, the rocker tip which bears on a valve stem may be deeply pitted, in which case the feeler will simply be bridging a depression. Thrust washers may also wear depressions in opposing faces to make accurate measurement difficult. End float is then easier to check by using a dial gauge. It is common practice to adjust end play in bearing assemblies, like front hubs with taper rollers, by doing up the axle nut until the hub becomes stiff to turn and then backing it off a little. Do not use this method with ballbearing hubs as the assembly is often preloaded by tightening the axle nut to its fullest extent. If the splitpin hole will not line up, file the base of the nut a little.

Steering assemblies often wear in the straight-ahead position. If any part is adjusted, make sure that it remains free when moved from lock to lock. Do not be surprised if an assembly like a steering gearbox, which is known to be carefully adjusted outside the car, becomes stiff when it is bolted in place. This will be due to distortion of the case by the pull of the mounting bolts, particularly if the mounting points are not all touching together. This problem may be met in other equipment and is cured by careful attention to the alignment of mounting points.

When a spanner is stamped with a size and A/F it means that the dimension is the width between the jaws and has no connection with ANF, which is the designation for the American National Fine thread. Coarse threads like Whitworth are rarely used on cars to-day except for studs which screw into soft aluminium or cast iron. For this reason it might be found that the top end of a cylinder head stud has a fine thread and the lower end a coarse thread to screw into the cylinder block. If the car has mainly UNF threads then it is likely that any coarse threads will be UNC, which are not the same as Whitworth. Small sizes have the same number of threads in Whitworth and UNC, but in the $\frac{1}{2}$ inch size for example, there are twelve threads to the inch in the former and thirteen in the latter.

7 After a major overhaul, particularly if a great deal of work has been done on the braking, steering and suspension systems, it is advisable to approach the problem of testing with care. If the braking system has been overhauled, apply heavy pressure to the brake pedal and get a second operator to check every possible source of leakage. The brakes may work extremely well, but a leak could cause complete failure after a few miles.

Do not fit the hub caps until every wheel nut has been checked for tightness, and make sure the tyre pressures are correct. Check the levels of coolant, lubricants and hydraulic fluids. Being satisfied that all is well, take the car on the road and test the brakes at once. Check the steering and the action of the handbrake. Do all this at moderate speeds on quiet roads, and make sure there is no other vehicle behind you when you try a rapid stop.

Finally, remember that many parts settle down after a time, so check for tightness of all fixings after the car has been on the road for a hundred miles or so.

8 It is useless to tune an engine which has not reached its normal running temperature. In the same way, the tune of an engine which is stiff after a rebore will be different when the engine is again running free. Remember too, that rocker clearances on pushrod operated valve gear will change when the cylinder head nuts are tightened after an initial period of running with a new head gasket.

Trouble may not always be due to what seems the obvious cause. Ignition, carburation and mechanical condition are interdependent and spitting back through the carburetter, which might be attributed to a weak mixture, can be caused by a sticking inlet valve.

For one final hint on tuning, never adjust more than one thing at a time or it will be impossible to tell which adjustment produced the desired result.

NOTES

GLOSSARY OF TERMS

Allen key — Cranked wrench of hexagonal section for use with socket head screws.

Alternator — Electrical generator producing alternating current. Rectified to direct current for battery charging.

Ambient temperature — Surrounding atmospheric temperature.

Annulus — Used in engineering to indicate the outer ring gear of an epicyclic gear train.

Armature — The shaft carrying the windings, which rotates in the magnetic field of a generator or starter motor. That part of a solenoid or relay which is activated by the magnetic field.

Axial — In line with, or pertaining to, an axis.

Backlash — Play in meshing gears.

Balance lever — A bar where force applied at the centre is equally divided between connections at the ends.

Banjo axle — Axle casing with large diameter housing for the crownwheel and differential.

Bendix pinion — A self-engaging and self-disengaging drive on a starter motor shaft.

Bevel pinion — A conical shaped gearwheel, designed to mesh with a similar gear with an axis usually at 90 deg. to its own.

bhp — Brake horse power, measured on a dynamometer.

bmep — Brake mean effective pressure. Average pressure on a piston during the working stroke.

Brake cylinder — Cylinder with hydraulically operated piston(s) acting on brake shoes or pad(s).

Brake regulator — Control valve fitted in hydraulic braking system which limits brake pressure to rear brakes during heavy braking to prevent rear wheel locking.

Camber — Angle at which a wheel is tilted from the vertical.

Capacitor — Modern term for an electrical condenser. Part of distributor assembly, connected across contact breaker points, acts as an interference suppressor.

Castellated — Top face of a nut, slotted across the flats, to take a locking splitpin.

Castor — Angle at which the kingpin or swivel pin is tilted when viewed from the side.

cc — Cubic centimetres. Engine capacity is arrived at by multiplying the area of the bore in sq cm by the stroke in cm by the number of cylinders.

Clevis — U-shaped forked connector used with a clevis pin, usually at handbrake connections.

Collet — A type of collar, usually split and located in a groove in a shaft, and held in place by a retainer. The arrangement used to retain the spring(s) on a valve stem in most cases.

Commutator — Rotating segmented current distributor between armature windings and brushes in generator or motor.

Compression ratio — The ratio, or quantitative relation, of the total volume (piston at bottom of stroke) to the unswept volume (piston at top of stroke) in an engine cylinder.

Condenser — See capacitor.

Core plug — Plug for blanking off a manufacturing hole in a casting.

Crownwheel — Large bevel gear in rear axle, driven by a bevel pinion attached to the propeller shaft. Sometimes called a 'ring gear'.

'C'-spanner — Like a 'C' with a handle. For use on screwed collars without flats, but with slots or holes.

Damper — Modern term for shock-absorber, used in vehicle suspension systems to damp out spring oscillations.

Depression — The lowering of atmospheric pressure as in the inlet manifold and carburetter.

Dowel — Close tolerance pin, peg, tube, or bolt, which accurately locates mating parts.

Drag link — Rod connecting steering box drop arm (pitman arm) to nearest front wheel steering arm in certain types of steering systems.

Dry liner — Thinwall tube pressed into cylinder bore

Dry sump — Lubrication system where all oil is scavenged from the sump, and returned to a separate tank.

Dynamo — See Generator.

Electrode — Terminal, part of an electrical component, such as the points or 'Electrodes' of a sparking plug.

Electrolyte — In lead-acid car batteries a solution of sulphuric acid and distilled water.

End float — The axial movement between associated parts, end play.

EP — Extreme pressure. In lubricants, special grades for heavily loaded bearing surfaces, such as gear teeth in a gearbox, or crownwheel and pinion in a rear axle.

Fade	Of brakes. Reduced efficiency due to overheating.
Field coils	Windings on the polepieces of motors and generators.
Fillets	Narrow finishing strips usually applied to interior bodywork.
First motion shaft	Input shaft from clutch to gearbox.
Fullflow filter	Filters in which all the oil is pumped to the engine. If the element becomes clogged, a bypass valve operates to pass unfiltered oil to the engine.
FWD	Front wheel drive.
Gear pump	Two meshing gears in a close fitting casing. Oil is carried from the inlet round the outside of both gears in the spaces between the gear teeth and casing to the outlet, the meshing gear teeth prevent oil passing back to the inlet, and the oil is forced through the outlet port.
Generator	Modern term for 'Dynamo'. When rotated produces electrical current.
Grommet	A ring of protective or sealing material. Can be used to protect pipes or leads passing through bulkheads.
Grubscrew	Fully threaded headless screw with screwdriver slot. Used for locking, or alignment purposes.
Gudgeon pin	Shaft which connects a piston to its connecting rod. Sometimes called 'wrist pin', or 'piston pin'.
Halfshaft	One of a pair transmitting drive from the differential.
Helical	In spiral form. The teeth of helical gears are cut at a spiral angle to the side faces of the gearwheel.
Hot spot	Hot area that assists vapourisation of fuel on its way to cylinders. Often provided by close contact between inlet and exhaust manifolds.
HT	High Tension. Applied to electrical current produced by the ignition coil for the sparking plugs.
Hydrometer	A device for checking specific gravity of liquids. Used to check specific gravity of electrolyte.
Hypoid bevel gears	A form of bevel gear used in the rear axle drive gears. The bevel pinion meshes below the centre line of the crownwheel, giving a lower propeller shaft line.
Idler	A device for passing on movement. A free running gear between driving and driven gears. A lever transmitting track rod movement to a side rod in steering gear.
Impeller	A centrifugal pumping element. Used in water pumps to stimulate flow.
Journals	Those parts of a shaft that are in contact with the bearings.
Kingpin	The main vertical pin which carries the front wheel spindle, and permits steering movement. May be called 'steering pin' or 'swivel pin'.
Layshaft	The shaft which carries the laygear in the gearbox. The laygear is driven by the first motion shaft and drives the third motion shaft according to the gear selected. Sometimes called the 'countershaft' or 'second motion shaft.'
lb ft	A measure of twist or torque. A pull of 10 lb at a radius of 1 ft is a torque of 10 lb ft.
lb/sq in	Pounds per square inch.
Little-end	The small, or piston end of a connecting rod. Sometimes called the 'small-end'.
LT	Low Tension. The current output from the battery.
Mandrel	Accurately manufactured bar or rod used for test or centring purposes.
Manifold	A pipe, duct, or chamber, with several branches.
Needle rollers	Bearing rollers with a length many times their diameter.
Oil bath	Reservoir which lubricates parts by immersion. In air filters, a separate oil supply for wetting a wire mesh element to hold the dust.
Oil wetted	In air filters, a wire mesh element lightly oiled to trap and hold airborne dust.
Overlap	Period during which inlet and exhaust valves are open together.
Panhard rod	Bar connected between fixed point on chassis and another on axle to control sideways movement.
Pawl	Pivoted catch which engages in the teeth of a ratchet to permit movement in one direction only.
Peg spanner	Tool with pegs, or pins, to engage in holes or slots in the part to be turned.
Pendant pedals	Pedals with levers that are pivoted at the top end.
Phillips screwdriver	A cross-point screwdriver for use with the cross-slotted heads of Phillips screws.
Pinion	A small gear, usually in relation to another gear.
Piston-type damper	Shock absorber in which damping is controlled by a piston working in a closed oil-filled cylinder.
Preloading	Preset static pressure on ball or roller bearings not due to working loads.
Radial	Radiating from a centre, like the spokes of a wheel.

Radius rod	Pivoted arm confining movement of a part to an arc of fixed radius.
Ratchet	Toothed wheel or rack which can move in one direction only, movement in the other being prevented by a pawl.
Ring gear	A gear tooth ring attached to outer periphery of flywheel. Starter pinion engages with it during starting.
Runout	Amount by which rotating part is out of true.
Semi-floating axle	Outer end of rear axle halfshaft is carried on bearing inside axle casing. Wheel hub is secured to end of shaft.
Servo	A hydraulic or pneumatic system for assisting, or, augmenting a physical effort. See 'Vacuum Servo'.
Setscrew	One which is threaded for the full length of the shank.
Shackle	A coupling link, used in the form of two parallel pins connected by side plates to secure the end of the master suspension spring and absorb the effects of deflection.
Shell bearing	Thinwalled steel shell lined with anti-friction metal. Usually semi-circular and used in pairs for main and big-end bearings.
Shock absorber	See 'Damper'.
Silentbloc	Rubber bush bonded to inner and outer metal sleeves.
Socket-head screw	Screw with hexagonal socket for an Allen key.
Solenoid	A coil of wire creating a magnetic field when electric current passes through it. Used with a soft iron core to operate contacts or a mechanical device.
Spur gear	A gear with teeth cut axially across the periphery.
Stub axle	Short axle fixed at one end only.
Tachometer	An instrument for accurate measurement of rotating speed. Usually indicates in revolutions per minute.

TDC	Top Dead Centre. The highest point reached by a piston in a cylinder, with the crank and connecting rod in line.
Thermostat	Automatic device for regulating temperature. Used in vehicle coolant systems to open a valve which restricts circulation at low temperature.
Third motion shaft	Output shaft of gearbox.
Threequarter floating axle	Outer end of rear axle halfshaft flanged and bolted to wheel hub, which runs on bearing mounted on outside of axle casing. Vehicle weight is not carried by the axle shaft.
Thrust bearing or washer	Used to reduce friction in rotating parts subject to axial loads.
Torque	Turning or twisting effort. See 'lb ft'.
Track rod	The bar(s) across the vehicle which connect the steering arms and maintain the front wheels in their correct alignment.
UJ	Universal joint. A coupling between shafts which permits angular movement.
UNF	Unified National Fine screw thread.
Vacuum servo	Device used in brake system, using difference between atmospheric pressure and inlet manifold depression to operate a piston which acts to augment brake pressure as required. See 'Servo'.
Venturi	A restriction or 'choke' in a tube, as in a carburetter, used to increase velocity to obtain a reduction in pressure.
Vernier	A sliding scale for obtaining fractional readings of the graduations of an adjacent scale.
Welch plug	A domed thin metal disc which is partially flattened to lock in a recess. Used to plug core holes in castings.
Wet liner	Removable cylinder barrel, sealed against coolant leakage, where the coolant is in direct contact with the outer surface.
Wet sump	A reservoir attached to the crankcase to hold the lubricating oil.

NOTES

CAR PERFORMANCE

Explanatory Definitions

On occasion, even the well-informed find it difficult to convey in simple language the meaning of commonplace technical terms. The following definitions may prove useful in such situations.

Horse-power (hp):

The unit of work; 1 hp is equal to 33,000 ft lb per min. This is the work done in lifting a weight of 33,000 lb through a distance of one foot in one minute, or any other quantities of pounds and feet which when multiplied give 33,000.

Brake horse-power (bhp):

The actual power developed at the engine-shaft, as measured on test by coupling the engine to a dynamometer or 'brake' for absorbing the power.

Torque:

The effort applied to a shaft or wheel which tends to turn it. When the torque is of sufficient value to rotate the shaft through a definite distance in a given time, work is done, which is then stated in hp.

Mean effective pressure (mep), or mean indicated pressure (mip):

The average pressure produced in the cylinders on the explosion stroke, and which results in the shaft-power. It is measured at the cylinder itself, by a scientific apparatus, or 'indicator'.

Brake mean effective pressure (bmep) or brake mean pressure (bmp):

A figure analogous to the above, but obtained by calculation from the actual bhp. The figure is imaginary, as it allows for the mechanical losses in the engine. It does however enable useful comparisons to be made between designs, in almost all relevant aspects.

Mechanical efficiency:

A factor expressed as a percentage, which shows how much of the explosion pressure is obtained as power at the engine-shaft; it is the percentage difference between the mep and the bmep. The loss is due to friction, inertia, etc., in the engine moving parts.

Thermal efficiency:

A factor expressed as a percentage which shows how much power is obtained from the heat energy in the fuel used; it is thus an indication of the effectiveness of the engine as an apparatus for converting heat into work.

Volumetric efficiency:

A factor showing the degree of completeness with which a cylinder is charged, exhausted and recharged as the operating cycle is performed; it is a measure of the adequacy of valves, ports, induction and exhaust systems, etc.

Catalogue information

The catalogues issued by reputable car makers are intended not only to show the vehicle in as attractive a light as possible, but also to provide the prospective buyer with the information he needs, in order for him to decide whether the mechanical characteristics are commensurate with his kind of motoring. Manufacturers however are by no means unanimous as regards their methods of obtaining performance data, and this has to be borne in mind when making comparison as between different models in a similar class.

Engine output

Engine output, given as maximum brake horse-power at a specified rate of rev/min, is obtained by coupling the engine to a power-absorbing dynamometer on a test-bed. Some makers when testing in this manner, disconnect accessories such as the fan, water pump and generator all of which, in practice, absorb a certain amount of engine power. Further methods of increasing the power obtained at the engine flywheel are to employ a special test-bed exhaust system which permits a much freer passage for the exhaust gases than is the case when the standard pipe and silencer are in use. The test-house temperature may also be kept at the best figure for maximum output, while cases are known whereby the carburetter and ignition timing have been adjusted to obtain maximum performance at each particular increment of engine rev/min when obtaining the bhp/torque curves. Performance figures which are obtained in the manner typified by the above, are commonly found in American car catalogues, but several British makers also use the method. The figures are then known as Gross, or SAE, the initials denoting the Society of Automotive Engineers whose headquarters are in New York. All continental cars, and many British ones, carry out their engine tests under conditions equivalent to those when installed in the car, with all accessories driven, and with the standard exhaust system. This is called the Nett figure, or DIN (Deutsche Industrie Norm) in the case of continental engines.

Obviously the nett figure is considerably below the gross, the reduction being as much as 15 to 20 per cent. There is also a minor difference between the nett figures for British and continental engines, as the latter equate 735 Watts with 1 hp instead of the British 746 W. Thus 1 hp is equal to 1.014 metric hp.

Torque and brake mean pressure

The figures given for maximum torque can be related to the acceleration and hill-climbing power of the car by taking in the laden weight and gear ratios. However, this requires a fairly expert appraisal, and it generally suffices to note the engine rev/min at which maximum torque and maximum bhp occur. If the former is obtained at a low engine speed, in comparison with the speed for maximum bhp, the engine will have been designed in general to pull strongly from fairly low speeds. This characteristic is useful in cars which are liable to be heavily laden or used for towing caravans and trailers. The maximum horse-power, however, will be limited in comparison with engines on which maximum torque occurs higher up the speed range. The latter condition indicates that the engine is built for brisk revving and free use of the gearbox, in which case a high performance is obtained. In general, engine design tends towards this type nowadays.

Compression ratio:

There has been a great improvement of late both in the quality of fuel and the variety available. Designers have taken advantage of these developments, which enable the compression ratio to be increased with a consequent increase in the thermal efficiency of the engine. Higher torque is also obtained, so long as the compression ratio is not increased beyond the maximum advised for any particular fuel grading. It is the rule nowadays for the car maker to specify the fuel to be used, particularly where alternative compression ratios are offered. In such cases, the lower ratio is usually intended for buyers who have to use the vehicle in countries where lower-grade fuel only is obtainable. For environments where motoring is well established, however, compression ratios of between 8 and 9:1 are quite normal on family-type saloons, while high-powered sports car engines may run on ratios from 10 to 12:1, when using the highest grades available.

INDEX

NOTES

Alfa Romeo Giulia 1600,
1750, 2000 1962 on
Aston Martin 1921-58
Auto Union Audi 70, 80,
Super 90, 1966-72
Audi 100 1969 on
Austin, Morris etc.
1100 Mk. 1 1962-67
Austin, Morris etc. 1100
Mk. 2, 3, 1300 Mk. 1, 2, 3
America 1968 on
Austin A30, A35, A40
Farina 1951-67
Austin A55 Mk. 2, A60
1958-69
Austin A99, A110 1959-68
Austin J4 1960 on
Austin Allegro 1973 on
Austin Maxi 1969 on
Austin, Morris 1800
1964 on
Austin, Morris 2200 1972 on
Austin Kimberley, Tasman
1970 on
Austin, Morris 1300, 1500
Nomad 1969 on
BMC 3 (Austin A50, A55
Mk. 1, Morris Oxford
2, 3 1954-59)
Austin Healey 100/6,
3000 1956-68
Austin Healey, MG
Sprite, Midget 1958 on
Bedford CA Mk. 2 1964-69
Bedford CF Vans 1969 on
Bedford Beagle HA Vans
1964 on
BMW 1600 1966 on
BMW 1800 1964-71
BMW 2000, 2002 1966 on
Chevrolet Corvair 1960-69
Chevrolet Corvette V8
1957-65
Chevrolet Corvette V8
1965 on
Chevrolet Vega 2300
1970 on
Chrysler Valiant V8
1965 on
Chrysler Valiant Straight
Six 1963 on
Citroen DS 19, ID 19
1955-66
Citroen ID 19, DS 19, 20,
21 1966 on
Citroen Dyane Ami 1964 on
Daf 31, 32, 33, 44, 55
1961 on
Datsun Bluebird 610 series
1972 on
Datsun Cherry 100A, 120A
1971 on
Datsun 1000, 1200 1968 on
Datsun 1300, 1400, 1600
1968 on
Datsun 240C 1971 on

Datsun 240Z Sport 1970 on
Fiat 124 1966 on
Fiat 124 Sport 1966 on
Fiat 125 1967-72
Fiat 127 1971 on
Fiat 128 1969 on
Fiat 500 1957 on
Fiat 600, 600D 1955-69
Fiat 850 1964 on
Fiat 1100 1957-69
Fiat 1300, 1500 1961-67
Ford Anglia Prefect 100E
1953-62
Ford Anglia 105E, Prefect
107E 1959-67
Ford Capri 1300, 1600 OHV
1968 on
Ford Capri 1300, 1600,
2000 OHC 1972 on
Ford Capri 2000 V4, 3000 V6
1969 on
Ford Classic, Capri
1961-64
Ford Consul, Zephyr,
Zodiac, 1, 2 1950-62
Ford Corsair Straight
Four 1963-65
Ford Corsair V4 1965-68
Ford Corsair V4 2000
1969-70
Ford Cortina 1962-66
Ford Cortina 1967-68
Ford Cortina 1969-70
Ford Cortina Mk. 3
1970 on
Ford Escort 1967 on
Ford Falcon 6 1964-70
Ford Falcon XK, XL
1960-63
Ford Falcon 6 XR/XA
1966 on
Ford Falcon V8 (U.S.A.)
1965-71
Ford Falcon V8 (Aust.)
1966 on
Ford Pinto 1970 on
Ford Maverick 6 1969 on
Ford Maverick V8 1970 on
Ford Mustang 6 1965 on
Ford Mustang V8 1965 on
Ford Thames 10, 12,
15 cwt 1957-65
Ford Transit V4 1965 on
Ford Zephyr Zodiac Mk. 3
1962-66
Ford Zephyr Zodiac V4,
V6, Mk. 4 1966-72
Ford Consul, Granada
1972 on
Hillman Avenger 1970 on
Hillman Hunter 1966 on
Hillman Imp 1963-68
Hillman Imp 1969 on
Hillman Minx 1 to 5
1956-65
Hillman Minx 1965-67

Hillman Minx 1966-70
Hillman Super Minx
1961-65
Jaguar XK120, 140, 150,
Mk. 7, 8, 9 1948-61
Jaguar 2.4, 3.4, 3.8 Mk.
1, 2 1955-69
Jaguar 'E' Type 1961-72
Jaguar 'S' Type 420
1963-68
Jaguar XJ6 1968 on
Jowett Javelin Jupiter
1947-53
Landrover 1, 2 1948-61
Landrover 2, 2a, 3 1959 on
Mazda 616 1970 on
Mazda 808, 818 1972 on
Mazda 1200, 1300 1969 on
Mazda 1500, 1800 1967 on
Mazda RX-2 1971 on
Mazda R100, RX-3 1970 on
Mercedes-Benz 190b,
190c, 200 1959-68
Mercedes-Benz 220
1959-65
Mercedes-Benz 220/8
1968 on
Mercedes-Benz 230
1963-68
Mercedes-Benz 250
1965-67
Mercedes-Benz 250
1968 on
Mercedes-Benz 280
1968 on
MG TA to TF 1936-55
MGA MGB 1955-68
MGB 1969 on
Mini 1959 on
Mini Cooper 1961-72
Morgan Four 1936-72
Morris Marina 1971 on
Morris (Aust) Marina
1972 on
Morris Minor 2, 1000
1952-71
Morris Oxford 5, 6 1959-71
NSU 1000 1963-72
NSU Prinz 1 to 4 1957-72
Opel Ascona, Manta
1970 on
Opel GT 1900 1968 on
Opel Kadett, Olympia 993 cc
1078 cc 1962 on
Opel Kadett, Olympia 1492,
1698, 1897 cc 1967 on
Opel Rekord C 1966-72
Peugeot 204 1965 on
Peugeot 304 1970 on
Peugeot 404 1960 on
Peugeot 504 1968 on
Porsche 356A, B, C 1957-65
Porsche 911 1964 on
Porsche 912 1965-69
Porsche 914 S 1969 on
Reliant Regal 1952-73

Renault R4, R4L, 4 1961 on
Renault 5 1972 on
Renault 6 1968 on
Renault 8, 10, 1100 1962-71
Renault 12, 1969 on
Renault 15, 17 1971 on
Renault R16 1965 on
Renault Dauphine
Floride 1957-67
Renault Caravelle 1962-68
Rover 60 to 110 1953-64
Rover 2000 1963-73
Rover 3 Litre 1958-67
Rover 3500, 3500S 1968 on
Saab 95, 96, Sport
1960-68
Saab 99 1969 on
Saab V4 1966 on
Simca 1000 1961 on
Simca 1100 1967 on
Simca 1300, 1301, 1500,
1501 1963 on
Skoda One (440, 445, 450)
1955-70
Sunbeam Rapier Alpine
1955-65
Toyota Carina, Celica
1971 on
Toyota Corolla 1100,
1200 1967 on
Toyota Corona 1500 Mk. 1
1965-70
Toyota Corona Mk. 2
1969 on
Triumph TR2, TR3, TR3A
1952-62
Triumph TR4, TR4A
1961-67
Triumph TR5, TR250,
TR6 1967 on
Triumph 1300, 1500
1965-73
Triumph 2000 Mk. 1, 2.5 PI
Mk. 1 1963-69
Triumph 2000 Mk. 2, 2.5 PI
Mk. 2 1969 on
Triumph Dolomite 1972 on
Triumph Herald 1959-68
Triumph Herald 1969-71
Triumph Spitfire, Vitesse
1962-68
Triumph Spitfire Mk. 3, 4
1969 on
Triumph GT6, Vitesse
2 Litre 1969 on
Triumph Stag 1970 on
Triumph Toledo 1970 on
Vauxhall Velox, Cresta
1957-72
Vauxhall Victor 1, 2, FB
1957-64
Vauxhall Victor 101
1964-67
Vauxhall Victor FD 1600,
2000 1967-72

Continued on following page

THE AUTOBOOK SERIES OF WORKSHOP MANUALS

Vauxhall Victor 3300,
  Ventora 1968-72
Vauxhall Victor FE
  Ventora 1972 on
Vauxhall Viva HA 1963-66
Vauxhall Viva HB 1966-70

Vauxhall Viva, HC Firenza
  1971 on
Volkswagen Beetle 1954-67
Volkswagen Beetle 1968 on
Volkswagen 1500 1961-66

Volkswagen 1600 Fastback
  1965-73
Volkswagen Transporter
  1954-67
Volkswagen Transporter
  1968 on

Volkswagen 411 1968-72
Volvo 120 series 1961-70
Volvo 140 series 1966 on
Volvo 160 series 1968 on
Volvo 1800 1960-73

NOTES

NOTES

NOTES

NOTES